Real-Resumes For Legal & Paralegal Jobs

...including real resumes used to change careers
and gain federal employment

Anne McKinney, Editor

PREP PUBLISHING

FAYETTEVILLE, NC

PREP Publishing
1110 ½ Hay Street
Fayetteville, NC 28305
(910) 483-6611

Library of Congress Cataloging-in-Publication Data

Real-resumes for legal & paralegal jobs--including real resumes used to change careers and gain federal employment / Anne McKinney, editor.
      p. cm. -- (Real-resumes series)
  ISBN 1-885288-38-7 (alk. paper)
  1. Resumes (Employment)--United States. 2. Lawyers--United States. 3. Legal Assistants-- Employment--United States. 4. Government attorneys--United States. 5. Law--Vocational guidance--United States. 6. Career changes--United States. I. Title: Real-resumes for legal and paralegal jobs. II. McKinney, Anne, 1948- III. Series.

  HF5383.R395867 2004
  650.14'2-dc22   2004041421

Printed in the United States of America

PREP Publishing

Business and Career Series:

RESUMES AND COVER LETTERS THAT HAVE WORKED, Revised Edition

RESUMES AND COVER LETTERS THAT HAVE WORKED FOR MILITARY PROFESSIONALS

GOVERNMENT JOB APPLICATIONS AND FEDERAL RESUMES

COVER LETTERS THAT BLOW DOORS OPEN

LETTERS FOR SPECIAL SITUATIONS

RESUMES AND COVER LETTERS FOR MANAGERS

REAL-RESUMES FOR COMPUTER JOBS

REAL-RESUMES FOR MEDICAL JOBS

REAL-RESUMES FOR FINANCIAL JOBS

REAL-RESUMES FOR TEACHERS

REAL-RESUMES FOR STUDENTS

REAL-RESUMES FOR CAREER CHANGERS

REAL-RESUMES FOR SALES

REAL ESSAYS FOR COLLEGE & GRADUATE SCHOOL

REAL-RESUMES FOR AVIATION & TRAVEL JOBS

REAL-RESUMES FOR POLICE, LAW ENFORCEMENT & SECURITY JOBS

REAL-RESUMES FOR SOCIAL WORK & COUNSELING JOBS

REAL-RESUMES FOR CONSTRUCTION JOBS

REAL-RESUMES FOR MANUFACTURING JOBS

REAL-RESUMES FOR RESTAURANT, FOOD SERVICE & HOTEL JOBS

REAL-RESUMES FOR MEDIA, NEWSPAPER, BROADCASTING & PUBLIC AFFAIRS JOBS

REAL-RESUMES FOR RETAILING, MODELING, FASHION & BEAUTY JOBS

REAL-RESUMES FOR HUMAN RESOURCES & PERSONNEL JOBS

REAL-RESUMES FOR NURSING JOBS

REAL-RESUMES FOR AUTO INDUSTRY JOBS

REAL RESUMIX & OTHER RESUMES FOR FEDERAL GOVERNMENT JOBS

REAL KSAS--KNOWLEDGE, SKILLS & ABILITIES--FOR GOVERNMENT JOBS

REAL BUSINESS PLANS & MARKETING TOOLS

REAL-RESUMES FOR ADMINISTRATIVE SUPPORT, OFFICE & SECRETARIAL JOBS

REAL-RESUMES FOR FIREFIGHTING JOBS

REAL-RESUMES FOR JOBS IN NONPROFIT ORGANIZATIONS

REAL-RESUMES FOR SPORTS INDUSTRY JOBS

REAL-RESUMES FOR LEGAL & PARALEGAL JOBS

Judeo-Christian Ethics Series:

SECOND TIME AROUND

BACK IN TIME

WHAT THE BIBLE SAYS ABOUT...Words that can lead to success and happiness

A GENTLE BREEZE FROM GOSSAMER WINGS

BIBLE STORIES FROM THE OLD TESTAMENT

Contents

Real-Resumes For Legal & Paralegal Jobs

Anne McKinney, Editor

A WORD FROM THE EDITOR:
ABOUT THE REAL-RESUMES SERIES

Welcome to the Real-Resumes Series. The Real-Resumes Series is a series of books which have been developed based on the experiences of real job hunters and which target specialized fields or types of resumes. As the editor of the series, I have carefully selected resumes and cover letters (with names and other key data disguised, of course) which have been used successfully in real job hunts. That's what we mean by "Real-Resumes." What you see in this book are *real* resumes and cover letters which helped real people get ahead in their careers.

We hope the superior samples will help you manage your current job campaign and your career so that you will find work aligned to your career interests.

The Real-Resumes Series is based on the work of the country's oldest resume-preparation company known as PREP Resumes. If you would like a free information packet describing the company's resume preparation services, call 910-483-6611 or write to PREP at 1110½ Hay Street, Fayetteville, NC 28305. If you have a job hunting experience you would like to share with our staff at the Real-Resumes Series, please contact us at preppub@aol.com or visit our website at http://www.prep-pub.com.

The resumes and cover letters in this book are designed to be of most value to people already in a job hunt or contemplating a career change. If we could give you one word of advice about your career, here's what we would say: Manage your career and don't stumble from job to job in an incoherent pattern. Try to find work that interests you, and then identify prosperous industries which need work performed of the type you want to do. Learn early in your working life that a great resume and cover letter can blow doors open for you and help you maximize your salary.

As the editor of this book, I would like to give you some tips on how to make the best use of the information you will find here. Because you are considering a career change, you already understand the concept of managing your career for maximum enjoyment and self-fulfillment. The purpose of this book is to provide expert tools and advice so that you *can* manage your career. Inside these pages you will find resumes and cover letters that will help you find not just a job but the type of work you want to do.

Overview of the Book
Every resume and cover letter in this book actually worked. And most of the resumes and cover letters have common features: most are one-page, most are in the chronological format, and most resumes are accompanied by a companion cover letter. In this section you will find helpful advice about job hunting. Step One begins with a discussion of why employers prefer the one-page, chronological resume. In Step Two you are introduced to the direct approach and to the proper format for a cover letter. In Step Three you learn the 14 main reasons why job hunters are not offered the jobs they want, and you learn the six key areas employers focus on when they interview you. Step Four gives nuts-and-bolts advice on how to handle the interview, send a follow-up letter after an interview, and negotiate your salary.

The cover letter plays such a critical role in a career change. You will learn from the experts how to format your cover letters and you will see suggested language to use in particular career-change situations. It has been said that "A picture is worth a thousand words" and, for that reason, you will see numerous examples of effective cover letters used by real individuals to change fields, functions, and industries.

The most important part of the book is the Real-Resumes section. Some of the individuals whose resumes and cover letters you see spent a lengthy career in an industry they loved. Then there are resumes and cover letters of people who wanted a change but who probably wanted to remain in their industry. Many of you will be especially interested by the resumes and cover letters of individuals who knew they definitely wanted a career change but had no idea what they wanted to do next. Other resumes and cover letters show individuals who knew they wanted to change fields and had a pretty good idea of what they wanted to do next.

Whatever your field, and whatever your circumstances, you'll find resumes and cover letters that will "show you the ropes" in terms of successfully changing jobs and switching careers.

Before you proceed further, think about why you picked up this book.
- Are you dissatisfied with the type of work you are now doing?
- Would you like to change careers, change companies, or change industries?
- Are you satisfied with your industry but not with your niche or function within it?
- Do you want to transfer your skills to a new product or service?
- Even if you have excelled in your field, have you "had enough"? Would you like the stimulation of a new challenge?
- Are you aware of the importance of a great cover letter but unsure of how to write one?
- Are you preparing to launch a second career after retirement?
- Have you been downsized, or do you anticipate becoming a victim of downsizing?
- Do you need expert advice on how to plan and implement a job campaign that will open the maximum number of doors?
- Do you want to make sure you handle an interview to your maximum advantage?

- Would you like to master the techniques of negotiating salary and benefits?
- Do you want to learn the secrets and shortcuts of professional resume writers?

Using the Direct Approach

As you consider the possibility of a job hunt or career change, you need to be aware that most people end up having at least three distinctly different careers in their working lifetimes, and often those careers are different from each other. Yet people usually stumble through each job campaign, unsure of what they should be doing. Whether you find yourself voluntarily or unexpectedly in a job hunt, the direct approach is the job hunting strategy most likely to yield a full-time permanent job. The direct approach is an active, take-the-initiative style of job hunting in which you choose your next employer rather than relying on responding to ads, using employment agencies, or depending on other methods of finding jobs. You will learn how to use the direct approach in this book, and you will see that an effective cover letter is a critical ingredient in using the direct approach.

The "direct approach" is the style of job hunting most likely to yield the maximum number of job interviews.

Lack of Industry Experience Not a Major Barrier to Entering New Field

"Lack of experience" is often the last reason people are not offered jobs, according to the companies who do the hiring. If you are changing careers, you will be glad to learn that experienced professionals often are selling "potential" rather than experience in a job hunt. Companies look for personal qualities that they know tend to be present in their most effective professionals, such as communication skills, initiative, persistence, organizational and time management skills, and creativity. Frequently companies are trying to discover "personality type," "talent," "ability," "aptitude," and "potential" rather than seeking actual hands-on experience, so your resume should be designed to aggressively present your accomplishments. Attitude, enthusiasm, personality, and a track record of achievements in any type of work are the primary "indicators of success" which employers are seeking, and you will see numerous examples in this book of resumes written in an all-purpose fashion so that the professional can approach various industries and companies.

Using references in a skillful fashion in your job hunt will inspire confidence in prospective employers and help you "close the sale" after interviews.

The Art of Using References in a Job Hunt

You probably already know that you need to provide references during a job hunt, but you may not be sure of how and when to use references for maximum advantage. You can use references very creatively during a job hunt to call attention to your strengths and make yourself "stand out." Your references will rarely get you a job, no matter how impressive the names, but the way you use references can boost the employer's confidence in you and lead to a job offer in the least time.

You should ask from three to five people, including people who have supervised you, if you can use them as a reference during your job hunt. You may not be able to ask your current boss since your job hunt is probably confidential.

A common question in resume preparation is: "Do I need to put my references on my resume?" No, you don't. Even if you create a references page at the same time you prepare your resume, you don't need to mail, e-mail, or fax your references page with the resume and cover letter. Usually the potential employer is not interested in references until he meets you, so the earliest you need to have references ready is at the first interview. Obviously there are exceptions to this standard rule of thumb; sometimes an ad will ask you to send references with your first response. Wait until the employer requests references before providing them.

An excellent attention-getting technique is to take to the first interview not just a page of references (giving names, addresses, and telephone numbers) but an actual letter of reference written by someone who knows you well and who preferably has supervised or employed you. A professional way to close the first interview is to thank the interviewer, shake his or her hand, and then say you'd like to give him or her a copy of a letter of reference from a previous employer. Hopefully you already made a good impression during the interview, but you'll "close the sale" in a dynamic fashion if you leave a letter praising you and your accomplishments. For that reason, it's a good idea to ask supervisors during your final weeks in a job if they will provide you with a written letter of recommendation which you can use in future job hunts. Most employers will oblige, and you will have a letter that has a useful "shelf life" of many years. Such a letter often gives the prospective employer enough confidence in his opinion of you that he may forego checking out other references and decide to offer you the job on the spot or in the next few days.

With regard to references, it's best to provide the names and addresses of people who have supervised you or observed you in a work situation.

Whom should you ask to serve as references? References should be people who have known or supervised you in a professional, academic, or work situation. References with big titles, like school superintendent or congressman, are fine, but remind busy people when you get to the interview stage that they may be contacted soon. Make sure the busy official recognizes your name and has instant positive recall of you! If you're asked to provide references on a formal company application, you can simply transcribe names from your references list. In summary, follow this rule in using references: If you've got them, flaunt them! If you've obtained well-written letters of reference, make sure you find a polite way to push those references under the nose of the interviewer so he or she can hear someone other than you describing your strengths. Your references probably won't ever get you a job, but glowing letters of reference can give you credibility and visibility that can make you stand out among candidates with similar credentials and potential!

The approach taken by this book is to (1) help you master the proven best techniques of conducting a job hunt and (2) show you how to stand out in a job hunt through your resume, cover letter, interviewing skills, as well as the way in which you present your references and follow up on interviews. Now, the best way to "get in the mood" for writing your own resume and cover letter is to select samples from the Table of Contents that interest you and then read them. A great resume is a "photograph," usually on one page, of an individual. If you wish to seek professional advice in preparing your resume, you may contact one of the professional writers at Professional Resume & Employment Publishing (PREP) for a brief free consultation by calling 1-910-483-6611.

What if you don't know what you want to do?

Your job hunt will be more comfortable if you can figure out what type of work you want to do. But you are not alone if you have no idea what you want to do next! You may have knowledge and skills in certain areas but want to get into another type of work. What *The Wall Street Journal* has discovered in its research on careers is that most of us end up having at least three distinctly different careers in our working lives; it seems that, even if we really like a particular kind of activity, twenty years of doing it is enough for most of us and we want to move on to something else!

Figure out what interests you and you will hold the key to a successful job hunt and working career. (And be prepared for your interests to change over time!)

That's why we strongly believe that you need to spend some time figuring out **what interests you** rather than taking an inventory of the skills you have. You may have skills that you simply don't want to use, but if you can build your career on the things that interest you, you will be more likely to be happy and satisfied in your job. Realize, too, that interests can change over time; the activities that interest you now may not be the ones that interested you years ago. For example, some professionals may decide that they've had enough of retail sales and want a job selling another product or service, even though they have earned a reputation for being an excellent retail manager. We strongly believe that interests rather than skills should be the determining factor in deciding what types of jobs you want to apply for and what directions you explore in your job hunt. Obviously one cannot be a lawyer without a law degree or a secretary without secretarial skills; but a professional can embark on a next career as a financial consultant, property manager, plant manager, production supervisor, retail manager, or other occupation if he/she has a strong interest in that type of work and can provide a resume that clearly demonstrates past excellent performance in *any* field and *potential* to excel in another field. As you will see later in this book, "lack of exact experience" is the last reason why people are turned down for the jobs they apply for.

How can you have a resume prepared if you don't know what you want to do?

You may be wondering how you can have a resume prepared if you don't know what you want to do next. The approach to resume writing which PREP, the country's oldest resume-preparation company, has used successfully for many years is to develop an "all-purpose" resume that translates your skills, experience, and accomplishments into language employers can understand. What most people need in a job hunt is a versatile resume that will allow them to apply for numerous types of jobs. For example, you may want to apply for a job in pharmaceutical sales but you may also want to have a resume that will be versatile enough for you to apply for jobs in the construction, financial services, or automotive industries.

"Lack of exact experience" is the last reason people are turned down for the jobs for which they apply.

Based on more than 20 years of serving job hunters, we at PREP have found that your best approach to job hunting is **an all-purpose resume** and **specific cover letters tailored to specific fields** rather than using the approach of trying to create different resumes for every job. If you are remaining in your field, you may not even need more than one "all-purpose" cover letter, although the cover letter rather than the resume is the place to communicate your interest in a narrow or specific field. An all-purpose resume and cover letter that translate your experience and accomplishments into plain English are the tools that will maximize the number of doors which open for you while permitting you to "fish" in the widest range of job areas.

Your resume will provide the script for your job interview.
When you get down to it, your resume has a simple job to do: Its purpose is to blow as many doors open as possible and to make as many people as possible want to meet you. So a well-written resume that really "sells" you is a key that will create opportunities for you in a job hunt.

This statistic explains why: The typical newspaper advertisement for a job opening receives more than 245 replies. And normally only 10 or 12 will be invited to an interview.

But here's another purpose of the resume: it provides the "script" the employer uses when he interviews you. If your resume has been written in such a way that your strengths and achievements are revealed, that's what you'll end up talking about at the job interview. Since the resume will govern what you get asked about at your interviews, you can't overestimate the importance of making sure your resume makes you look and sound as good as you are.

So what is a "good" resume?
Very literally, your resume should motivate the person reading it to dial the phone number or e-mail the screen name you have put on the resume. When you are relocating, you should put a local phone number on your resume if your physical address is several states away; employers are more likely to dial a local telephone number than a long-distance number when they're looking for potential employees.

If you have a resume already, look at it objectively. Is it a limp, colorless "laundry list" of your job titles and duties? Or does it "paint a picture" of your skills, abilities, and accomplishments in a way that would make someone want to meet you? Can people understand what you're saying? If you are attempting to change fields or industries, can potential employers see that your skills and knowledge are transferable to other environments? For example, have you described accomplishments which reveal your problem-solving abilities or communication skills?

How long should your resume be?
One page, maybe two. Usually only people in the academic community have a resume (which they usually call a *curriculum vitae*) longer than one or two pages. Remember that your resume is almost always accompanied by a cover letter, and a potential employer does not want to read more than two or three pages about a total stranger in order to decide if he wants to meet that person! Besides, don't forget that the more you tell someone about yourself, the more opportunity you are providing for the employer to screen you out at the "first-cut" stage. A resume should be concise and exciting and designed to make the reader want to meet you in person!

Should resumes be functional or chronological?
Employers almost always prefer a chronological resume; in other words, an employer will find a resume easier to read if it is immediately apparent what your current or most recent job is, what you did before that, and so forth, in reverse chronological order. A resume that goes back in detail for the last ten years of employment will generally satisfy the employer's curiosity about your background. Employment more than ten years old can be shown even more briefly in an "Other Experience" section at the end of your "Experience" section. Remember that your intention is not to tell everything you've done but to "hit the high points" and especially impress the employer with what you learned, contributed, or accomplished in each job you describe.

Your resume is the "script" for your job interviews. Make sure you put on your resume what you want to talk about or be asked about at the job interview.

The one-page resume in chronological format is the format preferred by most employers.

Once you get your resume, what do you do with it?

You will be using your resume to answer ads, as a tool to use in talking with friends and relatives about your job search, and, most importantly, in using the "direct approach" described in this book.

When you mail your resume, always send a "cover letter."

A "cover letter," sometimes called a "resume letter" or "letter of interest," is a letter that accompanies and introduces your resume. Your cover letter is a way of personalizing the resume by sending it to the specific person you think you might want to work for at each company. Your cover letter should contain a few highlights from your resume—just enough to make someone want to meet you. Cover letters should always be typed or word processed on a computer—never handwritten.

Never mail or fax your resume without a cover letter.

1. Learn the art of answering ads.

There is an "art," part of which can be learned, in using your "bestselling" resume to reply to advertisements.

Sometimes an exciting job lurks behind a boring ad that someone dictated in a hurry, so reply to any ad that interests you. Don't worry that you aren't "25 years old with an MBA" like the ad asks for. Employers will always make compromises in their requirements if they think you're the "best fit" overall.

What about ads that ask for "salary requirements?"

What if the ad you're answering asks for "salary requirements?" The first rule is to avoid committing yourself in writing at that point to a specific salary. You don't want to "lock yourself in."

What if the ad asks for your "salary requirements?"

There are two ways to handle the ad that asks for "salary requirements."

First, you can ignore that part of the ad and accompany your resume with a cover letter that focuses on "selling" you, your abilities, and even some of your philosophy about work or your field. You may include a sentence in your cover letter like this: "I can provide excellent personal and professional references at your request, and I would be delighted to share the private details of my salary history with you in person."

Second, if you feel you must give some kind of number, just state a range in your cover letter that includes your medical, dental, other benefits, and expected bonuses. You might state, for example, "My current compensation, including benefits and bonuses, is in the range of $30,000-$40,000."

Analyze the ad and "tailor" yourself to it.

When you're replying to ads, a finely tailored cover letter is an important tool in getting your resume noticed and read. On the next page is a cover letter which has been "tailored to fit" a specific ad. Notice the "art" used by PREP writers of analyzing the ad's main requirements and then writing the letter so that the person's background, work habits, and interests seem "tailor-made" to the company's needs. Use this cover letter as a model when you prepare your own reply to ads.

Date

Exact Name of Person
Title or Position
Name of Company
Address (no., street)
Address (city, state, zip)

Dear Exact Name of Person: (or Dear Sir or Madam if answering a blind ad.)

I would appreciate an opportunity to talk with you soon about how I could contribute my problem-solving and decision-making skills to an organization that can use a creative, well-organized professional with excellent written and oral communication skills.

As you will see from my enclosed resume, I was selected for a prestigious internship with the Rayham County Courthouse. I observed nearly every type of courtroom proceeding and gained valuable insight into courtroom procedures. As I made the acquaintance of many people within the legal system including judges, lawyers, legal assistants, and others, I developed an understanding of how judges arrive at their decisions and observed how they manage the courtroom, interact with lawyers, and instruct juries.

In a previous intern position with the Douglas Powell Probation Office, I acted as the "right arm" and "shadow" of a very skilled parole officer who spent extensive time teaching me the nuts and bolts of probation and parole. As I spent some time with several people on probation and parole, I earned the respect of senior probation/parole officers for my listening and counseling skills. I demonstrated my ability to interact with probationers and parolees in a poised and professional manner.

After four years at Boise State University, I recently graduated with a Bachelor of Science degree in Criminal Justice. I excelled in senior seminars related to Social Problems in Criminal Justice as well as Mediation and Arbitration as Problem-Solving Alternatives.

You would find me to be a congenial and poised young person who is known for having "maturity beyond my years." I hope you will welcome my call soon to arrange a brief meeting at your convenience to discuss your needs and goals and how I might serve them. Thank you in advance for your time.

Yours sincerely,

Elizabeth L. Chesnutt

Alternate last paragraph:
I hope you will call or write soon to suggest a time convenient for us to meet and discuss your current and future needs and how I might serve them. Thank you in advance for your time.

Employers are trying to identify the individual who wants the job they are filling. Don't be afraid to express your enthusiasm in the cover letter!

2. Talk to friends and relatives.

Don't be shy about telling your friends and relatives the kind of job you're looking for. Looking for the job you want involves using your network of contacts, so tell people what you're looking for. They may be able to make introductions and help set up interviews.

About 25% of all interviews are set up through "who you know," so don't ignore this approach.

3. Finally, and most importantly, use the "direct approach."

The "direct approach" is a strategy in which you choose your next employer.

More than 50% of all job interviews are set up by the "direct approach." That means you actually mail, e-mail, or fax a resume and a cover letter to a company you think might be interesting to work for.

To whom do you write?

In general, you should write directly to the *exact name* of the person who would be hiring you: say, the vice-president of marketing or data processing. If you're in doubt about to whom to address the letter, address it to the president by name and he or she will make sure it gets forwarded to the right person within the company who has hiring authority in your area.

How do you find the names of potential employers?

You're not alone if you feel that the biggest problem in your job search is finding the right names at the companies you want to contact. But you can usually figure out the names of companies you want to approach by deciding first if your job hunt is primarily geography-driven or industry-driven.

In a **geography-driven job hunt,** you could select a list of, say, 50 companies you want to contact **by location** from the lists that the U.S. Chambers of Commerce publish yearly of their "major area employers." There are hundreds of local Chambers of Commerce across America, and most of them will have an 800 number which you can find through 1-800-555-1212. If you and your family think Atlanta, Dallas, Ft. Lauderdale, and Virginia Beach might be nice places to live, for example, you could contact the Chamber of Commerce in those cities and ask how you can obtain a copy of their list of major employers. Your nearest library will have the book which lists the addresses of all chambers.

In an **industry-driven job hunt,** and if you are willing to relocate, you will be identifying the companies which you find most attractive in the industry in which you want to work. When you select a list of companies to contact **by industry,** you can find the right person to write and the address of firms by industrial category in *Standard and Poor's, Moody's,* and other excellent books in public libraries. Many Web sites also provide contact information.

Many people feel it's a good investment to actually call the company to either find out or double-check the name of the person to whom they want to send a resume and cover letter. It's important to do as much as you feasibly can to assure that the letter gets to the right person in the company.

On-line research will be the best way for many people to locate organizations to which they wish to send their resume. It is outside the scope of this book to teach Internet research skills, but librarians are often useful in this area.

What's the correct way to follow up on a resume you send?

There is a polite way to be aggressively interested in a company during your job hunt. It is ideal to end the cover letter accompanying your resume by saying, "I hope you'll welcome my call next week when I try to arrange a brief meeting at your convenience to discuss your current and future needs and how I might serve them." Keep it low key, and just ask for a "brief meeting," not an interview. Employers want people who show a determined interest in working with them, so don't be shy about following up on the resume and cover letter you've mailed.

It pays to be aware of the 14 most common pitfalls for job hunters.

STEP THREE: Preparing for Interviews

But a resume and cover letter by themselves can't get you the job you want. You need to "prep" yourself before the interview. Step Three in your job campaign is "Preparing for Interviews." First, let's look at interviewing from the hiring organization's point of view.

What are the biggest "turnoffs" for potential employers?

One of the ways to help yourself perform well at an interview is to look at the main reasons why organizations *don't* hire the people they interview, according to those who do the interviewing.

Notice that "lack of appropriate background" (or lack of experience) is the *last* reason for not being offered the job.

The 14 Most Common Reasons Job Hunters Are Not Offered Jobs (according to the companies who do the interviewing and hiring):

1. Low level of accomplishment
2. Poor attitude, lack of self-confidence
3. Lack of goals/objectives
4. Lack of enthusiasm
5. Lack of interest in the company's business
6. Inability to sell or express yourself
7. Unrealistic salary demands
8. Poor appearance
9. Lack of maturity, no leadership potential
10. Lack of extracurricular activities
11. Lack of preparation for the interview, no knowledge about company
12. Objecting to travel
13. Excessive interest in security and benefits
14. Inappropriate background

Department of Labor studies have proven that smart, "prepared" job hunters can increase their beginning salary while getting a job in *half* the time it normally takes. (4½ months is the average national length of a job search.) Here, from PREP, are some questions that can prepare you to find a job faster.

Are you in the "right" frame of mind?

It seems unfair that we have to look for a job just when we're lowest in morale. Don't worry *too* much if you're nervous before interviews. You're supposed to be a little nervous, especially if the job means a lot to you. But the best way to kill unnecessary fears about job hunting is through 1) making sure you have a great resume and 2) preparing yourself for the interview. Here are three main areas you need to think about before each interview.

Do you know what the company does?

Don't walk into an interview giving the impression that, "If this is Tuesday, this must be General Motors."

Research the company before you go to interviews.

Find out before the interview what the company's main product or service is. Where is the company heading? Is it in a "growth" or declining industry? (Answers to these questions may influence whether or not you want to work there!)

Information about what the company does is in annual reports, in newspaper and magazine articles, and on the Internet. If you're not yet skilled at Internet research, just visit your nearest library and ask the reference librarian to guide you to printed materials on the company.

Do you know what you want to do for the company?

Before the interview, try to decide how you see yourself fitting into the company. Remember, "lack of exact background" the company wants is usually the last reason people are not offered jobs.

Understand before you go to each interview that the burden will be on you to "sell" the interviewer on why you're the best person for the job and the company.

How will you answer the critical interview questions?

Anticipate the questions you will be asked at the interview, and prepare your responses in advance.

Put yourself in the interviewer's position and think about the questions you're most likely to be asked. Here are some of the most commonly asked interview questions:

Q: "What are your greatest strengths?"

A: Don't say you've never thought about it! Go into an interview knowing the three main impressions you want to leave about yourself, such as "I'm hard-working, loyal, and an imaginative cost-cutter."

Q: "What are your greatest weaknesses?"

A: Don't confess that you're lazy or have trouble meeting deadlines! Confessing that you tend to be a "workaholic" or "tend to be a perfectionist and sometimes get frustrated when others don't share my high standards" will make your prospective employer see a "weakness" that he likes. Name a weakness that your interviewer will perceive as a strength.

Q: "What are your long-range goals?"

A: If you're interviewing with Microsoft, don't say you want to work for IBM in five years! Say your long-range goal is to be *with* the company, contributing to its goals and success.

Q: "What motivates you to do your best work?"

A: Don't get dollar signs in your eyes here! "A challenge" is not a bad answer, but it's a little cliched. Saying something like "troubleshooting" or "solving a tough problem" is more interesting and specific. Give an example if you can.

Q: "What do you know about this organization?"

A: Don't say you never heard of it until they asked you to the interview! Name an interesting, positive thing you learned about the company recently from your research. Remember, company executives can sometimes feel rather "maternal" about the company they serve. Don't get onto a negative area of the company if you can think of positive facts you can bring up. Of course, if you learned in your research that the company's sales seem to be taking a nose-dive, or that the company president is being prosecuted for taking bribes, you might politely ask your interviewer to tell you something that could help you better understand what you've been reading. Those are the kinds of company facts that can help you determine whether or not you want to work there.

Go to an interview prepared to tell the company why it should hire you.

Q: "Why should I hire you?"

A: "I'm unemployed and available" is the wrong answer here! Get back to your strengths and say that you believe the organization could benefit by a loyal, hard-working cost-cutter like yourself.

In conclusion, you should decide in advance, before you go to the interview, how you will answer each of these commonly asked questions. Have some practice interviews with a friend to role-play and build your confidence.

STEP FOUR: Handling the Interview and Negotiating Salary

Now you're ready for Step Four: actually handling the interview successfully and effectively. Remember, the purpose of an interview is to get a job offer.

A smile at an interview makes the employer perceive of you as intelligent!

Eight "do's" for the interview

According to leading U.S. companies, there are eight key areas in interviewing success. You can fail at an interview if you mishandle just one area.

1. **Do wear appropriate clothes.**
   You can never go wrong by wearing a suit to an interview.

2. **Do be well groomed.**
   Don't overlook the obvious things like having clean hair, clothes, and fingernails for the interview.

3. **Do give a firm handshake.**
   You'll have to shake hands twice in most interviews: first, before you sit down, and second, when you leave the interview. Limp handshakes turn most people off.

4. **Do smile and show a sense of humor.**
   Interviewers are looking for people who would be nice to work with, so don't be so somber that you don't smile. In fact, research shows that people who smile at interviews are perceived as more intelligent. So, smile!

5. **Do be enthusiastic.**
   Employers say they are "turned off" by lifeless, unenthusiastic job hunters who show no special interest in that company. The best way to show some enthusiasm for the employer's operation is to find out about the business beforehand.

6. Do show you are flexible and adaptable.

An employer is looking for someone who can contribute to his organization in a flexible, adaptable way. No matter what skills and training you have, employers know every new employee must go through initiation and training on the company's turf. Certainly show pride in your past accomplishments in a specific, factual way ("I saved my last employer $50.00 a week by a new cost-cutting measure I developed"). But don't come across as though there's nothing about the job you couldn't easily handle.

7. Do ask intelligent questions about the employer's business.

An employer is hiring someone because of certain business needs. Show interest in those needs. Asking questions to get a better idea of the employer's needs will help you "stand out" from other candidates interviewing for the job.

8. Do "take charge" when the interviewer "falls down" on the job.

Go into every interview knowing the three or four points about yourself you want the interviewer to remember. And be prepared to take an active part in leading the discussion if the interviewer's "canned approach" does not permit you to display your "strong suit." You can't always depend on the interviewer's asking you the "right" questions so you can stress your strengths and accomplishments.

Employers are seeking people with good attitudes whom they can train and coach to do things their way.

An important "don't": Don't ask questions about salary or benefits at the first interview.
Employers don't take warmly to people who look at their organization as just a place to satisfy salary and benefit needs. Don't risk making a negative impression by appearing greedy or self-serving. The place to discuss salary and benefits is normally at the second interview, and the employer will bring it up. Then you can ask questions without appearing excessively interested in what the organization can do for you.

Now...negotiating your salary
Even if an ad requests that you communicate your "salary requirement" or "salary history," you should avoid providing those numbers in your initial cover letter. You can usually say something like this: "I would be delighted to discuss the private details of my salary history with you in person."

Once you're at the interview, you must avoid even appearing *interested* in salary before you are offered the job. Make sure you've "sold" yourself before talking salary. First show you're the "best fit" for the employer and then you'll be in a stronger position from which to negotiate salary. **Never** bring up the subject of salary yourself. Employers say there's no way you can avoid looking greedy if you bring up the issue of salary and benefits before the company has identified you as its "best fit."

Don't appear excessively interested in salary and benefits at the interview.

Interviewers sometimes throw out a salary figure at the first interview to see if you'll accept it. You may not want to commit yourself if you think you will be able to negotiate a better deal later on. Get back to finding out more about the job. This lets the interviewer know you're interested primarily in the job and not the salary.

When the organization brings up salary, it may say something like this: "Well, Mary, we think you'd make a good candidate for this job. What kind of salary are we talking about?" You may not want to name a number here, either. Give the ball back to the interviewer. Act as though you hadn't given the subject of salary much thought and respond something like this: "Ah, Mr. Jones, I wonder if you'd be kind enough to tell me what salary you had in mind when you advertised the job?" Or ... "What is the range you have in mind?"

Don't worry, if the interviewer names a figure that you think is too low, you can say so without turning down the job or locking yourself into a rigid position. The point here is to negotiate for yourself as well as you can. You might reply to a number named by the interviewer that you think is low by saying something like this: "Well, Mr. Lee, the job interests me very much, and I think I'd certainly enjoy working with you. But, frankly, I was thinking of something a little higher than that." That leaves the ball in your interviewer's court again, and you haven't turned down the job either, in case it turns out that the interviewer can't increase the offer and you still want the job.

Last, send a follow-up letter.
Mail, e-mail, or fax a letter right after the interview telling your interviewer you enjoyed the meeting and are certain (if you are) that you are the "best fit" for the job. The people interviewing you will probably have an attitude described as either "professionally loyal" to their companies, or "maternal and proprietary" if the interviewer also owns the company. In either case, they are looking for people who want to work for *that* company in particular. The follow-up letter you send might be just the deciding factor in your favor if the employer is trying to choose between you and someone else. You will see an example of a follow-up letter on page 16.

A cover letter is an essential part of a job hunt or career change.
Many people are aware of the importance of having a great resume, but most people in a job hunt don't realize just how important a cover letter can be. The purpose of the cover letter, sometimes called a **"letter of interest,"** is to introduce your resume to prospective employers. The cover letter is often the critical ingredient in a job hunt because the cover letter allows you to say a lot of things that just don't "fit" on the resume. For example, you can emphasize your commitment to a new field and stress your related talents. The cover letter also gives you a chance to stress outstanding character and personal values. On the next two pages you will see examples of very effective cover letters.

Special help for those in career change
We want to emphasize again that, especially in a career change, the cover letter is very important and can help you "build a bridge" to a new career. A creative and appealing cover letter can begin the process of encouraging the potential employer to imagine you in an industry other than the one in which you have worked.

As a special help to those in career change, there are resumes and cover letters included in this book which show valuable techniques and tips you should use when changing fields or industries. The resumes and cover letters of career changers are identified in the table of contents as "Career Change" and you will see the "Career Change" label on cover letters in Part Two where the individuals are changing careers.

Salary negotiation can be tricky.

A follow-up letter can help the employer choose between you and another qualified candidate.

A cover letter is an essential part of a career change.

Please do not attempt to implement a career change without a cover letter. A cover letter is the first impression of you, and you can influence the way an employer views you by the language and style of your letter.

**Addressing the Cover
Letter:** Get the exact
name of the person to
whom you are writing. This
makes your approach
personal.

First Paragraph: This
explains why you are
writing.

Second Paragraph: You
have a chance to talk
about whatever you feel is
your most distinguishing
feature.

Third Paragraph: You
bring up your next most
distinguishing qualities and
try to
sell yourself.

Fourth Paragraph: Here
you have another
opportunity to reveal
qualities or achievements
which will impress your
future employer.

Final Paragraph: She
asks the employer to
contact her. Make sure
your reader knows what
the "next step" is.

**Alternate Final
Paragraph:** It's more
aggressive (but not too
aggressive) to let the
employer know that you
will be calling him or her.
Don't be afraid to be
persistent. Employers are
looking for people who
know what they want to
do.

Date

Exact Name of Person
Title or Position
Name of Company
Address (no., street)
Address (city, state, zip)

Dear Exact Name of Person: (or Dear Sir or Madam if answering a blind ad.)

I would appreciate an opportunity to talk with you soon about how I could contribute to your organization through my education and skills as a paralegal.

As you will see from my resume, I am an ABA approved Graduate of the Paralegal Technology Program at Highland Community College where I completed courses in Debtor/Creditor Relationships, Family Law, Real Estate Law, Contracts, Computer Software, Legal Research, Criminal Law, Wills, Estates, Trusts, and Civil Litigation. I excelled academically and can provide outstanding references from instructors and faculty advisors with whom I have interacted.

Currently employed as a Customer Service Representative for Home Depot, I have become known for my sunny disposition while greeting customers, handling complaints, processing payroll, gift certificates, rainchecks, and other areas. In a previous position with JCPenney Department Store, I was responsible for handling all credit problems. I am confident that my strong interpersonal skills and attitude of "attention to detail" would be assets to a legal firm that is seeking a highly motivated young paralegal.

You would find me to be an energetic and reliable professional who prides myself on doing any job to the best of my ability. I can provide excellent personal references from my current employer at the appropriate time.

I hope you will call or write me soon to suggest a time convenient for us to meet and discuss your current and future needs and how I might serve them. Thank you in advance for your time.

Sincerely yours,

Kelly A. Fields

I hope you will welcome my call soon when I seek to arrange a brief meeting with you to discuss your current or future openings. Thank you in advance for your time.

Date

TO: Dade County Detention Center
FROM: Sergeant Carolyn Gonzalez
RE: Detention Officer II, Classification

Dear Sir or Madam:

This letter of interest is to formally communicate my interest in the position of Detention Officer II, Classification.

On November 11, 1998 I was hired by the Dade County Sheriff's Office (DCSO) as a Detention Officer. During my six years as a Detention Officer, I gained expert knowledge of Sheriff's Office operations while refining my written and oral communication skills. During that period, I gained a reputation as a outstanding Detention Officer. I excelled in numerous training programs which included intake and booking area, Housing Units B and C management stations, central control, and video visitation.

In July 2002, I was promoted to the rank of Corporal. Upon assuming that position, I was entrusted with the responsibility of Field Training Officer for most of the new officers assigned to B Platoon. During that time I worked closely with the lieutenants and sergeants on duty to familiarize myself with the procedures involved in in-processing inmates. I became skilled in classifying an inmate based on charges, bond, background history, and attitude, and I gained extensive experience in interviewing inmates to determine suitable housing and other matters. I also gained in-depth knowledge of the procedures involved in releasing an inmate from jail. As a Corporal, I was the "go-to" person for communicating with inmates to assist with any problems and, if necessary, to notify the immediate supervisor of any situation which posed a potential disturbance within the facility. During this period of time, I gained proficiency with the computer system "Pistol" utilized to run daily custody reports and pull up any inmate in the facility in order to identify current and previous record.

In December 2003, I was promoted to the rank of Sergeant. On a daily basis, sergeants ensure that the inmate "head count" is correct and that all keys are accounted for. I am involved in teaching and evaluating junior Detention Officers in order to help them develop their skills and knowledge to the fullest possible extent. I sign the disciplinary reports for my area, and make sure that reports are correct and that fair punishment is given according to the inmate violation rule book.

My written and oral communication skills have been refined through experience as well as training. I have completed courses including Developing Writing Skills for Detention and Law Enforcement Officers (Florida Justice Academy), Detention Field Training Officer (Justice Academy), 80 hours of In-Service and Direct Supervision Training (DCSO), Report Writing (DCSO), Interpersonal Communications (DCSO), and Subject Control (DCSO). I am known for my ability to exercise tact, firmness, compassion, and common sense in all situations, and I am also known for my ability to work effectively with inmates, the public, inmate families, courts, members of the local bar, law enforcement officers, and others.

I realize that this is a Jailer II position, and if given the position I would take a voluntary demotion in rank and pay. I am confident I could excel in this position.

This accomplished young jailer is responding to her county's request for "letters of interest" for a current opening. She analyzed the job vacancy opening very closely and she has made sure that she has tailored her letter of interest to the areas mentioned in the vacancy announcement. She is seeking this position because the new position would offer working hours more conducive to the needs of a "working mom."

Date

Exact Name of Person
Title or Position
Name of Company
Address (number and street)
Address (city, state, and zip)

Dear Exact Name:

I am writing to express my appreciation for the time you spent with me on December 9, and I want to let you know that I am sincerely interested in the position of Paralegal which we discussed.

I feel confident that I could skillfully interact with your 60-attorney staff, and I would cheerfully travel weekly to your Tennessee office, as we discussed.

As you described to me what you are looking for in the person who fills this position, I had a sense of "déjà vu" because my current employer was in a similar position when I went to work for his firm. The managing partner needed someone to come in and be his "right arm" and take on an increasing amount of his management responsibilities so that he could be freed up to do other things. I have played a key role in the growth and profitability of his practice, and his firm has come to depend on my sound advice as much as well as my proven ability to "cut through" huge volumes of work efficiently and accurately. Since this is one of the busiest times of the year in the real estate industry, I feel that I could not leave during that time. I could certainly make myself available by mid-January.

It would be a pleasure to work for your well-known and prestigious law firm, and I am confident that I could contribute significantly not only through my paralegal background but also through my strong qualities of loyalty, reliability, and trustworthiness. I am confident that I could quickly learn your style and procedures, and I would welcome being trained to do things your way.

Yours sincerely,

Jacob Evangelisto

In the following pages you will see examples of letters and essays written especially for applying for admission to law school.

In essays and personal statements viewed as part of an application process, you are often asked to reveal your philosophy, values, ideas, and goals. Although these samples are provided to give you some ideas and insights, it's very important to be yourself!

Usually an essay is a tool for conveying autobiographical information. In this section, you will see an essay used as part of the application process for law school which presents autobiographical information in an effort to explain slow academic progress. This letter is called a "personal statement" and is a formal part of the application process for many graduate schools. Personal statements often provide an opportunity to explain erratic periods in your past.

In essays and personal statements, you are trying to create a memorable, appealing image of yourself, and you are attempting to develop, in words, a "picture" of who you are and who you want to be. Avoid cliched expressions which will make you appear the same as everybody else. Use words and phrases, based on your unique life experiences and circumstances, that will make you "come alive" and appear unique.

Date

Exact Name of Person
Exact Title
Exact Name of Company
Address
City, State, Zip

APPLYING TO LAW SCHOOL

Actually this individual never gave a thought to applying to law school until he got out of college! Now he realizes that law school may be a way of achieving his career goals.

Dear Exact Name of Person: (or Dear Sir or Madam if answering a blind ad):

With the enclosed resume, I would like to make you aware of my desire to make application for enrollment in your law school in the fall.

As you will see from my resume, I earned a B.A. degree in Criminal Justice from the University of South Carolina where I excelled as a campus and fraternity leader. In my senior year, I was recruited by a senior executive of the General Motors Management Services Company for a part-time position which involved interacting with local clients of the company. The executive who recruited me (as a result of chance social meeting) thought that my outgoing personality would "go down well" with the company's clients, and I spent much of my senior year entertaining the company's local customers and cementing relationships. It was certainly a great part-time job for my senior year!

After college graduation, I was offered a full-time management position with General Motors Management Services Company. Prior to assuming my first position, I completed extensive training related to union labor laws, safety laws and regulations, and industrial plant operations. After assuming my position as a Program Manager, I assumed responsibility for managing a new start-up for General Motors, and I supervised up to 40 employees in the process.

During my senior year in college and afterward, I have become aware of my great need to understand the law as it affects labor and the business environment. It is my desire to specialize someday in the area of safety and environmental law, and it is my goal to make a significant contribution to writing legislation which will make the workplace a safer place for employees and the environment a safer place for us all while assuring that business is creating safe and environmentally friendly products for consumers.

I hope you will favorably consider my application for law school. I feel that I will be a significant credit to the profession one day.

Sincerely,

Dean F. Daschal

DEAN F. DASCHAL

1110½ Hay Street, Fayetteville, NC 28305 • preppub@aol.com • (910) 483-6611

OBJECTIVE	I seek admission to a law school that can use a resourceful problem solver and strategic thinker who offers an ability to work effectively with others through applying my outgoing personality, communication skills, and ability to help disputing parties resolve differences.
EDUCATION	Earned a **B.A. degree in Criminal Justice,** University of South Carolina, Columbia, SC, 2001. Made the Dean's List in my senior year.

- Elected Social Chairman of the fraternity Phi Delta Pi; provided strong leadership through my ability to organize social activities as well as philanthropic events which benefited children and the elderly. Was widely regarded as the "social conscience" of this fraternity. Discovered my knack for motivating others to participate in community service and charitable activities.
- Was active in intramural sports including volleyball, water polo, and surfing. During two summer vacations traveled with skilled amateur surfers to Mexico and other Central American countries.
- Partially financed my college education through part-time work as a carpenter.

Graduated from Graceland High School, Nashville, TN, 1995.

- Lettered in football, track, and wrestling. Served as an elected officer in the Key Club.

PROFESSIONAL TRAINING

Completed five months of executive training designed to increase my knowledge of contract law as it relates to a union shop; General Motors, Detroit, MI. Jan-May 2001.

- Gained insight into how an industrial plant operates. Was trained to audit employees' work, schedule payroll and job tasks, document employee hours, report daily incidents, and perform safety inspections "by the book" in hazardous areas.
- At General Motor's huge training complex, took classes in UAW law, safety law, and other areas. Developed an understanding of union shop laws.
- Interacted extensively with UAW lawyers and union employees, and gained insight into how the UAW employee handbook is considered the authority in matters of grievances.
- Was trained in the process of contract bidding and contract negotiation.

EXPERIENCE

PROGRAM MANAGER. General Motors Management Services, Charleston, SC (2001-present). Was aggressively recruited during my senior year in college by a senior vice president of a company which is the second largest manufacturer of automobile safety devices in the U.S. Major American companies outsource key functions to General Motors Services; for example, the company provides management services to automotive facilities in 13 states.

- **Sales and public relations:** Began working in my senior year in a part-time sales job; called on established accounts and entertained clients in order to cement relationships.
- **Consulting and relationship management:** During my intensive five-month training program after college graduation, the company won a major contract, and I worked with a senior corporate official to hire and train employees, design job tasks, equip the customer's facility with equipment, and develop relationships with union employees.
- **Contract and program management:** Relocated to Charleston, SC, in 2001 after the company won a major contract with Siemens Diesel Systems. Was promoted to Program Manager and assumed responsibilities for directing management services provided to a new facility built to surpass the rising EPA emission standards placed on the trucking industry by producing a new product: a virtually emission-free diesel fuel injector. Managed up to 40 employees.

REFERENCES

Can provide outstanding references including references from my current employer.

Personal Statement and Biographical Sketch
James Allen Collins
North Georgia University School of Law

PERSONAL STATEMENT AS PART OF AN APPLICATION TO LAW SCHOOL

Often an essay is an opportunity to "explain" a reckless or irresponsible period in one's life. This individual is seeking admission to law school at middle age, and he provides an intensely personal glimpse into who he is, where he's been, why he's done some of the things he's done, and what he wants to do now.

I respectfully ask the admissions committee to consider the following factors when evaluating my undergraduate academic record. After graduation from high school, I was financially unable to enter college. I worked in a local factory while continuing to work on the family farm. I came from a family of eight children and grew up in rural eastern Georgia. Most of my life—through age 16—we were sharecroppers. During my sophomore year in high school, my father obtained an entry-level civil service job. We then moved to our own family farm which my parents had bought when my father returned from World War II. This was the first opportunity we had to farm our own land rather than to sharecrop. The income from my father's job and our farm still barely kept us above the poverty level. I'm not sure that it did.

I am the third oldest child and the oldest son. When my father began working in the public job, I took over the running of the family farm. My parents believed strongly in education and sacrificed a great deal to see that we were provided with a quality education. We also sacrificed for each other. My oldest sister graduated from high school and went to work to help provide for us. When my next sister graduated, she was able to attend college a semester later. I enrolled at Georgia State University two years later with no outside financial aid. I worked part time and full time. I had six younger siblings who were still in school and who ranged in age from elementary through high school. I felt guilty, and my grades suffered. After dropping in and out of school several times, I decided to stay out of school and help the younger children. I knew that I would eventually return to college. In many respects, I'm glad that I made the decision to stay out of school and concentrate on helping support the family.

When my father died, my younger siblings needed my financial and moral support even more than before. Besides helping my family, I experienced a lot of personal growth during my absence from college. I completed the automotive mechanics course at the local community college and worked as a mechanic at a local dealership. I also repaired and serviced vehicles for many of the elderly and needy people in the community free of charge, because they needed the assistance. I still do some of this type of work when time permits.

After I entered military service, I experienced much of life that I never would have been able to experience otherwise. Besides serving my country, I also had the opportunity to provide for and help shape the lives of many individuals. I found a lifetime mate with like ideals and similar interests and who is also unselfish and dedicated to serving humanity. This time when I returned to college, I was able to work without the distractions of worrying about my family's basic needs. Five of the eight children in my family have earned bachelor's or advanced degrees and the other three have technical degrees and have done very well in their courses. I made the Dean's List each of my last four semesters even though I had a lot of earlier incompletes and failing grades to overcome. I am a hard worker and can excel in a rigorous curriculum.

WHAT IS YOUR PROFESSIONAL ORIENTATION?

My Professional Orientation

I have a passionate desire to work in the public service sector of criminal law. Though America is by far the greatest country in this world, we have a long way to go. I know first hand that we don't all start out in life on an equal footing. As a minority I know that I have a responsibility to help level the field. I have experienced first hand the obstacles and road blocks that too often impede the pursuit of the basic rights of all humans. I know what it's like to be under-represented or not represented at all. I know what it's like to overcome adversity. I know that adversity builds character. It also makes one a better advocate. Unless you really understand what it's like to be in another's situation, you cannot be the best advocate. I grew up financially strapped, but I know that lack of funds does not necessarily hinder one's success. I was born with an ear condition that left me deaf in one ear. It probably could have been corrected had we been able to afford proper treatment. Despite this setback, I overcame and often excelled.

There are many people with a lot to offer our society if given the slightest of opportunities. I began my military career as an enlisted man. I knew first hand what those at the lower ranks and pay grades must endure. When I became a non-commissioned officer and later a commissioned officer, I could better serve and lead because of understanding and being able to see all sides. Too many times I've been an "only" or "one of the few." I've been the "only" Chinese NCO in my section. I've been the "only" Chinese company commander in a battalion. I've been "one of the few" minority commissioned officers on a post. I've been the "only" Chinese profit center manager in a company I worked for, and later "one of the few" in each of these situations. I've tried to be a good advocate. I've personally helped many Chinese, blacks, whites, and other nationalities to succeed, despite the odds against them, and to realize their full potential—even though some of them would have been considered more "fortunate" than I. I've seen that many times some individuals in positions of authority place their personal agenda above the rights of others.

I want to be in a position to help insure "justice for all." I know that passion and commitment alone are not sufficient to do what I want to do. I need a legal education and a law degree to be equipped with the knowledge and credentials necessary for me to make a positive impact on our criminal justice system.

I am drawn to North Georgia School of Law because I know of its strong reputation in areas of advocacy. I personally know many North Georgia lawyers who set the standard for others to emulate. My personal lawyer is a North Georgia graduate. North Georgia is my undergraduate alma mater. I believe this fine institution's areas of expertise are an excellent fit for my goals.

ESSAY IN APPLICATION FOR ADMISSION TO LAW SCHOOL

This essay is intended to convey his passion for and commitment to the area of law which he wishes to study.

PERSONAL STATEMENT OF MICHAEL MCHALE
Northeastern University

What is your professional orientation?

I am particularly interested in specializing in environmental law, and this interest evolved in college and has strengthened since then. As you will see from my resume, since graduating from college I have worked in Tahoe Resort Company which is just 50 miles from Tahoe. As one of 28 professional ski patrollers, I participate in a wide variety of tasks related to keeping the mountains skiable and safeguarding guests.

While working in this winter paradise, I have become knowledgeable of environmental issues regarding wildlife endangerment, air pollution, overpopulation, and diminishing scarce resources as well as problems posed by hazardous wastes and toxic substances. Just recently I have seen first-hand the dangers posed by population growth as I have observed problems caused by the doubling of Tahoe County's population in the last five years. Furthermore, the population is expected to double again in five years; air pollution originating from Tahoe just 40 minutes away is noticeable; and species of wildlife such as mountain lions and black bears and even deer, which used to be abundant here, are scarce. I want to be a part of shaping and defending environmental policies in the U.S., and I believe my talent for working with people would make me an effective legal consensus builder between those who want to save all the land and those who want permission to build anything.

A lawyer from Washington State who befriended me when we discussed these issues recently said that he would gladly assist me in obtaining an internship with the Bureau of Land Management or the EPA during one of the summers after I enroll in law school.

I have a passionate desire to work in public service in the environmental area, and I believe that having a passion for something—such as I do for the environment—is a critical factor in becoming an effective advocate. I know, however, that passion and commitment are not sufficient by themselves to do what I want to do. I need a legal education and a law degree in order to be equipped with the knowledge and credential necessary for me to make a positive impact on environmental policy within the U.S. Again, that is why I am drawn to Northeastern University: I know of its strong reputation in the areas of environment law and advocacy, and I believe this fine institution's areas of expertise are an excellent fit with my strategic goals.

WHY SHOULD YOU BE SELECTED TO ATTEND LAW SCHOOL?

I am a hard worker with proven ingenuity and resourcefulness.

Using the resume I am enclosing with my application, I can demonstrate that I am a resourceful hard worker. I have worked since I was 15 years old in jobs that included setting up a business "from scratch" when I was a junior in high school. In that business called Your Helping Hand, Inc., I applied my entrepreneurial instincts as my best friend and I contracted with loggers for oak logs which my partner and I split, stacked, dried during the summer months, and then delivered during the winter months in a business from which we grossed $8,000 annually.

I have acquired excellent work habits.

From that experience I learned valuable lessons about what it takes to form a successful partnership. During the summers and college breaks, I also held jobs as a trim carpenter and as an aide/landscape technician in a large construction company. Through those jobs I learned that the productivity of every person in an organization is important; for example, it was my work as a landscape technician which was often the general public's "first impression" of a new development, and a poor outside appearance would have discredited even the finest inside operation. My favorite jobs, however, and those which most related to my professional interests, were those in which I cultivated a love for the outdoors and a reverence for nature.

I offer a respect for the outdoors and a desire to be a steward.

In the summer of 1995 I was a senior counselor at a well respected camp for boys called Camp Verity, and since graduating from college I have worked in Vail, Colorado, as a Professional Ski Patroller, a job which has required extensive training in areas related to search and rescue, medical emergency care, and other areas. I have become well acquainted with the day-to-day problems involving the environment and natural resources which I sincerely seek to protect through sensible actions that balance the need for growth with the need for conservation. Equipped with a law degree, I believe I can be a powerful tool for practical problem solving in the area of environmental stewardship in the 21st century.

WHY SHOULD YOU BE SELECTED TO ATTEND LAW SCHOOL?

This essay is intended to emphasize his capacity for hard work and ingenuity. Know the points you are trying to make in your essay. Don't just "drift" from thought to thought in an incoherent pattern.

DEVELOP A SUMMARY OF THE OVERALL GOAL YOU HAVE FOR YOUR LIFE.

DEVELOP A SUMMARY OF THE OVERALL GOAL YOU HAVE FOR YOUR LIFE.

Essays provide an opportunity for the admissions committee to see how you write, how you think, and how you feel. Don't be afraid of showing your emotion.
Note: This essay was written especially for a school which is strongly religious.

I feel that God is calling me toward a legal career which involves playing a role in shaping family law policy and intervention in the U.S.

I have a great respect for family values and the sanctity of familial bonds, and since earning my B.S. degree in Social Work, I have worked as a family counselor for the City of Detroit. Working with fractured families, families for whom crime is a daily reality, I have become knowledgeable of the legal system in a hands-on way. I have also seen how the law can unintentionally hurt the indigent.

Just recently a family that I have aided over an extended period of time has been able to send their eldest child to college. I have seen first-hand the dangers individuals encounter when they are without representation. I want to be part of shaping and defending children's rights policies in the U.S., and I believe my talent for working with people would make me an effective legal consensus builder between those who want to save family structure and those who want to provide the best environment for children.

A lawyer for a woman whom I have counseled has offered to assist me by providing an internship position with his firm, provided that I am accepted to law school. I have a passionate desire to work in the public service arena, but I know that passion alone is not enough. I know a legal education is the necessary tool I need in order to do the good I envision.

I have examined your university's second and third-year elective courses and feel that they, along with the Christian philosophy that your university endorses, are tailored to my spiritual needs and professional goals.

SPECIAL FACTORS AFFECTING MY
UNDERGRADUATE EDUCATION

I would respectfully ask the admissions committee to consider the following factors in evaluating my undergraduate academic record. After receiving a $1,000 academic scholarship to Georgia College and State University, I enrolled and began my academic career in my hometown of Milledgeville, Georgia. I got off to a good start academically and was elected a Senator in Student Government.

Then I made a poor decision to transfer to Georgia Perimeter College in Clarkston, Georgia, because my best friend was there and I wanted to "get away from home." After declaring my major as pre-med, I chose to enroll in some of the most difficult pre-med courses offered and joined a fraternity. My grades suffered as I began to realize that attending medical school was not my choice but the choice my parents had encouraged me to make. That realization was also the birth of my decision to apply to law school after college; I had "grown up" to a new level and had a fresh understanding of my professional goals.

I then transferred to Mercer University-Macon in Macon, Georgia, declared my major in Political Science and Political Philosophy, and went inactive in my fraternity after one semester in order to concentrate on academics. As a senior, I performed with distinction in a graduate-level course in International Law, for which I wrote and orally defended a 50-page paper on Cuban Refugees. Once I found my true academic "fit" and realized my career goal, my grades began to improve, although my GPA is not as strong as I would like it to be.

I ask that the admissions committee examine the attached resume because you will see that I am a hard worker who has held part-time and summer jobs since I was 15 years old. I am very proud of my parents and grateful to them for their parenting of me, but I feel that my uneasy undergraduate years also reflect my desire to seek my own identity apart from my two exceptionally talented parents—my mother owns and manages a large website business, and my father is a successful convenience store entrepreneur. In a way, I grew up under the shadow of two strong and successful business people and I believe my undergraduate years were a struggle to discover my own identity and God-given talents.

Going to law school is not the "easy way out" for me. The "easy way out" would be for me to accept a professional home in either my mother's or my father's company. But I feel strongly that the study of law is what will best equip me personally to combine my analytical skills, public speaking ability, capacity for hard work, and sincere instinct for public service. I am an individual who lives by high principles and morals, and I feel certain I would one day be a credit to the law profession as I make contributions in public sector policymaking.

SPECIAL FACTORS AFFECTING MY UNDERGRADUATE EDUCATION
If you are presented with such a question, view it as an opportunity to explain a weak area in your background.

REVIEW YOUR RESPONSES AND STATE ANY ADDITIONAL INFORMATION THAT MIGHT HELP TO GIVE AN ACCURATE PICTURE OF YOUR PERSONAL, SPIRITUAL, ACADEMIC, AND PROFESSIONAL GOALS.

REVIEW YOUR RESPONSES AND STATE ANY ADDITIONAL INFORMATION THAT MIGHT HELP TO GIVE AN ACCURATE PICTURE OF YOUR PERSONAL, SPIRITUAL, ACADEMIC, AND PROFESSIONAL GOALS.

Here is an essay written for a law school which is strongly religious in orientation.

I am a person who never gives up. Even when I hit a low point in college, wondering what I really needed to be doing with my life, I never felt like quitting for a moment. I am a tough, resilient, persevering individual and, indeed, even my current job as a Paramedic requires utmost discipline at all times. I take my commitments very seriously, and I am seriously committed to undertaking the study of law.

Although my personal, spiritual, academic and professional goals may seem eclectic if viewed from afar, they are closely tied by the underlying desire to achieve, become, and succeed.

My personal goals include bettering my rock-climbing skills and eventually scaling one of the highest peaks in my area. I am also an accomplished runner. I believe firmly in community commitment and volunteer time to teach inner city children self reliance as well as teamwork through learning to function in the wilderness.

Spiritual goals are so often difficult to define. I am firmly committed to growing spiritually and am convinced that God is leading me. My main spiritual goal is to do what is right according to my religious beliefs.

Academically I hope to graduate from your program near the top of my class. I am determined to absorb the law as fully as humanly possible. I also hope to become involved in student organizations that assist the local legal community in providing *pro bono* work for the elderly and impoverished.

Professionally I hope to one day be a leader in the field of law. Although I am currently not sure what area I wish to specialize in, I feel that my competitive spirit and drive to excel will aid in me in any endeavor that I undertake.

DO YOU FEEL THAT UNDERGRADUATE GPA IS A GOOD INDICATOR OF AN INDIVIDUAL'S CAPACITY FOR INTENSE STUDY?

I do not believe my undergraduate GPA is a good indicator of my intellect and capacity for intense study.

I would respectfully ask that the Admissions Committee look at my GPA and consider the fact that I was uncertain of my professional goals during my college years. I entered college at the very young age of seventeen. I was unprepared for the level of self-discipline and academic rigors with which I was faced. I suddenly found that, although I had the self-discipline required to maintain academic viability, I did not possess the desire to achieve my full potential. I felt aimless. I considered leaving college but I possess a tenacious personality not given to quitting. Although I struggled for the first half of my college career, a fact that my grade point average reflects, the second half of my college career was exemplary. As I matured, I was elected president of the college newspaper, The Source. Then, I took a class that changed my life. The class, Courts and Criminal Procedures, was required for my degree in journalism. I quickly became enthralled with the law. I changed my major to pre-law and suddenly found myself excelling academically. I found my strong communication and analytical skills could best be utilized in the legal arena. My initial lack of focus during my undergraduate career had a negative impact on my GPA, but out of that turbulence was born the firm conviction that I belong in the legal arena working to assure that we meet the responsibilities placed reverently on our shoulders by our forefathers when they signed the constitution that governs us to this day. I am a tireless worker with great intellectual acumen, and I regret that my GPA does not clearly reveal that. At age 25, I now have a clear vision of what my goals are and how they may be achieved. I ask the Admissions Committee to look beyond my cumulative GPA and see the fact that I was in the midst of a great personal and professional transition which is explained more fully in the next paragraph.

WHAT HAVE BEEN YOUR GREATEST BLESSINGS AND OBSTACLES?

I am very grateful to my parents and value the strong example they both have provided for me in being moral, hard-working individuals. They provided me with exceptional care, educational opportunities, and spiritual guidance. When I graduated at seventeen, they feared that I would not attend college if I did not enroll immediately. Living up to their high standards has always been important to me, but after beginning my college education, I realized that I should have taken a year to grow and mature before devoting myself to college. It was a hard lesson, but one that taught me that only I know the appropriate direction for my life. My undergraduate GPA reflects this struggle to find out who I was and what I wanted to do with my life. I think that this growth period in my life was essential, if difficult, and provided me with the gift of perspective that I had previously lacked. It enabled me to recognize the perfect fit my talents and goals have with the legal field when I first studied criminal law. I could have dropped out of college when I first encountered difficulties and thereby preserved my GPA. That would have been the easiest thing for me to do, but it would have betrayed my belief in perseverance in the face of uncertainty. My parents cast a long shadow, and I believe I was in their shadow until my sophomore year of college, when I began to find my own shadow and define my own career goals.

DO YOU FEEL THAT UNDERGRADUATE GPA IS A GOOD INDICATOR OF AN INDIVIDUAL'S CAPACITY FOR INTENSE STUDY?

This essay question could be viewed as an opportunity to wax philosophical or "sound like a lawyer," or it could be used as an opportunity to explain a low GPA in one's past academic record.

In this section, you will find resumes and cover letters of professionals seeking employmen᠊ or already employed, in the legal and paralegal field. How do these individuals diffe᠊ from other job hunters? Why should there be a book dedicated to people seeking jobs in the legal and paralegal field? Based on more than 20 years of experience in working with job hunters, this editor is convinced that resumes and cover letters which "speak the lingo" of the field you wish to enter will communicate more effectively than language which is not industry-specific. This book is designed to help people (1) who are seeking to prepare their own resumes and (2) who wish to use as models "real" resumes of individuals who have successfully launched careers in the legal and paralegal field or advanced in the field. You will see a wide range of experience levels reflected in the resumes in this book. Some of the resumes and cover letters were used by individuals seeking to enter the field; others were used successfully by senior professionals to advance in the field.

Newcomers to an industry sometimes have advantages over more experienced professionals. In a job hunt, junior professionals can have an advantage over their more experienced counterparts. Prospective employers often view the less experienced workers as "more trainable" and "more coachable" than their seniors. This means that the mature professional who has already excelled in a first career can, with credibility, "change careers" and transfer skills to other industries.

Newcomers to the field may have disadvantages compared to their seniors. Almost by definition, the inexperienced professional—the young person who has recently entered the job market, or the individual who has recently received respected certifications—is less tested and less experienced than senior managers, so the resume and cover letter of the inexperienced professional may often have to "sell" his or her potential to do something he or she has never done before. Lack of experience in the field she wants to enter can be a stumbling block to the junior employee, but remember that many employers believe that someone who has excelled in anything—academics, for example—can excel in many other fields.

Some advice to inexperienced professionals...
If senior professionals could give junior professionals a piece of advice about careers, here's what they would say: Manage your career and don't stumble from job to job in an incoherent pattern. Try to find work that interests you, and then identify prosperous industries which need work performed of the type you want to do. Learn early in your working life that a great resume and cover letter can blow doors open for you and help you maximize your salary.

Special help for career changers...
For those changing careers, you will find useful the resumes and cover letters marked "Career Change" on the following pages. Consult the Table of Contents for page numbers showing career changers.

CAREER CHANGE

Date

Exact Name of Person
Title or Position
Name of Company
Address (no., street)
Address (city, state, zip)

ASSISTANT BOOKKEEPER & COLLECTOR

for a finance company is seeking to transition into a law firm. Although she lacks experience in the legal environment, her skills and qualities are those typically sought by law firms.

Dear Exact Name of Person: (or Dear Sir or Madam if answering a blind ad.)

I would appreciate an opportunity to talk with you soon about how I could contribute to your organization through my experience as an Assistant Bookkeeper and Collector. I am responding to your recent advertisement for a collections specialist.

As you will see from my resume, I am employed as an Assistant Bookkeeper and Collector for Money Tree Finance. During my final year in high school, I began working for this finance company part-time as a Customer Service Representative and was immediately hired full-time upon high school graduation. I have been entrusted with the responsibility of opening and closing the office. I work with customers taking payments, clearing applications, and processing loans as well as performing collections, including outside collections of 30, 60, and 90 day accounts receivable. I am skilled in checking credit by CBI, Equifax, and TRW and have participated in a variety of telephone and mail solicitations. I have handled every type of office task including typing, filing, and operating a computer. After managing an increasing amount of responsibility, I was promoted to perform bookkeeping and accounting duties as well as end-of-month close outs.

You would find me to be a congenial and poised young person known for having "maturity beyond my years." I can provide an outstanding reference from my employer, who frequently commends my gracious manner of dealing with the public as well as my personal qualities of reliability, dependability, and loyalty to the company.

I hope you will welcome my call soon to arrange a brief meeting at your convenience to discuss your needs and how I might serve them. Thank you in advance for your time.

Yours sincerely,

Shanda E. Hamilton

Alternate last paragraph:
I hope you will call or write soon to suggest a time convenient for us to meet and discuss your current and future needs and how I might serve them. Thank you in advance for your time.

SHANDA E. HAMILTON

1110½ Hay Street, Fayetteville, NC 28305   •   preppub@aol.com   •   (910) 483-6611

OBJECTIVE   I want to contribute to an organization that can use a hardworking young professional who takes pride in my exceptional customer service, communication, and sales skills.

EXPERIENCE   **ASSISTANT BOOKKEEPER & COLLECTOR.** Money Tree Finance Company, Savannah, GA (2004-present). Began working for this finance company part-time as a Customer Service Representative during high school and was immediately hired full-time upon high school graduation.

- Was entrusted with the responsibility of opening and closing the office.
- Have worked with customers taking payments, clearing applications, and processing loans.
- Perform collections, mostly by telephone but sometimes outside collections as well, of 30, 60, and 90 day accounts receivable.
- Am skilled in checking credit by CBI, Equifax, and TRW.
- Participate in a variety of telephone and mail solicitations.
- Handle every type of office task including typing, filing, and operating a computer.
- Am knowledgeable of all aspects of finance company operations, and was commended for my attention to detail in handling bookkeeping and accounting activities.
- Can provide an outstanding reference from my employer, who frequently commends me for my gracious manner of dealing with the public as well as for my personal qualities of reliability, dependability, and loyalty to the company.
- Was increasingly promoted into responsibilities related to bookkeeping and accounting; handled the end-of-month close out and assisted the manager in various accounting tasks.
- Type nearly 80 words per minute.

EDUCATION   Graduated from Alice Byrney High School, Savannah, GA, 2003.
Completed numerous technical and management training programs sponsored by Money Tree Finance Company.

STRENGTHS
- Friendly, outgoing, very self-confident personality.
- Fast learner. Hard worker.
- Dependable and reliable.
- Highly intelligent and can rapidly master new tasks.
- Enjoy serving the public and working with people.

COMPUTERS   Proficient in utilizing a computer with a variety of software, including popular software and software and customized programs. Experienced with both Windows XP and Microsoft Office Suite.

PERSONAL   Am a very creative, energetic, and highly motivated individual. Enjoy painting, walking and fishing. Utilized my drama skills in my spare time with the Savannah College of Art and Design–Fine Arts Theatre.

CAREER CHANGE

Date

Exact Name of Person
Exact Title
Exact Name of Company
Address
City, State, Zip

BOOKING & INTAKE TECHNICIAN

for a sheriff's department is seeking a legal assistant or clerical position within a law firm

Dear Exact Name of Person: (or Dear Sir or Madam if answering a blind ad):

With the enclosed resume I would like to make you aware of my interest in any legal assistance or clerical/secretarial positions you may have available.

As you will see from my resume, I am employed as a Booking and Intake Technician for the Grayson County Sheriff's Department in Denison, TX. In charge of fingerprinting, photographing, and collecting biographical information for the completion of processing individuals in the criminal justice system, I maintain a daily log of individuals fingerprinted and perform criminal record checks on individuals brought in for arrest. Although I am excelling in my job, I would enjoy applying my administrative skills for the benefit of a law firm.

In multiple positions as an temporary employee for the U.S. Government, I refined my customer service and office automation skills. I also learned how to adapt quickly to new environments, and I was praised for my ability to rapidly master new software and computer systems.

I hope you will call or write me soon to suggest a time convenient for us to meet and discuss your current and future needs and how I might serve them. Thank you in advance for your time.

Sincerely yours,

Virginia N. Stokes

VIRGINIA N. STOKES

1110½ Hay Street, Fayetteville, NC 28305 • preppub@aol.com • (910) 483-6611

OBJECTIVE

I want to contribute to an organization that can use a dependable, hardworking professional with versatile skills related to office administration, computer operations, and data entry.

EDUCATION

Associate of Applied Science in Business Administration, Alvin Community College, Alvin, TX, 2002.
Completed training sponsored by the U.S. Government in software including Microsoft Word, Excel, Access, and PowerPoint.

EXPERIENCE

BOOKING & INTAKE TECHNICIAN. Grayson County Sheriff's Department, Denison, TX (2004-present). In charge of fingerprinting, photographing, and collecting biographical information for the completion of processing individuals in the criminal justice system; maintain daily log of individuals fingerprinted and perform criminal record checks on individuals brought in for arrest. Accurately and efficiently operate data conversion equipment in transforming information from source documents to computer input forms; demonstrate the ability to key data on a computer terminal at a prescribed rate and have successfully completed all assignments.

Refined my customer service and office automation skills while excelling in the following U.S. Government temporary assignments, Denison, TX (1999-04):
2003-04: DATA ENTRY TRANSCRIBER. Department of Labor, Denison, TX. Demonstrated exceptional skills in operating data transcription equipment while operating keyboard-controlled equipment to transcribe data entered onto disc in coded form for transfer to magnetic tape and input to digital computer; from memory, or by reference to code notebook or other guide, selected and entered program control code for desired format from 100 different variations.
2002-03: DATA ENTRY OPERATOR. Grayson County Finance Department, Denison, TX. Refined oral communication skills while researching financial discrepancies in multiple departments; contacted supervisors in various departments to verify time cards and produce paychecks.
2001-02: MEDICAL RECORDS CLERK. Grayson County Mental Health, Denison, TX. Maintained medical records; processed medical records release requests; pulled/logged charts; prepared daily schedules for each individual doctor.
1999-01: ADMINISTRATIVE SPECIALIST. Housing Authority of Alvin, Alvin, TX. Refined my written communication skills and exceptional proofreading capabilities preparing documents and materials in draft and final copy using Microsoft Word, Excel and Access.
- Typed confidential documents and correspondence including special reports, requisitions, forms, regulations, and directives.
- Assembled final product for review, signature, authentication, or other disposition.
- Opened, sorted, routed, and delivered incoming correspondence and messages; prepared suspense control documents and maintained suspense files; maintained publications.
- Determined proper functional files and file numbers posted to documents; destroyed or disposed of files in accordance with disposition instructors.
- Posted changes to regulations and directives; received and stocked blank forms.

COMPUTER SKILLS

Proficient with Windows XP, Microsoft Word, Excel, Access, PowerPoint, and PageMaker as well as Unisys terminal mainframes.

PERSONAL

Am a quick learner and a determined professional known for my cheerful disposition. Perform well under pressure. Excel at setting priorities. Take pride in a job well done.

CAREER CHANGE

Date

Exact Name of Person
Title or Position
Name of Company
Address (no., street)
Address (city, state, zip)

**CASHIER &
ASSISTANT
MANAGER**
for a gas station is
seeking to make a
career change into the
legal system.

Dear Exact Name of Person: (or Dear Sir or Madam if answering a blind ad.)

I would appreciate an opportunity to talk with you soon about how I could contribute to your organization through my paralegal training, investigative skills, and analytical ability as well as through my "common sense" and "street smarts."

As you will see from my resume, I have recently completed a degree in Paralegal Technology which I would like to put to use for your benefit. Previously I have excelled in jobs as a manager, inventory controller, and investigator, and I have always found resourceful ways to increase sales, efficiency, and customer satisfaction. I offer the ability to work well with people from all backgrounds and economic levels, and I enjoy the challenges associated with helping people, solving problems, and identifying new opportunities. I can provide outstanding references from my current and previous employers.

I decided to pursue training in paralegal technology because I have always been told that I have exceptional analytical and problem-solving skills. During the course of earning my degree, I refined my written communication skills as well as my ability to analyze large volumes of data in order to extract the "essence."

I hope you will welcome my call soon to arrange a brief meeting at your convenience to discuss your current and future needs and how I might serve them. Thank you in advance for your time.

Sincerely yours,

Gerald R. Samuels

Alternate last paragraph:
I hope you will call or write me soon to suggest a time convenient for us to meet and discuss your current and future needs and how I might serve them. Thank you in advance for your time.

GERALD R. SAMUELS

1110½ Hay Street, Fayetteville, NC 28305   •   preppub@aol.com   •   (910) 483-6611

OBJECTIVE

To contribute to an organization that can use a skilled paralegal who offers considerable experience in dealing with the public, managing business operations, investigating security problems, and controlling inventory and warehouse activities.

EDUCATION

Earned **Associate of Science** degree in **Paralegal Technology**, Tacoma Community College, Tacoma, WA, 2004.

COMPUTERS

Highly proficient with Word, Excel, Access, PowerPoint.

EXPERIENCE

CASHIER & ASSISTANT MANAGER. Exxon, Tacoma, WA (2003-present). Have excelled in this job while also pursuing my associate's degree; serve up to 500 customers in an eight-hour shift which produces $1,200 in revenue.
- Based on a customer survey conducted by the business, personally achieved an exceptionally high 97% customer satisfaction level in my dealings with customers.

MANAGER. Smokey's Barbecue, Tacoma, WA (2001-03). Increased revenue nearly 400% and created an atmosphere in this lounge which maximized repeat business in a town where there is much competition for the entertainment dollars spent by the consumer.
- Became skilled in "putting together" all the ingredients that go into creating a relaxed and friendly environment where people want to be.

INVENTORY CONTROLLER/STOCK CHECKER. Piccadilly's, Tacoma, WA (1999-01). Was frequently commended for my ability to handle large work loads with poise and to excel under pressure; learned the inventory control system used by Piccadilly's Cafeteria and also learned the importance of maintaining the stock room in a sanitary condition.
- Prepared food items for various chefs.
- Was a versatile and adaptable worker who was always willing to do whatever task needed to be done, from unloading trucks to accounting for outgoing items.

MANAGER. Visions Elite, Tacoma, WA (1997-99). Handled all aspects of managing this club including paying bills, preparing payroll, ordering and purchasing stock, monitoring memberships, and even cleaning the building when necessary.
- Often worked up to 16 hours a day in a club which produced $10,000 a week in revenue.
- Developed a management style that I could vary according to the types of personalities I needed to motivate; thoroughly enjoyed working with the fine staff I managed.

INVESTIGATOR & GUARD. Morgan Stanley & Dean Witter, Tacoma, WA (1997). Discovered that I have exceptionally strong investigative skills while working as an investigator and guard. During a strike, protected replacement workers and identified potentially violent situations with the union.
- Refined my public relations skills working in highly emotional situations.

ROUTE DRIVER. The Tacoma Daily, Tacoma, WA (1993-96). Through hard work, rapidly doubled my commission sales on this route while delivering wholesale magazines, books, games, and other items to retail outlets.
- Became skilled in managing my time for maximum efficiency; invented methods of delivery that led to coverage of this route in 3 1/2 days compared to the normal five days.

PERSONAL

Enjoy working with the public. Work well under pressure. References available upon request.

CAREER CHANGE

Date

Exact Name of Person
Exact Title
Exact Name of Company
Address
City, State, Zip

CIVIL EXECUTIONS CLERK

is seeking to use her newly minted degree in "Office Systems Technology with a concentration in Legal Studies" in order to make a career change as a Legal Assistant. This letter is designed to be "all purpose" so that she can send the letter introducing herself and her resume to nearly all the law firms in the city where she works.

Dear Exact Name of Person (or Dear Sir or Madam if answering a blind ad):

With the enclosed resume, I would like to make you aware of my interest in seeking employment with your organization. As you will see, I have recently earned an Associate's degree in Office Systems Technology with a concentration in Legal Studies, and I am eager to put that degree to work for your benefit!

In my current position, I have earned a promotion to increased responsibilities with the Bossier City Police Department. In addition to planning and organizing public auctions of personal and real properties, I supervise the sale of assets by deputies. I compose a variety of legal documents and work closely with deputies as I advise them of legal protocol involved in serving criminal and civil papers. I have acquired many skills and competencies usually possessed by a paralegal and legal assistant, and I have established a very valuable network of contacts within the police department and legal system which could be useful to you.

In my previous position as a Sales Representative, I earned a promotion to a higher level of responsibility while excelling in sales. I was cross-trained in the responsibilities of the Parts Manager and supervised up to eleven people. I can provide excellent references from all my employers.

Known for my strong personal initiative, I have become a valued and respected employee in every job I have held. I am a conscientious worker with outstanding problem-solving ability who always seeks resourceful ways to contribute to my employer's reputation and profitability. If you can use my versatile abilities, I would enjoy an opportunity to talk with you in person. I hope you will welcome my call soon when I try to arrange a brief meeting.

Sincerely,

Amy L. Beringer

AMY L. BERINGER

1110½ Hay Street, Fayetteville, NC 28305   •   preppub@aol.com   •   (910) 483-6611

OBJECTIVE

I want to contribute to an organization that can use a versatile and outgoing professional who has excelled in environments which required outstanding customer service and public relations skills as well as dedicated hard work and attention to detail.

EDUCATION

Associate of Science degree in Office Systems Technology with a concentration in Legal Studies, Bossier Parish Community College, Bossier City, LA, 2004.
- Earned this degree in my spare time at night while excelling in my full-time job.

EXPERIENCE

Have been promoted in this progression with Bossier City Police Department, Bossier City, LA (1999-present):

2003-present: CIVIL EXECUTIONS CLERK. Handle legal paperwork as well as financial collections; process and collect Civil Writs of Execution and State and County Tax Warrants. Am placed in charge of the county desk sergeant's station in his absence.
- Process 200 new executions and tax warrants monthly; recently collected $145,000 in an 11-month period after calculating monies owed (collected more monies than any predecessor). Plan and organize public auctions of levied personal and real properties, and then supervise the conduct of sales by deputies.
- Perform background checks on judgment debtors to assist deputies in locating them.
- Handle data entry of executions/tax warrants into the county's mainframe computer.
- Compose and type sheriff's legal documents including Notices of Hearing, Reports of Sale, and Orders; perform title searches as well as criminal and background checks.
- Supervise inventories of businesses and personal estates which the sheriff closed under order of seizure; advise 18 deputies of legal protocol in serving criminal and civil papers.

1999-02: LEGAL CLERK/DATA ENTRY SPECIALIST. Performed data entry related to most legal processes handled by the sheriff's office including civil and criminal summons, criminal warrants, subpoenas, and notices; operated a two-way radio base unit to assist deputies and also graciously assisted the public and handled telephone inquiries.
- Became skilled in using Clerk of Court computers and the county's mainframe.
- On my own initiative, played a valuable role in assisting the county's data processing department in modifying our tracking system program.

AUTO PARTS SALES REPRESENTATIVE. Rick Hendricks Toyota, Bossier City, LA (1996-98). Earned a promotion with increasing responsibilities because of my dedication, hard work and superior results; began as a Secretary and after five months moved into sales.
- Was cross-trained to perform as the Parts Manager, supervised up to eleven employees.
- Excelled in sales and earned maximum award points based on an incentive system; continuously earned promotion and corresponding increases in my commission structure.
- Utilized the ADP computer system for parts location and inventory control.

Other experience:
- On a temporary six-month job, handled the preparation and mailing of press releases, sales brochures, and souvenir orders for the Bossier Parish Visitor Center.
- As an assembler/packer for Simmons Ice House, frequently acted as assistant supervisor. Created a new form which the warehouse manager adopted as a form for all supervisors to use for their monthly production reports, and also created a new format for recording materials inventory which was implemented warehouse wide.

PERSONAL

Excellent personal and professional references are available upon request.

Date

Exact Name of Person
Title or Position
Name of Company
Address (no., street)
Address (city, state, zip)

CLERK OF COURT
for a district court
in Kentucky

Dear Exact Name of Person: (or Dear Sir or Madam if answering a blind ad.)

I would appreciate an opportunity to talk with you soon about how I could contribute to your organization. I am particularly interested in the position of General Manager of your law firm which you recently advertised in the "Frankfort Gazette."

In my current position as a Clerk of Court for the 6th District Court in Frankfort, I support the work of judges who are involved in rendering judgments in court cases after carefully listening to and considering testimony and evidence. I determine probable cause for the issuance of criminal processes and set conditions for pre-trial release.

Although I am excelling in my current position, I am anticipating a change in administrations next year during the election. Since my job is a politically appointed one, I am anticipating the possibility that I will be asked to resign if a different political party comes into power. I am confident that I could excel in managing a law firm, and I have established a strong network of valuable contacts in the legal community which could be put to work for you. I offer a reputation as a strong administrator and congenial colleague, and I am a well known for my ability to establish and maintain warm working relationships.

I hope you will welcome my call soon to arrange a brief meeting at your convenience to discuss your current and future needs and how I might serve them. Thank you in advance for your time.

Sincerely yours,

Harold I. Houlton

Alternate last paragraph:
I hope you will call or write me soon to suggest a time convenient for us to meet and discuss your current and future needs and how I might serve them. Thank you in advance for your time.

HAROLD I. HOULTON

1110½ Hay Street, Fayetteville, NC 28305 • preppub@aol.com • (910) 483-6611

OBJECTIVE

To offer my management skills and knowledge of legal operations to a law firm which can use a skilled problem-solver who understands the court system.

EXPERIENCE

CLERK OF COURT. 6th District Court, Frankfort, KY (2002-present). Am entrusted with supporting the work of judges who are rendering judgments in court cases after carefully listening to and considering testimony and evidence.

- Prepare the court schedule and advise judges on upcoming cases.
- Coordinate with attorneys and their staffs in assuring that the judicial system works efficiently for the general public.
- This position is a politically appointed one; I was chosen for the position by Sheriff Randy Boswell, after his successful re-election campaign.
- **Private Farmer:** Griffin Produce, Frankfort, KY (1992-present). Simultaneously with the job above, single-handedly farm 20 acres of produce and handle the commercial sale and distribution of goods; established business with Piggly Wiggly and Publix.

REGIONAL MANAGER. Shoe Carnival, Louisville, KY (1995-02). Rapidly achieved a track record of promotions with this popular shoe store and earned a promotion to Regional Manager in 2001; supervised eight district managers in the 40-plus store region.

- Supervised and reviewed hiring and training procedures for all 400 regional employees, overseeing promotion and transfer of store managers and district managers.
- Maintained regional sales quotas as set by the corporate office.
- Controlled payroll and budgeting according to company standards.
- Reviewed and ensured proper merchandise availability in all stores.
- Recommended store remodelings and was responsible for 17 new store openings.

Accomplishments:

- Operated the largest-volume region in the Shoe Carnival company, consistently rated as the first or second region for increased sales.
- Rated "number one" district in the Shoe Carnival company.
- Store achieved the largest dollar increase for Shoe Carnival Shoes.
- Was honored as "Regional Manager of the Year."

Highlights of earlier experience:

- Gained valuable experience through many years of dedication to Phillips Shoe Corp., Louisville, KY; began working part time as a stocker and advanced to sales representative, to assistant manager, to store manager, to district manager, to regional sales manager/ vice president.
- Was born and raised on commercial hog, tobacco, and cotton farms.

EDUCATION

Graduated with **Bachelor of Science** degree in Political Science, University of Kentucky, 1995.
Completed management courses at Frankfort Technical College, Frankfort, KY.
Have attended numerous seminars and workshops related to management with the Phillips Shoe Corporation.

PERSONAL

Outstanding references upon request. Offer a reputation as a strong leader and gifted problem solver. My administrative skills are highly refined.

CAREER CHANGE

Date

Exact Name of Person
Title or Position
Name of Company
Address (number and street)
Address (city, state, and zip)

CORPORATE PARALEGAL

for a law office in Washington, DC, seeks to transition to a political position in an election campaign.

Dear Exact Name of Person: (or Sir or Madam if answering a blind ad.)

I would appreciate an opportunity to talk with you soon about how I could contribute to your upcoming election campaign in some administrative capacity. As you will see from my resume, I worked as a Congressional Intern for two years, and I am knowledgeable of the workings of the U.S. Congress.

Currently employed with Morgan & Bradley Law Offices as a Corporate Paralegal, I work with up to 70 attorneys while organizing, maintaining, and supervising corporate closings including post-closing matters. Respected for my attention to detail, I consistently excel in conducting and analyzing corporate documents and maintaining financial statements. In my Congressional Intern position with Congressman Allen C. Arundel, I researched and answered constituent mail while proficiently operating a computer research program.

As you will see from my resume, I earned a Bachelor of Arts degree in History from the University of Maryland. You would find me to be a hard-working, energetic, and reliable professional who prides myself on doing any job to the best of my ability. I can provide excellent personal and professional references if you request them.

I believe strongly in the electability of Candidate Marilyn Jones, and I hope you will call or write me soon to suggest a time convenient for us to meet and discuss your current and future needs and how I might serve them. Thank you in advance for your time.

Sincerely yours,

Carl P. McHugh

CARL P. McHUGH

1110½ Hay Street, Fayetteville, NC 28305 • preppub@aol.com • (910) 483-6611

OBJECTIVE

To contribute to an organization that can use a skilled corporate paralegal who offers a proven ability to handle multiple simultaneous tasks as well as an outgoing personality which allows me to establish warm working relationships with others.

EXPERIENCE

CORPORATE PARALEGAL. Morgan & Bradley Law Offices, P.A., Washington, DC (2003-present). Was aggressively recruited by this prestigious law firm with 70 attorneys. Am involved in organizing, maintaining, and supervising corporate closings, including post-closing matters.
- Am specially requested by senior attorneys to assist in due diligence.
- Have become known for my attention to detail while preparing closing document binders.
- File and maintain UCC financing statements. Conduct and analyze UCC searches and litigation searches.
- Obtain and analyze corporate documents. Prepare and file corporate documents.
- Maintain corporate minute books.
- Prepare and file copyright, patent, and trademark registrations.
- Prepare and file corporate tax returns and escheat forms.
- Spend approximately 80% of time on large financial transactions.
- Proficient in Microsoft Word. Familiar with WESTLAW.

CONGRESSIONAL INTERN. Congressman Allen C. Arundel, Washington, DC (2001-03). Researched and answered constituent mail and then recommended solutions for constituent problems. Composed letters for the signature of the Councilman.
- Operated a computer research program.

LOAN OFFICER. National Bank of Maryland, Baltimore, MD (1999-01). In a part-time job while earning my college degree, refined my sales and customer service skills while working in the downtown office of one of Maryland's largest banks.
- Executed customer transactions.
- Was commended on my sunny disposition while performing customer service tasks.

EDUCATION

Bachelor of Arts degree in History, University of Maryland, College Park, MD, December 2001
Sigma Gamma Mu Fraternity; member
- Prepared pledge class for initiation.
- Membership Committee; 2003.
- Received recommendations for prospective members.
- Member of the Political Action Committee.

COMPUTERS

Proficient with software including Microsoft Word, Excel, Access, and PowerPoint. Have been exposed to numerous specialized databases used by the legal and law enforcement community.

AFFILIATION

Junior League of Baltimore, Inc.
Member, Young Republicans of Washington, DC

CAREER CHANGE

Date

Exact Name of Person
Exact Title
Exact Name of Company
Address
City, State, Zip

Dear Exact Name of Person: (or Dear Sir or Madam if answering a blind ad):

I would appreciate an opportunity to talk with you soon about how I could contribute to your organization through my versatile skills related to court security and law enforcement.

While working for the United States Marshal Service (USMS), I have established excellent working relationships with individuals from the USMS as well as other law enforcement agencies. I advanced into a supervisory position which involved training and managing other wildlife officers while enforcing state and federal laws related to hunting, fishing, and boating.

In a previous position as a Director for the Oklahoma Wildlife Commission, I refined my leadership ability and problem-solving skills while supervising and directing several wildlife officers in the enforcement of Oklahoma and federal laws related to hunting, fishing, other game activities, and boating. I trained numerous officers in organizing, scheduling, coordinating and inventory control. I also planned and administered budgets of varying sizes for the Wildlife Commission.

Known for my strong personal initiative, I have become a valued and respected employee in every job I have held. I can assure you that I am a conscientious worker with outstanding problem-solving ability, and I always seek resourceful ways to contribute to my employer's reputation and profitability. If you can use my versatile abilities, I would enjoy an opportunity to talk with you in person. I hope you will welcome my call soon when I try to arrange a brief meeting.

Sincerely yours,

Belinda Wuest

BELINDA WUEST

1110½ Hay Street, Fayetteville, NC 28305   •   preppub@aol.com   •   (910) 483-6611

OBJECTIVE	To serve as the United States Marshal for the Western District of Oklahoma.
EXPERIENCE	**COURT SECURITY OFFICER**. United States Marshal Service (USMS), Lawton, OK (2002-present). Have developed excellent working relationships with individuals from the Marshal Service, law enforcement agencies, U.S. attorneys, and the judiciary while involved in a wide range of activities related to providing security and protection.

- *entrance control*: Operate and enforce a system of personal identification which includes checking handbags, packages, and other items to detect weapons and contraband.
- *roving patrol*: Conduct roving patrols of the court area in accordance with schedules.
- *fixed post*: Maintain a fixed, stationary position outside and inside the chambers of courtroom judges and jury rooms in order to prevent unauthorized entrance.
- *personal escort*: Provide a personal escort for judges, court personnel, attorneys, jurors, and witnesses when directed to do so in order to assure their personal safety.
- *law and order*: Am responsible for the detection and detention of any person(s) seeking to gain unauthorized access to court proceedings.

DIRECTOR. Oklahoma Wildlife Commission, Lawton, OK (1996-02). Refined my leadership ability and problem-solving skills while supervising and directing several wildlife officers in a geographical area in the enforcement of OK and federal laws related to hunting, fishing, other game activities, and boating.

- *employee training/supervision*: Trained numerous officers in the wildlife field; evaluated their performance.
- *organizing/scheduling/coordinating*: Set up work details to handle wildlife activities; worked with state and federal law enforcement agencies; assisted in search and rescue missions.
- *inventory control*: Procured new equipment and monitored its maintenance and care.
- *budgeting and finance*: Planned and administered budgets of varying sizes.

WILDLIFE ENFORCEMENT OFFICER. Oklahoma Wildlife Commission, Lawton, OK (1990-96). Enforced game, fish, and boating laws in an assigned area and assisted other officers in high violation locations; maintained equipment in top condition.

EDUCATION & TRAINING	**Court Security Officer School** (law enforcement training), Lawton, OK, 2001. **Oklahoma Justice Academy** (OK Criminal Code), Lawton, OK, 2000. **University of Tulsa** (leadership training), Tulsa, OK 1999. **Basic, Intermediate, and Advanced Law Enforcement Course** (each was an annual course), University of Tulsa, Tulsa, OK, 1998. Other training in wildlife enforcement/hunter safety; disarming/defensive tactics; firearms.
DISTINCTIONS & HONORS	• Received letters of commendation from a federal judge for outstanding work • Was the recipient of numerous awards from clubs and civic organizations • Received the State Conservation Award • Was named Officer of the Month
AFFILIATIONS	*Professional*: Fraternal Order of Police; Lifetime Member, OK Wildlife Officers Association *Religious*: Member of Highland Presbyterian Church
PERSONAL	Have a strong desire to strengthen law enforcement in Lawton, Oklahoma. Can provide outstanding letters of recommendation and references upon request.

CAREER CHANGE

Date

Exact Name of Person
Exact Title
Exact Name of Company
Address
City, State, Zip

Dear Exact Name of Person: (or Dear Sir or Madam if answering a blind ad):

With the enclosed resume, I would like to make you aware of my interest in any legal assistant or secretarial positions you may have available.

As you will see from my resume, I offer extensive secretarial and customer service experience. In my current position as a Deputy Clerk with the Marion County Juvenile Court, I provide support services related to probate and guardianships. I have gained in-depth knowledge of the judicial system within the county, and I have established a network of strong working relationships with various law firms, police departments throughout the state, and numerous related organizations. I am known for my sunny disposition and positive attitude.

In previous positions with a financial institution and a real estate company, I refined my interpersonal skills while dealing with the public on financial issues. I refined my customer service skills in positions as a Registrar for a local community college and as a Customer Service Representative for a uniform rental company.

With a reputation as a hardworking and reliable professional who prides myself on doing any job to the best of my ability, I am confident that my professional skills and personal qualities could be valuable additions to your firm. A fast typist, I type nearly 80 wpm accurately.

I hope you will call or write me soon to suggest a time convenient for us to meet and discuss your current and future needs and how I might serve them. Thank you in advance for your time.

Sincerely yours,

Alfreda P. McCullough

ALFREDA P. McCULLOUGH

1110½ Hay Street, Fayetteville, NC 28305   •   preppub@aol.com   •   (910) 483-6611

OBJECTIVE

To benefit an organization that can use a skilled assistant with outstanding interpersonal abilities along with excellent analytical and research skills.

EXPERIENCE

DEPUTY CLERK. Marion County Juvenile Court, Marion, SC (2003-present). Type legal documents, and prepare court minutes. Interview clients to determine the necessity of a probate procedure.
- Involved in the administration of guardianships. Provide clients with power of attorney in the best interest of the child.
- Schedule court dates.

SECRETARY. Century 21, Marion, SC (2000-03). Researched the feasibility of estate title transfers. Also performed research for creditors if an estate had been open so that a claim could be placed on the estate.
- Answered a 12-line switchboard.
- Received a Certificate in Real Estate from the Marion Board of Realtors.
- Provided outstanding secretarial support for eight real estate brokers.
- Became experienced in qualifying clients for housing according to income and debt.
- Collected rent money for the houses in which the firm rented.
- Completed bookkeeping transactions and banking procedures.

BANK TELLER II. The Bank of South Carolina, Marion, SC (1996-00). Provided customer service and relations for the financial institution. Collected large deposits from commercial and personal accounts
- Sold and cashed savings bonds, money orders, personal checks, as well as Travelers Cheques.
- Became experienced in all duties pertaining to automated teller machine.

CUSTOMER SERVICE REPRESENTATIVE. Textilease Uniform Services, Marion, SC (1994-96). For a major uniform services company which served dozens of major employers throughout South Carolina, handled telephone orders and performed liaison with the production department.

REGISTRAR. Marion County Technical Community College, Marion, SC (1993-94). Enrolled students in semester courses for a two-year college. Entered customer orders by way of phone into computer terminal.

CARE GIVER. Manor Care Nursing Home, Givens, SC (1992-1993). In a geriatric facility, became known as a caring and compassionate individual. Helped elderly individuals become familiar with the facility after they arrived.

EDUCATION

Shelby State Community College, 1997 to 1998
Marion High School, Marion, SC; excelled in college preparatory courses, 1992

PERSONAL

Excellent references furnished upon request

Date

Exact Name of Person
Title or Position
Name of Company
Address (no., street)
Address (city, state, zip)

FILE CLERK
for a small law
firm outside of
Boulder, CO is
seeking a summer
internship

Dear Exact Name of Person: (or Dear Sir or Madam if answering a blind ad.)

I would appreciate an opportunity to talk with you soon about how I could contribute to your organization through my analytical and research skills, public relations and client relations ability, as well as the intellectual and conceptual abilities I offer.

As you will see from my resume, I am a prospective honors graduate at a prestigious public university, and it is my goal to apply to law schools after graduating from college. I speak Spanish fluently and spent the fall semester of 2003 living and studying abroad in Bogota, Colombia.

I am interested in an internship with your firm in the upcoming year, and I can assure you that you would be impressed with the intellect, creativity, and research skills I could bring to your organization. I can provide outstanding personal and professional references upon request.

I hope you will call or write me soon to suggest a time when we can talk in person to discuss the summer needs of your firm and how I might become involved in meeting those needs.

Sincerely yours,

Chase T. Sabari

CHASE T. SABARI

1110½ Hay Street, Fayetteville, NC 28305   •   preppub@aol.com   •   (910) 483-6611

OBJECTIVE
To contribute to and learn from an organization that can use an industrious and resourceful young scholar with foreign language fluency, experience in living abroad, and a wide range of skills gained from working in a variety of business and academic organizations.

LANGUAGE
Fluently read, write, and speak Spanish
- Spent the Fall 2003 semester abroad living in Bogota, Colombia; excelled academically in competition with international students and traveled extensively in South America.

COMPUTERS
Offer the ability to rapidly master new software/hardware; am proficient in Microsoft Works, Word, Excel, and Microsoft Windows XP and skilled in using Printshop and Quicken.

EDUCATION
Completing a **Bachelor of Arts degree in Spanish Language and Culture and in Sociology,** University of Colorado at Boulder, CO; degree expected 2005.
- By faculty recommendation was accepted into the honors program in Sociology: This involved completing a major analysis of a company and presenting the analysis to the Sociology faculty.
- Am planning to apply to law schools upon graduation from college.

EXPERIENCE
FILE CLERK/INTERN. Phillip & McNeally, Attorneys-at-Law, Boulder, CO (2003-present). At one of this town's oldest and most respected law firms, have acquired technical knowledge in drafting documentation related to wills, estates, and bankruptcies.
- Helped reduce a backlog of filing in the tax/bankruptcy library.

RESIDENT ADVISOR, CIRCULATION ASSISTANT, and **TUTOR.** University of Colorado at Boulder, Boulder, CO (2002-03). Worked in three different jobs simultaneously while excelling in all academic courses.
- **Resident Advisor.** Planned and organized educational and cultural programs for a group of 36 upperclassmen and 26 freshmen; led the nine-person team of resident advisors that I work with to be named "Staff of the Year."
- **Circulation Assistant/Researcher, School of Law.** Conducted legal research based on requests phoned in by lawyers and UC professors; after the law library moved to a new building, handled a huge volume of filing.
- **Tutor.** As a tutor in the Learning Assistance Program, provided help to students needing assistance in understanding Spanish grammar and composition.

SUMMER CONFERENCE ASSISTANT. University of Colorado, Denver, CO (2000-01). Was specially chosen for this highly sought-after summer job which requires staff members "to serve as role models, resource people, and as reliable and effective administrators."
- Excelled in working with an eight-person team that essentially provided services for various summer camps and programs attended by people from all over the world.

MANAGEMENT ASSISTANT. Gerald's Tires and Brakes, Denver, CO (1999-00). Learned to expertly perform every job in the office of this busy tire retailer including typing correspondence, filing invoices and statements, answering and directing phone calls, and selling tire products and warranties.
- Rewrote and updated the company Employee Handbook.

PERSONAL
Cheerful hard worker with outstanding personal and professional references.

CAREER CHANGE

Date

Exact Name of Person
Exact Title
Exact Name of Company
Address
City, State, Zip

**GENERAL
MANAGER
& ENTREPRENEUR**
for a trucking service
in Sacramento, CA
seeks to return to the
legal field, where she
worked previously.

Dear Exact Name of Person (or Dear Sir or Madam if answering a blind ad):

With the enclosed resume, I would like to make you aware of my interest in exploring employment opportunities with your organization.

Experience related to the legal and criminal justice system
As you will see from my resume, I offer experience as a Legal Assistant with two different law firms. I am accustomed to working in environments in which attention to detail is a requirement at all times, and I am comfortable in working with the public. I have completed two years of college studies related to Paralegal Technology.

Excellent problem-solving skills
For the past six years, I have succeeded in an entrepreneurial job as part of a two-person transportation business which my husband and I operated together. We had a lot of fun traveling throughout the country together until he succumbed to cancer a year ago. We provided hauling of freight for Atlas Van Lines which included freight from other companies such as JCPenney, Office Depot, and United Express. I negotiated with shippers, dispatchers, receivers, terminal personnel, and corporate decision makers in the process of resolving a wide range of problems which occur when freight is shipped cross country. I received an award for three years of driving with no accidents, and we also received an award as one of the company's top five teams corporate wide. That experience has made me very comfortable in most aspects of the travel and transportation business.

Prior experience in bookkeeping
Prior to working as a Legal Secretary, I served as the "right arm" of a respected school principal (Carlie Mouzone) in the capacity of school bookkeeper and secretary.

I took a year off from work after my husband's death to settle matters related to his estate, but I am now enthusiastically eager to re-enter the work force, and I am confident that I can become a valuable asset to a firm that appreciates intelligence and initiative. If you can use an outgoing and dedicated self-starter to join your organization, I would appreciate an opportunity to meet with you to discuss your needs. I can provide outstanding personal and professional references.

Yours sincerely,

Alma Q. Gooden

ALMA Q. GOODEN

1110½ Hay Street, Fayetteville, NC 28305   •   preppub@aol.com   •   (910) 483-6611

OBJECTIVE

I want to contribute to an organization that can use a loyal and dedicated individual who offers a proven ability to organize and manage activities which require outstanding business management and customer service skills.

EXPERIENCE

GENERAL MANAGER & ENTREPRENEUR. Sneider Trucking Services, Sacramento, CA (2000-04). Traveled throughout the country with my husband-partner until he succumbed to cancer in 2004. We managed an incorporated business which provided for the hauling of freight for Atlas Van Lines located in Van Nuys, CA which includes freight from JCPenney, Office Depot, and United Express.
- Worked as a driver on long-haul driving trips throughout the U.S. and Canada.
- Negotiated with shippers, dispatchers, receivers, terminal personnel, and corporate decision makers in the process of coordinating the pickup and delivery of freight.
- Managed the scheduling of all shipments; increase profit by developing the most cost-efficient routes.
- Became highly skilled at map reading and at all aspects of navigation.
- Worked closely with a bookkeeper and accountant for tax reporting. Personally maintained all records for taxes.
- Received an award for three years of safe driving with no accidents. Also received a team award given to one of the company's top five teams.
- Have become skilled in developing itineraries for long-distance travel. Am adept at solving the myriad of problems which tend to crop up on over-the-road trips by vehicle.

LEGAL ASSISTANT. Willis & Willis Law Firm, Sacramento, CA (1996-00). Was specially recruited to become the "right arm" and legal assistant to an attorney who specialized in domestic law and personal injury law.
- Met with and interviewed clients while assisting in the process of preparing documents for domestic and personal injury cases.
- Assisted in maintaining trust and office financial accounts, interacted daily with opposing counsel, and other demanding activities.
- Worked with caseloads involving divorce law, traffic law bankruptcy, personal injury, general civil litigation as well as criminal and juvenile law.

LEGAL ASSISTANT & RECEPTIONIST. Bader & Brooks Law Offices, Sacramento, CA (1993-96). Began as a receptionist and rapidly assumed responsibilities as a legal secretary.
- Became knowledgeable of legal instruments related to wills and estates, corporate bill collections, and other areas.

Highlights of other experience:
ASSISTANT MANAGER. Began in an entry-level position with this fast-food giant and was rapidly promoted to assistant manager in charge of 10 employees.
BOOKKEEPER & SECRETARY. Worked for Principal Carlie Mouzone at Burnes Elementary School. Coordinated with teachers as well as with all other personnel including kitchen and janitorial staff. Assisted teachers with office needs.

EDUCATION & LICENSE

Attended California State University and studied two years of college studies concentrating in Paralegal Studies, Sacramento, CA.
Commercial Driver's License (CDL)

PERSONAL

Self-starter with strong personal initiative. Outstanding references upon request.

CAREER CHANGE

Date

Exact Name of Person
Exact Title
Exact Name of Company
Address
City, State, Zip

**GENERAL MANAGER
& PARALEGAL**

is relocating to
another city with his
wife and is seeking a
position with an
established firm

Dear Exact Name of Person: (or Dear Sir or Madam if answering a blind ad):

With the enclosed resume, I would like to make you aware of my strong background as a paralegal and acquaint you with desire to apply my knowledge and skills for the benefit of your law firm. My wife and I are in the process of relocating to South Carolina, where she will work as a Divisional General Manager for a Fortune 500 company, and I am seeking employment as a Paralegal.

After completing my Associate degree in Paralegal Technology, I applied my entrepreneurial spirit by establishing "from scratch" a firm which provides title insurance to attorneys in Nashville. I interview, hire, and now supervise the 15 paralegals and office professionals who work in my company, and I personally am an acknowledged expert in searching titles as well as in instructing paralegal staff in the methods for conducting title searches.

In previous experience, I excelled in handling responsibilities equivalent to those of a General Merchandise Manager while supervising a 20-store operation. In the process of generating sales and gross margin, merchandise mix, and advertising, I achieved eight percent average annual sales growth with no sacrifice of margin percent.

If you can use a self-motivated, enthusiastic individual with top-notch paralegal skills, I hope you will write or call me soon to suggest a time when we might meet to discuss your needs and goals and how my background might serve them. I can provide outstanding references at the appropriate time.

Sincerely,

Jason Sanders

JASON SANDERS

1110½ Hay Street, Fayetteville, NC 28305   •   preppub@aol.com   •   (910) 483-6611

OBJECTIVE

To benefit an organization that can use an articulate professional with an outgoing personality, exceptional organizational skills, and strong attention to detail.

EDUCATION

Associate of Applied Science degree in Paralegal Technology, Labette Community College, Parsons, KS, 2000; graduated with a 3.9 cumulative GPA.
Completed courses in Debtor/Creditor Relationships, Family Law, Real Estate Law, Corporations, Computer Literacy, Legal Research, Criminal Law, Wills, Estates, and Trusts and Civil Litigation.

LANGUAGE

Fluently read, write, and speak Spanish.
- Spent the fall, 1999 semester abroad living in Spain; excelled academically in competition with international students and traveled extensively in Europe.

COMPUTERS

Offer the ability to rapidly master new software/hardware; am proficient in Microsoft Works, and Microsoft Word, Excel and Windows XP. Skilled in using Westlaw and PageMaker.

EXPERIENCE

GENERAL MANAGER. Bilbraut Insurance Agency, Inc., Nashville, TN (2001-present). After completing my paralegal education, launched my own company providing title insurance to attorneys in the area.
- Interview, hire, and supervise as many as 15 paralegals and office professionals while establishing and managing multiple offices.
- An acknowledged expert in searching titles, instruct paralegal staff in the proper methods for conducting accurate title searches.
- Known for my outgoing personality, personally oversaw all marketing efforts, present the company's services to local attorneys and law firms.
- Learned to adapt and interact effectively with a wide range of personalities, from builders, to real estate agents, to attorneys.
- Honed my ability to make sound judgments, negotiate contracts, and commit to decisions under tight deadlines and in stressful situations.
- Personally perform a large number of title searches, in addition to monitoring the performance of my staff in an industry in which no mistakes can be tolerated.

DIVISIONAL MERCHANDISE MANAGER. Macy's Department Store, Home Store Division and Children's Division, Nashville, TN (1995-00). Excelled in handling responsibilities equivalent to those of a General Merchandise Manager while supervising a 20-store operation; received a Macy's Award of Excellence for my community leadership as a member of the Board of Directors of the Habitat for Humanity.
- Supervised a staff of buyers, associate buyers, and a Pool Stock Supervisor.
- Was responsible for generating sales and gross margin, merchandise mix, and advertising.

LICENSES

Hold TN Title Insurance License
Licensed Notary Public for the state of Tennessee

AFFILIATIONS

Past member, Nashville Area Chamber of Commerce

PERSONAL

Am willing to travel extensively to meet the needs of my employer. Excellent personal and professional references are available upon request.

CAREER CHANGE

Date

Exact Name of Person
Title or Position
Name of Company
Address (no., street)
Address (city, state, zip)

Dear Exact Name of Person: (or Dear Sir or Madam if answering a blind ad.)

I would appreciate an opportunity to talk with you soon about how I could contribute my problem-solving and decision-making skills to an organization that can use a creative, well-organized professional with excellent written and oral communication skills.

As you will see from my enclosed resume, I was selected for a prestigious internship with the Rayham County Courthouse. I observed nearly every type of courtroom proceeding and gained valuable insight into courtroom procedures. I made the acquaintance of many people within the legal system including judges, lawyers, legal assistants, and others as well as developed an understanding of how judges arrive at their decisions and observed how they manage the courtroom, interact with lawyers, and instruct juries.

In a previous intern position with the Douglas Powell Probation Office, I acted as the "right arm" and "shadow" of a very skilled parole officer who spent extensive time teaching me the nuts and bolts of probation and parole. I spent some time with several people on probation and parole, and earned the respect of senior probation/parole officers for my listening and counseling skills. I demonstrated my ability to interact with probationers and parolees in a poised and professional manner.

After studying four years at Boise State University, I recently graduated with a Bachelor of Science degree in Criminal Justice. I excelled in numerous seminars and courses related to these and other areas: social problems in criminal justice mediation and arbitration as problem-solving alternatives. I have worked full-time at Sam's during college in order to finance my education.

You would find me to be a congenial and poised young person who is known for having "maturity beyond my years." I am a hard worker who understands the importance of working with others as a team. I hope you will welcome my call soon to arrange a brief meeting at your convenience to discuss your needs and goals and how I might serve them. Thank you in advance for your time.

Yours sincerely,

Elizabeth L. Chesnutt

Alternate last paragraph:
I hope you will call or write soon to suggest a time convenient for us to meet and discuss your current and future needs and how I might serve them. Thank you in advance for your time.

ELIZABETH L. CHESNUTT

1110½ Hay Street, Fayetteville, NC 28305   •   preppub@aol.com   •   (910) 483-6611

OBJECTIVE

I want to contribute my problem-solving and decision-making skills to an organization that can use a creative, well-organized professional with excellent written and oral communication skills.

EDUCATION

Bachelor of Science in Criminal Justice, Boise State University, Boise, ID 2004.
Have excelled in numerous seminars and courses related to these and other areas:
    Social problems in criminal justice
    Mediation and arbitration as problem-solving alternatives

EXPERIENCE

INTERN, *RAYHAM COUNTY COURT HOUSE.* Boise, ID (2004). As part of my criminal justice curriculum, was selected for a prestigious internship with the Court House.
- Observed nearly every type of courtroom proceeding and gained valuable insight into courtroom procedures.
- Made the acquaintance of many people within the legal system including judges, lawyers, legal assistants, and others.
- Developed an understanding of how judges arrive at their decisions and observed how they manage the courtroom, interact with lawyers, and instruct juries.

INTERN, *DOUGLAS POWELL PROBATION OFFICE.* Boise, ID (2003). Acted as the "right arm" and "shadow" of a very skilled parole officer who spend extensive time teaching me the nuts and bolts of probation and parole.
- Spent some time with several people on probation and parole, and earned the respect of senior probation/parole officers for my listening and counseling skills; demonstrated my ability to interact with probationers and parolees in a poised and professional manner.
- Became knowledgeable about the paperwork and documentation required of probation and parole officers; assist in completing paperwork.
- Coordinated with other law enforcement agencies about particular cases.
- Made visits to court and conducted home visits.
- Was invited to apply for a permanent job here upon college graduation.

SALES CLERK. Sam's Wholesale, Boise, ID (2000-present). Have become a valued employee and trusted co-worker of this retail giant while working to finance my college education.
- Was complimented numerous times for my excellent listening and customer service skills.
- Through my sales experience, have gained insights into consumer behavior and have learned how to "read" people in sales situations.
- Am often in situations where I must educate and counsel people about the expected benefits of certain products.
- Because of my strong analytical skills and attention to detail, have been invited to apply to the management training program of this corporation, and have been evaluated as possessing proven executive potential and outstanding communication skills.
- Have developed a business style that emphasizes listening carefully to the customer.

PERSONAL

Can provide outstanding personal and professional references upon request. Am known as a hard worker who always gives 110% to any job I take on. Can provide outstanding personal and professional references upon request. Truly enjoy a situation where I can make a positive difference in someone's life.

Date

Exact Name of Person
Title or Position
Name of Company
Address (no., street)
Address (city, state, zip)

INTERN
for a law office
in Nebraska is
exploring full-time
career opportunities
after college
graduation

Dear Exact Name of Person: (or Dear Sir or Madam if answering a blind ad.)

I would appreciate an opportunity to talk with you soon about how I could contribute my problem-solving and decision-making skills to an organization that can use a creative, well-organized professional with excellent written and oral communication skills.

As you will see from my enclosed resume, I was selected for a prestigious internship with the Law Offices of John Upright where I conducted criminal case research for attorneys while also interviewing witnesses for DWI and criminal cases. I completed court documents while strictly observing court deadlines and updated client case files after assisting with client consultations.

By the end of December 2005, I will have earned a Bachelor of Science degree in Criminal Justice from Wayne State College. With double minors in Sociology and Psychology, I currently have a GPA of 3.7 and am a member of the Wayne State College Dean's List, Delta Psi Phi Criminal Justice Honors Society and the Student Government Legislator.

You would find me to be a congenial and poised young person who is known for having "maturity beyond my years." I am a hard worker who understands the importance of working with others as a team in order to maximize profitability and market share in an industry. I hope you will welcome my call soon to arrange a brief meeting at your convenience to discuss your needs and goals and how I might serve them. Thank you in advance for your time.

Yours sincerely,

Lisa Stuckey

Alternate last paragraph:
I hope you will call or write soon to suggest a time convenient for us to meet and discuss your current and future needs and how I might serve them. Thank you in advance for your time.

LISA STUCKEY

1110½ Hay Street, Fayetteville, NC 28305 • preppub@aol.com • (910) 483-6611

OBJECTIVE
To benefit an organization that can use a flexible, hard-working, knowledgeable young professional with proven skills in the legal field along with exceptionally strong written and oral communication abilities.

EDUCATION
College: Pending Bachelor of Science degree (December 2005) in Criminal Justice with double minors in Sociology and Psychology from Wayne State College, Wayne, NE. Current G.P.A. of 3.7.
- Member of the Wayne State College Dean's List
- Crimestoppers (student chapter)
- Student Government Legislator (Wayne State College-Wayne, NE)
- Member of Delta Psi Phi Criminal Justice Honor Society

LEGAL EXPERIENCE
INTERN. The Law Offices of John Upright, Wayne, NE
Summer 2004
Kevin Moniz, Supervisor
- Conducted criminal case research for attorneys.
- Interviewed witnesses for DWI and criminal cases.
- Completed court documents by court deadlines.
- Updated client case files.
- Assisted with client consultations.

OTHER EXPERIENCE
SERVER. Carey Hilliards, Wayne, NE
Aug. 2003-present
David Gutrick, Proprietor
- Deliver impeccable service to guests.
- Responsible for opening and closing restaurant—supervise waitstaff during this time.
- Direct and train new staff members.
- Received Employee of the Month Award.

SERVER. Sticky Fingers, Wayne, NE
Jun. 2001-Mar. 2003
Brian Nulf, Manager
- Provided stellar customer service to guests.
- Was responsible for opening and closing restaurant.
- Rated as top server by management.

COMPUTER SKILLS
Up-to-date knowledge of Windows XP, Microsoft Word, Excel, and PowerPoint.

PERSONAL
Professional references available upon request

CAREER CHANGE

Date

Exact Name of Person
Title or Position
Name of Company
Address (no., street)
Address (city, state, zip)

**LAW OFFICE
ASSISTANT**

for a real estate
attorney seeks a career
in the property field

Dear Exact Name of Person: (or Dear Sir or Madam if answering a blind ad.)

Can you use a highly motivated young professional who offers proven management ability and executive potential? I am responding to your recent advertisement for a Property Manager for the Hollywood Hills complex.

As you will see from my enclosed resume, I excelled academically in earning a B.A. degree in Pre-Law from University of Iowa while excelling in demanding part-time jobs in banking and sales in order to finance my college education. While working in various jobs as a college student, I gained valuable insights into internal banking operations and legal/real estate/loan procedures.

In my current position as a Law Office Assistant with a firm of real estate attorneys, I am involved in researching foreclosures, conducting title searches and analyzing courthouse records. Although I am excelling in my position and can provide outstanding references, I am seeking a position such as the one described in your ad in which I can utilize my leadership ability and management skills.

You would find me to be a congenial and poised young person known for having "maturity beyond my years." I am a hard worker who understands the importance of working with others as a team in order to maximize profitability and market share in an industry.

I hope you will welcome my call soon to arrange a brief meeting at your convenience to discuss your needs and goals and how I might serve them. Thank you in advance for your time.

Yours sincerely,

Susan McFarlane

Alternate last paragraph:
I hope you will call or write soon to suggest a time convenient for us to meet and discuss your current and future needs and how I might serve them. Thank you in advance for your time.

SUSAN McFARLANE

1110½ Hay Street, Fayetteville, NC 28305   •   preppub@aol.com   •   (910) 483-6611

OBJECTIVE

To contribute to an organization that can use a highly motivated young professional who offers excellent communication skills, a proven ability to serve the public graciously, as well as sales and banking experience which demonstrates my unlimited executive potential.

EDUCATION

Bachelor of Arts degree in **Pre-Law**, University of Iowa, Iowa City, IA, 2003.
- Extensively refined my written and oral communication skills in this degree program which stressed the development of top-notch writing, research, analytical, and public speaking ability.
- Excelled academically; was inducted into University of Iowa Political Science Honor Society and was named to the Dean's List several semesters.

COMPUTER KNOWLEDGE

Other software: Am experienced in utilizing Windows XP, Microsoft Works, Word and Excel software; offer the ability to rapidly master new software and hardware.

EXPERIENCE

LAW OFFICE ASSISTANT. McDowell & Douglass, Iowa City, IA (2003-present). Am gaining insight into legal procedures and learning the mechanics of the loan process while assisting real estate attorneys with business transactions.
- Research foreclosures, conduct title searches, and analyze courthouse records.
- Write numerous kinds of letters, and was commended for my excellent written communication skills.

BANK TELLER/DOCUMENTS ANALYST. Iowa Federal Credit Union, Iowa City, IA (2000-02). While excelling academically as a college student, worked part-time at two different locations of this financial institution and also worked at another job on the weekends; learned to manage my time wisely for maximum effectiveness in every activity.
- As a **Bank Teller**, greeted customers, introduced and sold new services, performed data entry and transactions on the computer, consolidated the day's paperwork, and balanced a drawer with thousands of dollars in credits and debits.
- As a **Documents Analyst**, worked in a busy operations center where I performed multiple duties including researching bank documents from all branches to solve account problems, retrieving account records, and stocking cancelled checks.
- Gained an understanding of internal bank operations.

Other experience: *Worked in these jobs in Des Moines, Cedar Rapids and Waterloo, IA, during high school and while in college in order to help finance my college education:*
DRY CLEANER CLERK. Took pride in serving customers in a cheerful manner at all times while acting as a counter clerk, operating a cash register, tagging clothes, and assisting dissatisfied customers.
SALES REPRESENTATIVE. Was commended for my "natural" sales ability while becoming the highest-volume salesperson; developed a new credit policy for the store which is still in use today after becoming skilled in calculating credit accounts and accounting for large amounts of cash.
WAITRESS. For the popular Red Lobster in Iowa City, learned to perform every job in this 150-person restaurant, and became a valuable part of the restaurant's catering business.

LANGUAGE

Proficient in speaking and understanding German.

PERSONAL

In high school, was captain of my basketball and tennis teams, and gained valuable confidence and leadership experience — including the ability to motivate others — from athletics.

Date

Exact Name of Person
Title or Position
Name of Company
Address (no., street)
Address (city, state, zip)

LEGAL ASSISTANT

for a firm that specializes
in consumer fraud

Dear Exact Name of Person: (or Dear Sir or Madam if answering a blind ad.)

In response to your advertisement for a Legal Secretary in the Orlando News Daily, enclosed please find my resume and accept this letter as a enthusiastic expression of interest in the position.

As you will see from my resume, I am currently employed as a Legal Assistant for Attorney Michael Bell at Bell & Associates. With a reputation for efficiency and accuracy, I perform post-petition bankruptcy work, including negotiations with creditors, attend all creditors meetings, draft pleadings, and formulate debtor repayment plans.

In a prior position with Filmore, Cox, & Wright, I worked as a Legal Secretary to Richard Lancaster and Lance Pullman performing general secretarial responsibilities and overflow legal assistant functions, such as deposition summaries and drafting pleadings.

I would appreciate your review and consideration of my experience and qualifications. If you feel you can use an individual with my skills and talents, I hope you will contact me to suggest a time when we might meet to discuss your needs in detail I can provide outstanding references at the appropriate time.

Very truly yours,

Tasha Bellomy

TASHA BELLOMY

1110½ Hay Street, Fayetteville, NC 28305　·　preppub@aol.com　·　(910) 483-6611

OBJECTIVE　　　To contribute to an organization that can use an accomplished administrative assistant who has excelled in demanding assignments in the legal field.

EXPERIENCE

2003-present　　**Legal Assistant** to Michael Bell
Bell & Associates, Attorneys at Law (Consumer Fraud)
2229 English Oaks Lane, Orlando Florida 33141, (111) 111-111
Post-petition bankruptcy work, including negotiations with creditors, attendance at creditors meetings, drafting pleadings, and formulation of debtor repayment plans.

2001-2003　　**Legal Secretary** to Richard Lancaster and Lance Pullman
Filmore, Cox & Wright, P.C., Attorneys at Law
332 Martha Drive, Orlando FL, 33142, (222) 222-2222
General secretarial responsibilities and overflow legal assistant functions, such as deposition summaries and drafting pleadings.

1999-2001　　**Legal Secretary** to Andrew L. Thomas
Andrew L. Thomas, Attorney at Law
128 Dowling Street, Orlando, FL, 33143, (333) 333-3333
Secretarial and legal assistant duties, including client communications, drafting, and preparing pleadings and trial exhibits.

1998-1999　　**Legal Secretary**
Frederick, Gooden & Lewis, LLP
812 Pittman Road, Orlando, FL, 33144, (444) 444-4444
General secretarial functions for six attorneys. Also, relief for receptionist and two legal assistants.

EDUCATION　　Completed two years of college studies, Frank Phillips College, Borger, Texas; maintained a 3.8 GPA, 1998.
Completed one year of secretarial studies, Valencia Community College, Orlando, Florida, 1997.
Graduated from Burke High School, Orlando, Florida — graduated May, 1995 in top 10% of my class. Lettered in three sports: softball, tennis, and soccer, and was named Most Valuable Player on the tennis team in my senior year.

COMPUTERS　　Proficient with software including Microsoft Word, Excel, Access, and PowerPoint.

TYPING SKILLS　　Highly fast and accurate typist who can type more than 85 wpm.

PERSONAL　　Outstanding references and letters of recommendation available upon request.

Date

Exact Name of Person
Title or Position
Name of Company
Address (no., street)
Address (city, state, zip)

LEGAL ASSISTANT
for a firm that
specializes
in consumer, family,
immigration and
divorce law

Dear Exact Name of Person: (or Dear Sir or Madam if answering a blind ad.)

I would appreciate an opportunity to talk with you soon about how I could contribute to your organization as an attorney.

As you will see from my resume, I am currently a Legal Assistant for the Richards, Cauldwell & Wheeler law firm. I have gained valuable work experience in the areas of consumer, family, immigration, and divorce law. I assert, negotiate, and settle cases under provisions of the Minnesota Law.

I hold a Bachelor of Science degree in Political Science and Biology from the University of St. Thomas, where I was named to Dean's List for several semesters, elected President of the Sociology Club, and became well known for my strong public speaking skills.

You would find me to be a dynamic communicator who is known for my capacity for hard work and long hours.

I hope you will welcome my call soon to arrange a brief meeting at your convenience to discuss your current and future needs and how I might serve them. Thank you in advance for your time.

Sincerely yours,

Dana K. Evans

Alternate last paragraph:
I hope you will call or write me soon to suggest a time convenient for us to meet and discuss your current and future needs and how I might serve them. Thank you in advance for your time.

DANA K. EVANS

1110½ Hay Street, Fayetteville, NC 28305   •   preppub@aol.com   •   (910) 483-6611

OBJECTIVE

I want to contribute to an organization that can use a polished young professional who offers excellent written and oral communication skills, strong research and analytical abilities, proven leadership strengths, as well as the capacity for hard work and long hours.

EDUCATION

Bachelor of Science (B.S.) degree, Political Science and Biology, University of St. Thomas, St. Paul, MN, 2003.
- Was named to Dean's List several semesters.
- Was elected President of the Sociology Club, 2003; well-known because of my public speaking skills.
- Member of the Political Science Club, 2003..
- Elected Secretary of the Science Club in a school-wide competition.
- Volunteered my time generously to activities of the World Harvest Ministries.
- Worked during the summers and while in college to finance my education.

SKILLS

Offer experience with software including Microsoft Word, Excel and Access as well as for Windows XP.

EXPERIENCE

LEGAL ASSISTANT. Richards, Cauldwell & Wheeler, St. Paul, MN (2003-present). Through this internship, gained valuable work experience in the areas of consumer, family, immigration, and divorce law.

Worked in these part-time jobs in St. Paul, MN, and was commended in each one for my exceptional planning and organizational abilities as well as my knack for dealing with the public in a tactful and gracious manner:
WORD PROCESSING SECRETARY (Part-time). The Finance Department of SunTrust Bank (2003-present). Began as a receptionist and was selected to handle responsibilities not normally assigned to summer workers; handle responsibilities for updating and keeping tracking of budgeting files assigned to the Finance Department.
- Praised for my initiative and willingness to take charge of disorganized areas.

LEGAL SECRETARY (Part-time). The Law Offices of Schuler and Schuler (2001-03). Was a secretary for one of the nine lawyers in this legal department, and handled a wide range of responsibilities as a personal assistant and legal secretary.
- Took dictation; for all nine lawyers, logged pertinent information regarding court dates and pending litigation.
- Booked flights, reserved hotel rooms, and arranged automobile travel.
- Handled responsibilities related to case management including updating files with all information pertinent to litigation. Routinely handled privileged information.
- Participated in the development of a new database program.
- Prepared a wide range of written communication including memos and letters.

SECRETARY. Department of Social Services (Summers 2000 and 2001). Performed receptionist/secretarial duties and assisted in the recruitment of managerial employees; prepared and sent letters to recruit personnel; collected and organized data for presentation to top management.

PERSONAL

Enjoy tennis and piano. Also thoroughly enjoy applying my talent for planning and organizing activities. Have acquired excellent personal time management skills. Can provide outstanding personal and professional references.

CAREER CHANGE

Date

Exact Name of Person
Exact Title
Exact Name of Company
Address
City, State, Zip

LEGAL ASSISTANT
is seeking a position
with a legal aid office.
Although she is not
communicating the
fact that her career
goal is to become a
lawyer, her goal is to
gain a couple of years
of experience in the
legal field and then
apply to law school.

Dear Exact Name of Person (or Dear Sir or Madam if answering a blind ad):

With the enclosed resume, I would like to make you aware of my interest in seeking employment with your organization. I am responding to your advertisement for a Project Manager to serve in your Legal Aid Office.

You will see from my resume that I have earned a Bachelor of Science degree in Pre-Law from the College of Lake County in Grayslake. I maintained a cumulative GPA of above 3.0 while excelling in course work in these areas: political science, social work, psychology, journalism, research procedures, economics, law — including criminal and business law, business writing, communications — writing, speaking, and acting as well as sound, filming, and editing. I wrote articles for the college newspaper and contributed my organizational and leadership abilities while coordinating functions, arranging for speakers, and planning festivals, pageants, and other social functions.

In my current position as a Legal Assistant for The Office of the District Attorney, I have gained valuable exposure to the workings of the law while aiding assistant district attorneys in such activities as contacting witnesses to remind them of court appearances. I am familiar with the court system and legal procedures and have learned to work with elected officials. Part of my responsibility is to ensure that persons pleading "not guilty" are aware of how to respond to questioning, and I have become skilled at writing guilty pleas.

While earning my college education, I worked part-time as a Client Services Representative for the Grayslake Federal Bank. I consistently placed at the top of my peer group within the region according to the bank's system of internal performance ratings.

Known for my strong personal initiative, I have become a valued and respected employee in every job I have held. I can assure you that I am a conscientious worker with outstanding problem-solving ability, and I always seek resourceful ways to contribute to my employer's reputation and profitability. If you can use my versatile abilities, I would enjoy an opportunity to talk with you in person. I hope you will welcome my call soon when I try to arrange a brief meeting.

Sincerely,

Paula K. Logan

PAULA K. LOGAN

1110½ Hay Street, Fayetteville, NC 28305 • preppub@aol.com • (910) 483-6611

OBJECTIVE

To offer my strong verbal and written communication skills along with my ability to translate ideas and concepts into interesting and informative materials.

EDUCATION

Bachelor of Science degree in Pre-Law, College of Lake County, Grayslake, IL, 2003.
- Maintained a cumulative GPA of above 3.0 while excelling in course work in these areas:

  political science   social work

  psychology   journalism

  research procedures   economics

  law — including criminal and business law   business writing

  communications — writing, speaking, and acting as well as sound, filming, and editing
- Wrote articles for the college newspaper.
- Contributed my organizational and leadership abilities while coordinating functions, arranging for speakers, and planning festivals, pageants, and other social events as the elected secretary of the student government's committee.

Attended Illinois State University, Normal, IL for two years of studies in Liberal Arts.
- Selected by faculty advisors to edit the college yearbook during my sophomore year, applied my communication skills and creativity to write copy for and produce a well-organized and attractive publication.
- Polished skills gained while editing my high school yearbook.

EXPERIENCE

LEGAL ASSISTANT. The Office of the District Attorney, Normal, IL (2003-present). Gained valuable exposure to the workings of the law while aiding assistant district attorneys in such activities as contacting witnesses to remind them of court appearances; became familiar with the court system and legal procedures while learning to work with elected officials.
- Ensured persons pleading "not guilty" were aware of how to respond to questioning; learned to write guilty pleas.
- Earned a reputation for my maturity and judgment displayed while relating to a variety of people from all socioeconomic and age groups.

CLIENT SERVICES REPRESENTATIVE. Grayslake Federal Bank, Grayslake, IL (2001-2003). Worked part-time in this job while earning my college degree. Gained experience as a Teller before advancing to this highly visible role as the public's first contact with the bank and its services.
- Consistently placed at the top of my peer group within the region according to the bank's system of internal performance ratings.
- Displayed the ability to listen to people's financial needs and requirements in order to recommend products such as Certificates of Deposit, MasterCard and VISA credit cards, and savings accounts and to open accounts.

CIVIC INVOLVEMENT

Involved in the activities of the Grayslake Junior League, as chairman of the Public Relations committee. Prepare and approve all news releases concerning league activities. Serve on the Grayslake Chamber of Commerce as a member of the Board of Directors.

COMPUTERS

Completed training in Microsoft Word; am skilled in preparing spreadsheets.

PERSONAL

Am an articulate speaker and skilled writer. Offer a creative and enthusiastic approach to project development and the organizational skills to see them to completion. Enjoy dealing with the public and making contributions to my community.

Exact Name of Person
Title or Position
Name of Company
Address (no., street)
Address (city, state, zip)

LEGAL ASSISTANT
for a fast-paced
legal practice

Dear Exact Name of Person: (or Dear Sir or Madam if answering a blind ad.)

Can you use a highly motivated young professional who offers proven management ability and executive potential?

As you will see from my enclosed resume, I am currently employed as a Legal Secretary with the Collins, Ross & Wagner in Phoenix, AZ. For this fast-paced legal firm which handles a vast number of medical malpractice cases, I answer six-line phone systems, process accounts receivable statements, type correspondence in addition to preparing various legal documents.

In a prior position as an Office Assistant III for Palmer Medical Services, Medical Records department, I provided clerical support to the clinical staff including performing transcription of clinical notes, progress notes, and evaluations. I maintained medical records and reviewed and checked charts to ensure that all documents in records were in compliance with policy and procedures.

You would find me to be a congenial and poised young person who is known for having "maturity beyond my years." I am a hard worker who understands the importance of working with others as a team.

I hope you will welcome my call soon to arrange a brief meeting at your convenience to discuss your needs and goals and how I might serve them. Thank you in advance for your time.

Yours sincerely,

Shirley Pait

Alternate last paragraph:
I hope you will call or write soon to suggest a time convenient for us to meet and discuss your current and future needs and how I might serve them. Thank you in advance for your time.

SHIRLEY PAIT

1110½ Hay Street, Fayetteville, NC 28305 • preppub@aol.com • (910) 483-6611

OBJECTIVE

I offer my clerical and secretarial skills to an organization that can use a hard-working young professional with exceptional public relations, planning, and organizing abilities.

EDUCATION
Clerical
and
Secretarial
Skills

Successfully completed courses in Executive Secretary Skills and Business Administration, at the Cochise College, Mesa, AZ, 1999.
- Can take dictation and transcribe shorthand.
- Have acquired expertise with this and other equipment:

Microsoft Word	Calculators	Typewriters (75 wpm)
PowerPoint	Access	Excel

- Developed business operations knowledge through courses in Business Law, Business Math, Economics, and Business English/Terminology.

EXPERIENCE

LEGAL SECRETARY. Collins, Ross & Wagner, Phoenix, AZ (2000-present). For this fast-paced legal practice which handled a vast number of medical malpractice cases, answer a six-line phone system. Process accounts receivable statements. Type correspondence in addition to preparing various legal documents including but not limited to foreclosures, bankruptcies, and personal injury.
- Excel in filing supplements in law library including AZ General Statutes.
- Provide backup for other secretaries.
- Refine my communication skills and develop an excellent eye-for-detail.
- Schedule appointments and keep up with deadlines. Perform monthly billings.

OFFICE ASSISTANT III (Medical Records). Palmer Development Services, Phoenix, AZ (1998-99). Provide clerical support to the clinical staff including performing transcription of clinical notes, progress notes, and evaluations. Maintained medical records; review and check charts to ensure that all documents are in compliance with policy and procedures.

LEAD WORKER III. Bethune Therapy Center, Phoenix, AZ (1996-98). While working two jobs simultaneously for both Palmer Development and Bethune Therapy Center, provided clerical and administrative services to the staff including processing phone calls, taking messages, coordinating a variety of resources in acquiring information, greeting clients/ visitors, typing, and maintaining administrative files.

WAITRESS and **HOSTESS.** Dino's Pizza, Mesa, AZ (1994-96). Through my public relations skills and cheerful disposition, played a key role in producing satisfied customers and repeat business for this firm operating in a very competitive industry.
- Was chosen for the special responsibility of opening and closing the restaurant.
- Was trusted to account for daily revenues of up to $700.

TELEMARKETING SPECIALIST. Highland Resorts, Mesa, AZ (1992-94). Learned to organize persuasive sales presentations and was praised for my "exceptional" telephone voice while arranging appointments for clients potentially interested in resort properties.
- Learned valuable prospecting and sales techniques while refining my skills in planning, organizing, and "following through." Compiled an unusually high new-client success rate of 90%, and was praised by my employer for my natural sales ability.

PERSONAL

Am a highly skilled organizer and achievement-oriented young professional. Welcome the opportunity to contribute to my employer's "bottom line."

Date

Exact Name of Person
Title or Position
Name of Company
Address (no., street)
Address (city, state, zip)

LEGAL ASSISTANT

for a criminal law
firm in Illinois

Dear Exact Name of Person: (or Dear Sir or Madam if answering a blind ad.)

With the enclosed resume, I would like to make you aware of my interest in and strong qualifications for the position of Office Supervisor which you recently advertised in the Dekalb Daily Journal.

As you will see from my resume, I offer experience in every aspect of office management, and I am extremely experienced in the bookkeeping and accounting function as well as in automated operations, personnel management, and the supervision of efficient workflows. My computer skills are top-notch, and I offer experience with MS Word, Excel, PowerPoint, Access, and many other programs.

While working as an Accounting Manager with the Air Force Audit Agency, I gained considerable experience in problem solving and managing in an environment in which priorities were constantly changing. I supervised budget analysts involved in formulating, executing, and reconciling monthly and yearly annual reports. I am skilled at budget preparation and proficient in formulating, justifying, determining corrective action needed, and implementing small budgets of less than $1 million up to multimillion-dollar budgets. I played a key role in automating manual functions, and I was instrumental in revamping financial/management systems into a process which increased control over cash flow and management reports.

I can assure you that I can provide outstanding personal and professional references; however I would prefer that you not contact my current employer until after we talk since he is embroiled in a fast-paced murder trial.

I hope you will contact me to suggest a time when we might meet to discuss your needs and how I might be suited to them. I am a highly energetic professional who is known for my ability to work well with others and to solve stubborn productivity and efficiency problems. Thank you in advance for your time.

Sincerely,

Caleb D. Smalls

CALEB D. SMALLS

1110½ Hay Street, Fayetteville, NC 28305 • preppub@aol.com • (910) 483-6611

OBJECTIVE

I want to contribute to an organization that can use an experienced office supervisor who offers outstanding computer know-how, excellent written and oral communication skills, as well as strong abilities related to office management and administrative practices.

EDUCATION & COMPUTER SKILLS

Bachelor of Arts degree in Business Administration, Northern Illinois University, DeKalb, IL, 2002.
Highly computer literate, and offer expertise in using Windows XP, Word, Access, PowerPoint, and Excel spreadsheets as well as other software programs and applications.

EXPERIENCE

LEGAL ASSISTANT. Leroy Thompson of the law firm Thompson & Associates, DeKalb, IL (2004-present). For a firm specializing in criminal law, am in constant communication statewide utilizing a sophisticated computer system as well as telephones.
- Prepare motions/orders for judges' signatures as well as assorted correspondence.
- Coordinate with judges, clients, and relevant agencies.
- Was recruited for this position by Attorney Leroy Thompson when he learned that the JCPenney office was closing.

BOOKKEEPER, MERCHANDISING ASSISTANT, & SPECIAL ASSISTANT. JCPenney, Inc., Dekalb, IL (2001-04). Began with JCPenney as a bookkeeper for seven stores, and then was asked to work in merchandising and handle the ordering function; worked with top JCPenney officials.
- Completed 13 separate courses in order to learn JCPenney's sophisticated computer system when I moved into the merchandising area; this job required an individual who could work with perfect accuracy since ordering errors were costly to the bottom line.
- After excelling in my role in merchandising, was recruited internally within JCPenney for a job as Special Assistant to the Manager of Sales Promotion; in that capacity, was constantly communicating by e-mail, telephone, letter, and personal contact within the JCPenney system to resolve problems.

ACCOUNTING MANAGER. Air Force Audit Agency, Boxdale, IL (1999-01). Became highly proficient in accounting and bookkeeping responsibilities, as I managed and provided guidance to military and other civilian budget analysts involved in formulating, executing, and reconciling monthly and yearly financial reports related to multimillion-dollar budgets.
- Supervised five budget analysts.
- Became proficient in formulating, justifying, determining corrective action needed, and implementing small budgets of less than $1 million to multimillion-dollar budgets.
- Gained the ability to prioritize an expanded workload to meet stringent deadlines while experiencing constant interruptions and adjusting to frequent changes in priorities.
- Assisted a comptroller in the development of a budgeting, forecasting, and reporting system; participated in the resolution of financial issues discovered in the development of the automated system.
- Was selected to troubleshoot a computer software package designed to facilitate reporting requirements at three functional levels.

PUBLICATIONS

Two published articles in a professional magazine: one illustrating methods of increasing productivity through efficient workflow of administrative operations; the other illustrating a complex multi-functional environment operating efficiently through planning.

PERSONAL

Outstanding personal and professional references available on request.

Date

Exact Name of Person
Title or Position
Name of Company
Address (no., street)
Address (city, state, zip)

LEGAL ASSISTANT Dear Exact Name of Person: (or Dear Sir or Madam if answering a blind ad.)

now acting as a
Billing Administrator   I would appreciate an opportunity to talk with you soon about how I could contribute
for a large law firm   to your organization as a Senior Legal Assistant.
seeks position as a
Senior Legal   While completing training programs in Legal Assistance as well as a Legal Office
Assistant. This   Services Program, I gained specialized skills which I have refined through on-the-job
individual has held   experience as a Paralegal.
various positions in
law firms and has an   I was aggressively recruited for my current position by a prestigious law firm with
excellent   18 attorneys. As Billing Administrator, I work on a specialized billing system while
understanding of her   handling vast responsibility for accounts receivables, billing, and cost accounting.
"best fit" in the   Although I am excelling in my job and can provide outstanding references at the
paralegal   appropriate time, I am selectively exploring opportunities as a Legal Assistant in other
environment.   law firms. An experienced Paralegal, I miss the analytical and research responsibilities
I have handled in previous jobs, and I am seeking a responsible Legal Assistant position
with a firm that seeks a highly intelligent individual who understands the fast pace of
law firms.

     You would find me to be a hard-working, energetic, and reliable professional who
prides myself on doing any job to the best of my ability. I can provide excellent personal
and professional references from all my employers.

     I hope you will call or write me soon to suggest a time convenient for us to meet
and discuss your current and future needs and how I might serve them. Thank you in
advance for your time.

Sincerely yours,

Sheila Wiggins

SHEILA WIGGINS

1110½ Hay Street, Fayetteville, NC 28305   •   preppub@aol.com   •   (910) 483-6611

OBJECTIVE

To benefit an organization through my oral and written communication skills as well as my proven administrative and interpersonal abilities.

EDUCATION

- **Legal Assistant Program**, American Bar Association (A.B.A.) approved, 82 semester hours, Glenville State College, Glenville, WV 2000-02.
- **Legal Assistant Program,** A.B.A. approved, 69 semester hours, Cuyahoga Community College, Cleveland, OH, 1992-95.
- **Legal Office Services Program,** earned Diploma, 40 hours, Christopher Newport University, Newport News, VA 1995.

EXPERIENCE

BILLING ADMINISTRATOR. Piedmont Law Offices, Glenville, WV (2001-present). Was recruited by one of the firm's senior partners. Generate billing for a firm of 18 attorneys. Manage accounts receivable and billing. Input expenses, time, and cost to individual files.

- Open and assign numbers to incoming files. Run monthly and end-of-the-year reports. Research files to ascertain status and balance of accounts. Work on Legal Management Alpine Billing system.
- Print work-in-process reports and monthly reports for individual attorneys. Process statements weekly and printed overdue bills monthly. Determine, separate, and calculate percentage of monies going to each partner and process billing statements.

PARALEGAL & LEGAL ASSISTANT. Newmann-Carr, LLP, Bluefield, WV (1999-2001). Opened, organized, and maintained personal injury case files. Interviewed new clients, screening and analyzing information pertinent to each case. Maintained business relationships with professionals (doctors, hospitals, psychologists, etc.).

- Researched legal precedents and case law in firms and West Virginia University School of Law Libraries. Kept attorney advised on statutes of limitations and other deadlines.
- Wrote legal memorandums and digest depositions. Interfaced with clients throughout their cases, answering and researching inquiries. Composed various legal business letters.
- Prepared settlement sheet when case was settled. Closed out files. Performed miscellaneous administrative tasks as needed. Used Microsoft Word software.

PARALEGAL. Athens Courthouse, Athens, GA (1996-98). Fulfilled internship requirements set by college while working for the Judge Advocate Division. Responsibilities included meeting and dealing with the public in addition to receiving and routing incoming telephone calls. Screened prospective clients while determining the nature of need and priority, made appropriate referrals or took action to schedule appointments.

- Held initial interviews to determine whether individuals had a need for an attorney or if needs could be better met by another organization. If need was determined, prepared the case file, providing details of the interview, and then scheduled appointments with the attorney who could best handle an individual client's needs.
- Prepared, edited, revised and finalized legal documents and contracts, including personal wills, passport applications, medical powers of attorney, adoptions, letters of credit resolutions, separation agreements, divorce agreements, real estate transactions, battery complaints, landlord complaints and a variety of other documents.
- Provided administrative assistance in typing technical and nontechnical legal documents for seven attorneys. Developed and maintained working relationships with 16 national and international organizations.

REFERENCES

Outstanding references available upon request.

Exact Name of Person
Title or Position
Name of Company
Address (no., street)
Address (city, state, zip)

**LEGAL ASSISTANT &
OFFICE MANAGER**

for three lawyers in
Missouri

Dear Exact Name of Person: (or Dear Sir or Madam if answering a blind ad.)

Can you use a highly motivated young professional who offers proven management ability and executive potential?

As you will see from my enclosed resume, I am currently employed as a Legal Assistant for Shinault, Wymer, & Britt. I have been often commended for my attention to detail and my ability to work without supervision in a job that involves my composing extensive written correspondence, updating and maintaining a large filing system, and performing light bookkeeping and client billing. I am skilled in communicating by telephone with people from all over the world.

In a previous position with Rachel Auburn, Attorney at Law, I excelled academically in a tough, two-year technical training program for legal assistants while assisting one of St. Louis's most respected lawyers. I became skilled in all aspects related to the administration of this busy firm and earned a reputation as a hard working individual willing to assume responsibility and take charge of problems. I also became known for my thorough reliability and punctuality.

You would find me to be a congenial and poised young person who is known for having "maturity beyond my years." I am a hard worker who understands the importance of working with others as a team in order to maximize profitability and market share in an industry.

I hope you will welcome my call soon to arrange a brief meeting at your convenience to discuss your needs and goals and how I might serve them. Thank you in advance for your time.

Yours sincerely,

Natalie W. Koller

Alternate last paragraph:
I hope you will call or write soon to suggest a time convenient for us to meet and discuss your current and future needs and how I might serve them. Thank you in advance for your time.

NATALIE W. KOLLER

1110½ Hay Street, Fayetteville, NC 28305   •   preppub@aol.com   •   (910) 483-6611

OBJECTIVE

I want to contribute to an organization that can use a hardworking young professional who offers excellent office skills, sales and customer service experience, along with proven problem-solving and decision-making abilities.

LANGUAGE

Fluently speak, write, and read Spanish

EXPERIENCE

LEGAL ASSISTANT/OFFICE MANAGER. Shinault, Wymer, & Britt, St. Louis, MO (2004-present). Am often commended for my attention to detail and my ability to work without supervision in a job that involves my composing extensive written correspondence, updating and maintaining a large filing system, and performing light bookkeeping and client billing.

- Am skilled in communicating by telephone with people calling from all over the world.
- On my own initiative, took over a dysfunctional filing operation and made simple changes which led to a much more efficient locating system.

LEGAL ASSISTANT. Rachel Auburn, Attorney at Law, St. Louis, MO (2002-04). Excelled academically in a tough, two-year technical training program for legal assistants while also working three days a week in a job assisting one of St. Louis's most respected lawyers.

- Became skilled in all aspects related to the administration of this busy firm:
  - Customer relations   Legal correspondence
  - Client billing   Filing/document maintenance
  - Bookkeeping   English/Spanish translation
- Earned a reputation as a hardworking willing to assume responsibility and take charge of problems.
- Became known for my thorough reliability and punctuality.

SALESPERSON/CASHIER. The Gap, St. Louis, MO (2001-02). After graduating from high school, became a valued employee of a local fashion retailer.

**EDUCATION &
TRAINING**

Graduated from two-year school for legal assistants, St. Louis Community College at Florissant Valley, St. Louis, MO, 2004.
- Was certified in typing and shorthand as producing 190 letters per minute and 120 syllables per minute.
- Was expertly trained to perform every aspect of legal assisting including bookkeeping and billing.

PERSONAL

Am a very responsible person who can always be counted on to perform under pressure. Am well organized.

Exact Name of Person
Title or Position
Name of Company
Address (no., street)
Address (city, state, zip)

LEGAL CLERK
for a district
attorney's office

Dear Exact Name of Person: (or Dear Sir or Madam if answering a blind ad.)

With the enclosed resume, I would like to make you aware of my interest in exploring employment opportunities with your organization.

As you will see from my enclosed resume, I am currently employed as a Legal Clerk with the Augusta District Attorney's Office. I have developed skills and gained experience handling several office procedures such as: researching cases to be sure they were completed and records were closed, logging new court dates, distributing documentation on new cases to the correct people in the appropriate divisions, and performing clerical functions including data entry, filing, making copies, and answering phones.

Through my work experience and training, I am skilled at working with two new automated operating systems: All-in-One and a specialized case management programs. I earned recognition for my polite and helpful attitude toward clients as well as other employees and am well-known as a very dependable hard worker who could be counted on to provide efficient support to a staff of legal professionals. I received official praise which stated, in part, "due to her organizational skills, work was always current" and "she could always be counted on to produce a high volume of work."

You would find me to be a congenial and poised young person who is known for having "maturity beyond my years."

I hope you will welcome my call soon to arrange a brief meeting at your convenience to discuss your needs and goals and how I might serve them. Thank you in advance for your time.

Yours sincerely,

Kiara McNeal

Alternate last paragraph:
I hope you will call or write soon to suggest a time convenient for us to meet and discuss your current and future needs and how I might serve them. Thank you in advance for your time.

KIARA McNEAL

1110½ Hay Street, Fayetteville, NC 28305   •   preppub@aol.com   •   (910) 483-6611

OBJECTIVE

To contribute through my secretarial skills and knowledge of office procedures to an organization that can use a detail-oriented young professional who works well with others.

SPECIAL SKILLS

- Offer experience in using computers with numerous popular software programs.
- Am familiar with software and operating systems including:

  Microsoft Word   All-in-One
  Case management systems unique to law offices   Westlaw

- Operate office equipment including calculators, multiline phone systems, and copy machines.

EXPERIENCE

LEGAL CLERK. District Attorney's Office, Augusta, GA (2002-present). Have developed skills and gained experience handling office procedures including the following:
Researching cases to be sure they were completed and records were closed
Logging new court dates
Distributing documentation on new cases to the correct people in the appropriate divisions
Making sure all cases were tracked through the system
Performing clerical functions including data entry, filing, making copies, and answering phones

- Am skilled at working with two new automated operating systems: All-in-One and specialized case management programs.

- Earned recognition for my polite and helpful attitude toward clients as well as other employees.

- Am known as a very dependable hard worker who could be counted on to provide efficient support to a staff of legal professionals.

- Received official praise which stated, in part, "due to her organizational skills, work was always current" and "she could always be counted on to produce a high volume of work."

CUSTOMER SERVICE SPECIALIST and **CASHIER.** Golden Corral, Augusta, GA (2000-01). Provided friendly and helpful service to restaurant customers while seating them and assuring they were taken care of properly.

- Gained a great deal of experience in how to work with others as a team.

- Was very careful when handling cash receipts from customers in order to be perfectly balanced at the end of each shift.

TRAINING

Completed a 40-hour orientation program sponsored by the State of Georgia emphasizing legal system operations.

LANGUAGES

Am completely bilingual in English and German.

PERSONAL

Completed a high school program emphasizing business courses. Am especially well organized. Outstanding references upon request.

Date

Exact Name of Person
Title or Position
Name of Company
Address (no., street)
Address (city, state, zip)

LEGAL SECRETARY
for an attorney
in Boston

Dear Exact Name of Person: (or Dear Sir or Madam if answering a blind ad.)

Can you use a poised young office professional who offers specialized experience and training as a paralegal and who is dedicated to ensuring top quality client relations?

In my current job as a Legal Secretary, I have been entrusted with researching data and preparing all documents for lawyers to try cases. I have earned a reputation as a hard-working and dedicated professional committed to quality and client relations.

You will see from my resume that I grew up in Florida and earned an Associate of Science degree in Secretarial Studies from Jensen Beach Community College. After relocating to Boston to live near my extended family, I became employed with a law firm, and that experience ignited my desire to pursue a degree in Paralegal Technology. Although I am highly regarded by my current employer, I am selectively seeking other opportunities while I am only two courses short of my degree.

I hope you will call or write me soon to suggest a time convenient for us to meet and discuss your current and future needs and how I might serve them. Thank you in advance for your time.

Sincerely your,

Jane Carnes

JANE CARNES

1110½ Hay Street, Fayetteville, NC 28305   •   preppub@aol.com   •   (910) 483-6611

OBJECTIVE   To contribute to an organization that can use a poised young office professional who offers specialized experience and training as a paralegal and legal assistant and is dedicated to ensuring top-quality client relations.

EDUCATION   Am only two classes from a Associate of Science degree with a ***Paralegal*** certificate, St. Leo's Community College, Boston, MA; degree expected 2005.
- Worked in full-time challenging positions as a Legal Secretary while pursuing this degree. Am excelling academically with a 3.8 GPA.

Previously received an Associate of Science degree in Secretary Studies, Jensen Beach Community College, Jensen Beach, FL, 1998.

EXPERIENCE   **LEGAL SECRETARY**. Peter M. Carlton, LLP, Boston, MA (2004-present). Was recruited for this position by an acquaintance whom I met in church. Interview clients for factual information and assume total responsibility for preparing all legal documents and cases for the attorney to try in court.
- While handling all domestic cases, maintain contact with clients and track case progress. Have demonstrated strong time management skills while handling multiple simultaneous responsibilities.
- Prepare accounting documents and compute daily bank deposits.

LEGAL SECRETARY. Michaels & Barnes, Attorneys at Law, Boston, MA (2003-04). Drafted pleadings, initiated and responded to discovery, and conducted in-depth research and investigations on cases. It was my experience in this job which motivated me to return to college to pursue paralegal studies.
- Routinely corresponded with clients, tracked case progress, and prepared final accounting documents.
- Kept track of and ordered office supplies.
- Maintained accurate and up-to-date ledgers on all clients.
- Was entrusted with computing and making daily bank deposits.

EXECUTIVE ASSISTANT. Florida Department of Law, Jensen Beach, FL (1998-03). Entered daily financial reports and budgets to keep track of fiscal spending; typed monthly and quarterly financial statements.
- Introduced and maintained a new and improved, proficient filing system.
- Managed accounts and payroll.

SPECIAL SKILLS   An excellent typist and word processor with exceptional attention to detail. 80 wpm. Skilled in a variety of software programs including Microsoft Word, Excel, Access and PowerPoint.
Offer experience using dictating equipment and various switchboards.

PERSONAL   Relocated to Massachusetts to be with my family and am a permanent resident. A very flexible and adaptable professional, am always willing to go the extra mile to ensure excellence. Always commit myself 100% to each and every project I work on.

Exact Name of Person
Title or Position
Name of Company
Address (no., street)
Address (city, state, zip)

LEGAL SECRETARY
for a legal office in
Albuquerque, NM

Dear Exact Name of Person: (or Dear Sir or Madam if answering a blind ad.)

Can you use a highly motivated young professional who offers proven management ability and executive potential?

As you will see from my enclosed resume, I am currently employed as a Legal Secretary with the Carter, Layman & Stewart in Albuquerque. For this fast-paced legal office, I answer six-line phone systems, process accounts receivable statements, type correspondence in addition to preparing various legal documents including but not limited to foreclosures, bankruptcies, and personal injury.

In a previous position as a Word Processor and an Administrative Aide for Players Inc., a toy manufacturing company in Gallup, I used my office skills while typing and word processing while attending college full-time. I handled the public with consistent poise and tact. On my own initiative, I reduced a backlog of paperwork through organized, efficient office management and learned inventory control skills setting up and maintaining files.

You would find me to be a congenial and poised young person who is known for having "maturity beyond my years." I am a hard worker who understands the importance of working with others as a team in order to maximize profitability and market share in an industry.

I hope you will welcome my call soon to arrange a brief meeting at your convenience to discuss your needs and goals and how I might serve them. Thank you in advance for your time.

Yours sincerely,

Clara Sigmon

Alternate last paragraph:
I hope you will call or write soon to suggest a time convenient for us to meet and discuss your current and future needs and how I might serve them. Thank you in advance for your time.

CLARA SIGMON

1110½ Hay Street, Fayetteville, NC 28305 • preppub@aol.com • (910) 483-6611

OBJECTIVE

I offer my clerical and secretarial skills to an organization that can use a hard-working young professional with exceptional public relations, planning, and organizing abilities.

EXPERIENCE
Legal
Expertise

LEGAL SECRETARY. Carter, Layman & Stewart, LLP, Albuquerque, NM (2003-present). For this fast-paced legal office, answer six-line phone system. Process accounts receivable statements. Type correspondence in addition to preparing various legal documents including but not limited to foreclosures, bankruptcies, and personal injury.
- Excel in filing supplements in law library including NM General Statutes.
- Have become experienced in supporting attorneys involved in civil litigation.
- Provide backup for other secretaries.
- Refined my communication skills and developed an excellent eye-for-detail.
- Schedule appointments and keep up with deadlines. Prepare and mail monthly billings.
- Hold a Notary Public Commission with the state of New Mexico.

WAITRESS and **HOSTESS.** Hungry Howie's, Albuquerque, NM (2001-03). Through my public relations skills and cheerful disposition, played a key role in producing satisfied customers and repeat business for this firm operating in a very competitive industry.
- Was chosen for the special responsibility of opening and closing the restaurant.
- Was trusted to account for daily revenues of up to $700. Greeted, seated, and served up to 120 customers daily. Planned and implemented special projects and private parties.
- Refined my skills in problem solving and in satisfying even "difficult" customers.
- Polished my communication skills through motivating fellow employees and creating a sense of teamwork. Developed a reputation for honesty and "common sense" while accounting for finances and inventory.

Office
Operations &
Know-how

WORD PROCESSOR and **ADMINISTRATIVE AIDE.** Players, Inc. (Toy Manufacturing Co.), Gallup, NM (1998-01). While a full-time student, used my office skills in this organization while performing typing and word processing. Handled the public with poise and tact.
- On my own initiative, reduced a backlog of paperwork through organized, efficient office management. Learned inventory control skills setting up and maintaining files.

TELEMARKETING SPECIALIST. Ocean Plaza, Gallup, NM (1995-98). Learned to organize persuasive sales presentations and was praised for my "exceptional" telephone voice while arranging appointments for clients potentially interested in resort properties.
- Learned valuable prospecting and sales techniques while refining my skills in planning, organizing, and "following through." Compiled an unusually high new-client success rate of 90%, and was praised by my employer for my natural sales ability.

EDUCATION

Successfully completed courses in Executive Secretary Skills and Business Administration, at the University of New Mexico, Gallup, NM.

Clerical
and
Secretarial
Skills

- Can take dictation and transcribe shorthand.
- Have acquired expertise with this and other equipment:

Microsoft Word	Calculators	Typing (75 wpm)
PowerPoint	Access	Excel

- Developed business operations knowledge through courses in Business Law, Business Math, Economics, and Business English/Terminology.

PERSONAL

Am a highly skilled organizer and achievement-oriented young professional. Welcome the opportunity to contribute to my employer's "bottom line."

Date

Exact Name of Person
Title or Position
Name of Company
Address (no., street)
Address (city, state, zip)

**LOAN CLOSING
SPECIALIST &
LEGAL ASSISTANT**
for a private
real estate practice

Dear Exact Name of Person: (or Dear Sir or Madam if answering a blind ad.)

I would appreciate an opportunity to talk with you soon about how I could contribute to your organization through my training as a Loan Closing Specialist/Legal Assistant.

Currently employed as a Loan Closing Specialist/Legal Assistant for Kevin H. Fuller, a well-known Attorney in Springfield with a private real estate practice, I assist in preparing loan packages and closings while preparing legal documents, conducting title searches, and providing customer service. In a previous position as a Loan Processing Clerk for the Springfield Federal Reserve Bank, I became skilled in all aspects of loan processing while handling mortgage banking and loan processing within a budget of over one million dollars. I submitted loans, coordinated appraisals, prepared legal documents, and compiled loan packages as well as interviewed loan applicants and prepared applications. I also coordinated with a wide range of real estate attorneys, appraisers, residential and commercial sales professionals, and VA/FHA officials.

While earning a Bachelor of Arts degree in English from the Chaminade University of Honolulu, Hawaii, I completed courses in Public Speaking, Business Writing, and English Literature. I am also skilled in utilizing various accounting and banking programs being proficient with Windows XP, Microsoft Word, Excel and PowerPoint.

I hope you will welcome my call soon to arrange a brief meeting at your convenience to discuss your needs and goals and how I might serve them. Thank you in advance for your time.

Yours sincerely,

Tina M. Shaver

Alternate last paragraph:
I hope you will call or write soon to suggest a time convenient for us to meet and discuss your current and future needs and how I might serve them. Thank you in advance for your time.

TINA M. SHAVER

1110½ Hay Street, Fayetteville, NC 28305   •   preppub@aol.com   •   (910) 483-6611

OBJECTIVE

To benefit an organization that can use a hard-working professional experienced in office operations with specialized knowledge of loan closing procedures, accounting/bookkeeping, and marketing/publicity.

EDUCATION

Earned **B.A. in English**, Chaminade University of Honolulu, Honolulu, HI, 1999.
In my spare time, am completing courses toward a B.S. degree, University of Illinois, Springfield, Illinois.

COMPUTERS

Skilled in utilizing various accounting and banking programs; proficient with Windows XP, Microsoft Office, and MLS.

EXPERIENCE

LOAN CLOSING SPECIALIST & LEGAL ASSISTANT. Kevin H. Fuller, Attorney-at-Law, Springfield, IL (2003-present). For a private real estate practice, assist in preparing loan packages and closings while also preparing legal documents, conduct title searches, and provide customer service.
• Use Windows operating system with specialized software.

LOAN PROCESSING CLERK. Springfield Federal Reserve Bank, Springfield, IL (2002-03). Became skilled in all aspects of loan processing while handling mortgage banking and loan processing within a budget of over one million dollars.
• Submitted loans, coordinated appraisals, prepared legal documents, and compiled loan packages.
• Interviewed loan applicants and prepared applications; provided customer service.
• Coordinated with a wide range of real estate attorneys, appraisers, residential and commercial sales professionals, and VA/FHA officials.

ACCOUNTING SPECIALIST. Morrison Business Services, Honolulu, HI (1997-02). Played a key role in the substantial growth of this small business which provided accounting services for small businesses.
• On my own initiative, developed and implemented aggressive marketing programs which coordinated telemarketing and direct mail activities with persistent follow-up.
• Provided all accounting support for small businesses: prepared P&Ls, payroll, general ledgers, and journals.
• Trained small businesses in recordkeeping procedures and performance reporting activities.

MARKETING COORDINATOR. Felder-Marcum, Inc., Honolulu, HI (1995-97). Developed and implemented national and local marketing programs for restaurants in Honolulu, Kahului & Laie.

MARKETING REPRESENTATIVE. Hampton Golf Club, Springfield, IL (1993-95). Excelled in a key position in marketing and public relations and worked closely with Hampton's founder and Springfield native Michael Bradford.
• Was instrumental in the development of the company's first marketing manual.
• Designed and published a golf course magazine; coordinated national tournaments and reporting results.

PERSONAL

Excellent references. Possess excellent written and verbal communication skills and work well with people at all ages. Congenial personality.

Exact Name of Person
Title or Position
Name of Company
Address (no., street)
Address (city, state, zip)

MAGISTRATE
for a district court in
Lake Charles, LA

Dear Exact Name of Person: (or Dear Sir or Madam if answering a blind ad.)

I would appreciate an opportunity to talk with you soon about how I could contribute to your organization through the decision-making and problem-solving skills I have refined as a Magistrate.

As you will see from my resume, I received a B.S. in Criminal Justice degree in 1999 and also hold a Bachelor of Science degree in Psychology.

In my current position as a Magistrate for the Macomb-Hines District Court Office, I determine probable cause for the issuance of criminal processes and set conditions for pre-trial release. I accept guilty pleas for traffic and misdemeanor offense. I also try small claims actions up to $2,000 in controversy and summary ejectment cases involving landlord and tenant laws.

In previous experience as Guardian Ad Litem for the Hager County Juvenile Court, I acted as a volunteer, conducted investigations on behalf of children identified as being neglected or abused. I interviewed professionals in support of the child and served as spokesperson for the child in juvenile court.

You would find me to be a dynamic communicator who is known for my capacity for hard work and long hours. I am a highly adaptable professional who offers exceptionally research skills along with the proven ability to master difficult cases and persuasively argue them to judges and juries.

I hope you will welcome my call soon to arrange a brief meeting at your convenience to discuss your current and future needs and how I might serve them. Thank you in advance for your time.

Sincerely yours,

Edward Dodger

Alternate last paragraph:
I hope you will call or write me soon to suggest a time convenient for us to meet and discuss your current and future needs and how I might serve them. Thank you in advance for your time.

EDWARD DODGER

1110½ Hay Street, Fayetteville, NC 28305 • preppub@aol.com • (910) 483-6611

OBJECTIVE	To contribute my management and supervisory experience along with my talents in customer service and human relations to an organization that can use a dedicated and loyal professional.
EDUCATION	Received a **Bachelor in Criminal Justice degree,** Louisiana State University, New Orleans, LA, 1999. **B.S., Psychology**, McNeese State University, Lake Charles, LA, 1996. Have completed 12 semester hours in the Guidance Counseling Master's Program, Northeast Louisiana University, Monroe, LA, 1997.

EXPERIENCE

MAGISTRATE. 4th District Court Office, Lake Charles, LA (2000-present). Determine probable cause for the issuance of criminal processes; set conditions for pre-trial release.
- Accept guilty pleas for traffic and misdemeanor offense.
- Try small claims actions up to $2,000 in controversy and summary ejectment cases involving landlord and tenant laws.
- Conduct civil marriage ceremonies.

GUARDIAN AD LITEM. Hager County Juvenile Court, Lake Charles, LA (1998-99). As a volunteer, conducted investigations on behalf of children identified as being neglected or abused.
- Interviewed professionals in support of the child.
- Prepared written court reports.
- Served as spokesperson for the child in juvenile court.

SALES REPRESENTATIVE. Bayonet, Inc., Lake Charles, LA (1997-98). Supervised sales and distribution and served as a brand manager.

COMMAND SERGEANT MAJOR. U.S. Army Supply Division, Fort Carson, CO (1977-97). Served as senior enlisted advisor to commanding officers; also served as senior instructor in various military schools.

STRENGTHS
- Highly motivated to achieve and dedicated to excellence.
- Demonstrated work ethic with proven initiative and dedication.
- Effective writer and speaker with strong interpersonal communication skills.
- Work well in a team-oriented setting and/or independently to meet deadlines.
- Results oriented; able to expedite and delegate effectively.
- Strong time-management skills; highly creative and intuitive problems solver.
- Goal-oriented; seek new challenges; offer excellent leadership and organizational skills.
- Computer skills in Windows compatible systems and software.

AFFILIATIONS

Member, Board of Directors, Osborne Community Developments, Inc.
Treasurer of the PTA, Haven Hill High School.
Vice President for Programs, Draughton Outreach, Lake Charles Chapter.
Member, Board of Directors, Guardian Ad Litem Program.

Personal and Professional References Available Upon Request

Date

Exact Name of Person
Title or Position
Name of Company
Address (no., street)
Address (city, state, zip)

Dear Exact Name of Person: (or Dear Sir or Madam if answering a blind ad.)

I would appreciate an opportunity to talk with you soon about how I could contribute to your organization as a Magistrate.

In my current position as a Magistrate Court Administrator for the Northwestern District Court Office in Seattle, I have received a prestigious medal for the exceptional managerial skills and legal knowledge. I am the "internal expert" on legal processes, procedures, and practices in a staff section that sees frequent attorney turnover. I obtain and review criminal citations, prepare and file all criminal information, court dockets, notice letters, discovery requests, warrants, and pre-trial agreements. I also supervise and train a paralegal and legal specialist while assisting three attorneys in preparation and trial of cases. On a daily basis, I expertly apply my knowledge of the procedures required to assemble misdemeanor and petty offense cases and ensure the correct legal review of cases, the filing of charges in Federal District Court, and the informing of defendants of court dates.

As you will see from my enclosed resume, I earned a Bachelor of Science degree in Criminal Justice from Seattle University. I completed the Legal Specialist Course which provided in-depth training in areas including application of rules of law, microcomputer applications, drafting documents, legal writing/correspondence, claims, and legal assistance. As a Legal Specialist, I gained hands-on training in legal research, civil litigation practices, legal practices, and legal office management. I completed a Leadership Development Course which emphasized public speaking as well as management/supervisory techniques.

You would find me to be a dynamic communicator who is known for my capacity for hard work and long hours. I am a highly adaptable professional who offers exceptionally research skills along with the proven ability to work effectively with judges and attorneys.

I hope you will welcome my call soon to arrange a brief meeting at your convenience to discuss your current and future needs and how I might serve them. Thank you in advance for your time.

Sincerely yours,

Patricia D. Howard

PATRICIA D. HOWARD

1110½ Hay Street, Fayetteville, NC 28305   •   preppub@aol.com   •   (910) 483-6611

OBJECTIVE

To contribute to an organization that can use a poised communicator and well organized young professional who offers extensive experience in supervising administrative operations within an extremely busy legal jurisdiction.

EDUCATION

Earned a **Bachelor of Science degree in Criminal Justice**, Seattle University, Seattle, WA, 2000.

Completed the **Legal Specialist Course** which provided in-depth training in areas including application of rules of law, microcomputer applications, drafting documents, legal writing/ correspondence, claims, and legal assistance.

As a **Legal Specialist,** gained hands-on training in legal research, civil litigation practices, legal practices, and legal office management.

Completed a **Leadership Development Course** which emphasized public speaking as well as management/supervisory techniques.

COMPUTERS

Proficient at Microsoft Word, Excel, Enable, LAAWS, PageMaker, and Windows XP

EXPERIENCE

MAGISTRATE COURT ADMINISTRATOR and **LEGAL ASSISTANT.** Northwestern District Court Office, Seattle, WA (2002-present). Have received a prestigious award for the exceptional managerial skills and legal knowledge demonstrated in this job; am the "internal expert" on legal processes, procedures, and practices in a staff section that sees many officer/ attorney rotations.

- Obtain and review criminal citations, prepare and file all criminal information, court dockets, notice letters, discovery requests, warrants, and pre-trial agreements.
- Supervise and train a paralegal and legal specialist while assisting three attorneys in preparation and trial of cases.
- On a daily basis, expertly apply my knowledge of the procedures required to assemble misdemeanor and petty offense cases; ensure the correct legal review of cases, the filing of charges in Federal District Court, and the informing of defendants of court dates.
- Oversee actions taken toward juvenile defendants who commit crimes on the base.
- Practice legal processes in alternate forms of justice, such as the voluntary Shoplifters Alternative Program and the Pre-Trial Diversion which requires investigation into a defendant's background to determine eligibility for the program.
- Write letters for attorneys informing defendants of court dates, missed appearances, and status of their offense; write letters to parents of juvenile offenders.
- Conduct interviews on behalf of attorneys to differentiate clients that require their assistance from those that need a quick answer.
- Answer hundreds of phone calls weekly from defendants and from agencies/offices including the Federal Marshals Office, Federal Probation Office, and the Federal Public Defenders Office; always maintain a professional and courteous attitude.

ADMINISTRATIVE CLERK. Federal Public Defenders Office, Seattle, WA (2001-02). Supported the administrative needs of the Public Defender; controlled travel vouchers, ordered supplies, distributed information, ordered printed material including books and software, maintained the law library, and purchased furnishings.

LEGAL CLERK. Williams & Williams Law Firm, Seattle, WA (2000). Assisted two attorneys in will preparation, powers of attorney, payment of foreign claims, and other matters.

PERSONAL

Am known for my clear and courteous style of expressing myself, orally and in writing.

Date

Exact Name of Person
Title or Position
Name of Company
Address (number and street)
Address (city, state, and zip)

PARALEGAL

for a respected firm
in South Carolina is
relocating to
another state and is
attempting to set up
interviews with
potential employers

Dear Exact Name of Person: (or Sir or Madam if answering a blind ad.)

With the enclosed resume, I would like to initiate the process of being considered for employment within your organization as a Paralegal.

As you will see from my resume, I earned my Associate of Applied Science in Paralegal Technology from Trident Technical College. With a 3.7 GPA, I was selected as a Legal Research Assistant at my college because of my academic standing and personal reputation. In that capacity I tutored students and assisted faculty in projects that involved legal writing and research.

In prior employment, I excelled as a Legal Specialist for the Legal Services Division of the Charleston Air Force Base, and I became a trusted advisor to military executives. I routinely provided legal advice to military executives and senior managers as I received special recognition for my accomplishments and success in office management and leadership abilities. I was also entrusted with the responsibility for supervising the legal work performed at numerous organizations.

You would find me in person to be a congenial individual, and I can assure you that my legal research and legal writing skills are top-notch. If you can use a hard-working, resourceful, and thorough paralegal in your firm, I hope you will contact me to suggest a time when we might meet after I arrive in the Denver area on May 15. Feel free to call my current number to suggest a time for us to meet.

If you can use a hard worker who could become a valuable part of your organization, I hope you will call to suggest a time when I can make myself available for a personal interview at your convenience. Thank you in advance for your time.

Sincerely,

Gary Coaxum

GARY COAXUM

1110½ Hay Street, Fayetteville, NC 28305   •   preppub@aol.com   •   (910) 483-6611

OBJECTIVE

To become a contributing member of a law firm that can use a versatile Paralegal who offers experience with real estate law, corporate law, civil litigation, personal injury, and criminal defense along with outstanding analytical, research, and communication skills.

EDUCATION

Associate of Applied Science in Paralegal Technology (an ABA Approved Program), Trident Technical College, North Charleston, SC, 2003.
- With a 3.7 GPA, graduated *summa cum laude*.
- Named to Sigma Theta Psi Fraternity, which requires a GPA above 3.5.
- Consistently named to President's and Dean's Lists; Active member, Paralegal Club.
- Coursework completed:

Legal Research	Partnership/Corporate Law	Civil Litigation
Tort Law	Investigations	Family Law
Case Analysis/Reasoning	Contract Law and the UCC	Criminal Procedures

Other college: Previously completed courses at College of Charleston, SC, 1997.

Other legal training: While employed as a Legal Research Assistant for the Legal Services Division at the Charleston Air Force Base in Charleston, SC, completed extensive legal training in addition to a five-week Legal Specialist Training Program.

EXPERIENCE

PARALEGAL. Bayman & Crouch, Attorneys at Law, Charleston, SC (2003-present). Have been successful in being selected for this Paralegal Internship with one of the city's most respected law firms; excelled in this part-time job while I retained my #1 position in my graduating class, and can provide outstanding references from this firm.
- Assist Attorney Rogers with his real estate and corporate law practice.
- Assist Attorney Phillips in civil litigation, personal injury, and criminal defense.
- Was commended by both attorneys for significantly reducing their research time through my excellent analytical skills and research ability.
- Learned how to title search and how to prepare loan closing packages.

LEGAL RESEARCH ASSISTANT. Trident Technical College, Charleston, SC (2002-03). Was selected for this honorary role at my college because of my personal reputation and GPA; tutored students in legal research methodology.
- Assisted faculty members with projects which required excellent legal writing skills.

LEGAL SPECIALIST. Charleston Air Force Base, Legal Services Division, Charleston, SC (1999-02). Provided legal services for a 500-soldier organization while working under the supervision of numerous military attorneys.
- Supervised two employees while managing legal work performed in three organizations.
- Prepared correspondence for the signature of military executives.
- Was specially selected to manage the legal office for a 2,000-person unit when the Senior Legal Specialist was absent; this responsibility was usually reserved for someone with more authority.
- Became a trusted advisor to military executives, and routinely provided legal advice to military executives and senior managers received special recognition for my accomplishments and success in office management and leadership abilities.

COMPUTERS

Proficient with Westlaw, Microsoft Word, PowerPoint, Excel and Adobe PageMaker.

PERSONAL

Excellent references available upon request.

CAREER CHANGE

Date

Exact Name of Person
Title or Position
Name of Company
Address (no., street)
Address (city, state, zip)

PARALEGAL

for a law firm seeks
another position in the
legal field

Dear Exact Name of Person: (or Dear Sir or Madam if answering a blind ad.)

I would appreciate an opportunity to talk with you soon about how I could contribute to your organization through my experience as a Paralegal.

In my current position as a Paralegal for Carlson & Buckley Law Firm, I perform various tasks such as title searching, preparing title insurance applications, preparing loan closing packages, recording documents, and observing loan closings. I was responsible for setting up personal injury files, preparing subpoenas, organizing medical correspondence, and accident reports.

In a previous position as an Underwriter for Brodman Title Services, I picked up, disbursed and logged in mail as well as figure premiums. I underwrote applications for Title Insurance and I typed and assembled policies as well as figure weekly, monthly, quarterly, and yearly reports. I also assumed managerial duties when the supervisor is out of the office.

As you will see from my resume, I have specialized skills and abilities that could make me a valuable part of your team. I can provide excellent personal and professional references if you request them.

I hope you will call or write me soon to suggest a time convenient for us to meet and discuss your current and future needs and how I might serve them. Thank you in advance for your time.

Sincerely yours,

Alechia Cummings

ALECHIA CUMMINGS

1110½ Hay Street, Fayetteville, NC 28305   •   preppub@aol.com   •   (910) 483-6611

OBJECTIVE:
I want to contribute to an organization that can use a Paralegal with outstanding analytical skills.

JOB EXPERIENCE:
Paralegal and Paralegal Intern
Carlson & Buckley Law Firm
3764 Fairfax Avenue
Milwaukee, WI 78273
2003-present
Completed internship program with this firm and was offered a full-time Paralegal position. I perform various tasks such as title searching, preparing title insurance applications, preparing loan closing packages, recording documents and observing loan closings; setting up personal injury files, preparing subpoenas, organizing medicals, correspondence, accident reports; participating in general office duties.

Underwriter
Brodman Title Services
5613 Main Street
Milwaukee, WI 78173
1999-03
Picked up, disbursed, and logged in mail; figured premiums; underwrote applications for Title Insurance; typed policies and assembled policy packets; figured weekly, monthly, quarterly, and yearly reports; answered telephone; assumed managerial duties when supervisor was out of the office.

Waitress
Ryan's Steakhouse
8311 Paisley Avenue
Milwaukee, WI 78516
1995-99
Assisted customers, cashier. Part-time employment while attending Averett High School.

COMPUTERS:
Proficient with personal computers and with software including Excel, Access, and PowerPoint; familiar with Westlaw.

EDUCATION:
Associate Degree in Paralegal Technology, Western Wisconsin Technical College, 1998.
Graduated from Averett High School, 1996 honor graduate.

COMMUNITY INVOLVEMENT:
As a resident of Milwaukee, Wisconsin, I attended New Zion AME, played on the Averett High School basketball and softball teams.

PERSONAL:
Outstanding personal and professional references available on request.

CAREER CHANGE

Date

Exact Name of Person
Title or Position
Name of Company
Address (no., street)
Address (city, state, zip)

PARALEGAL
is seeking his first
full-time position in
a law firm

Dear Exact Name of Person: (or Dear Sir or Madam if answering a blind ad.)

I would like to discuss with you how I could benefit your organization through my skills as a Paralegal.

While earning my degree in Paralegal Technology, I worked for the Valencia County Public Library as a Library Page and Library Technician. In spite of the fact that I worked full-time while excelling in a demanding job, I excelled academically and achieved a 3.9 GPA.

I was promoted by the library because of my outstanding performance as a Library Page, and I am respected for my attention to detail as well as my outstanding analytical skills. I am confident that those strengths will be appreciated in a legal environment as well. In previous experience as an Industrial Technician for Hydraulic Industrial Resources in Albuquerque, I received extensive training in quality assurance and safety.

I can provide outstanding personal and professional references from previous employers, who would describe me, I am certain, as a cheerful and adaptable office professional who can be counted on to meet tight deadlines and produce quality work under pressure. You would find me to be an intelligent person who is good at problem solving in office environments.

I hope you will call or write me soon to suggest a time convenient for us to meet and discuss your current and future needs and how I might serve them. Thank you in advance for your time.

Sincerely yours,

Richard LaFlam

RICHARD LAFLAM

1110½ Hay Street, Fayetteville, NC 28305 • preppub@aol.com • (910) 483-6611

OBJECTIVE

To benefit an organization that can use a versatile and dedicated hard worker who possesses excellent written and oral communication skills along with experience in customer service, research, and computer operations.

EDUCATION

Associate of Science degree in Paralegal Technology, Dona Ana Branch Community College, Las Cruces, NM, 2004.
- Was cited by professors for my exceptional writing skills.

Bachelor of Arts degree in History with a concentration in Political Science, University of New Mexico, Albuquerque, NM, 1999.
- Earned a spot on the Dean's List, 1997-1998.

HONORS

College: Dean's List, Membership in the National Honor Society for Political Science, Advisor of the History Club
High School: Honor Roll and Perfect Attendance Certificates for two years

EXPERIENCE

Worked for the Valencia County Public Library in two different positions:
2000-present: LIBRARY TECHNICIAN I. Collier Branch of the Valencia County Public Library, Albuquerque, NM.
Was promoted to this position because of my outstanding performance as a Library Page. Checked library materials in and out for patrons; answered customer inquiries over a multi-line phone system; collected fines from library patrons for overdue materials; counted fees in cash registers and opened/closed the library; collected materials from the book drop; handled the shelving of books according to strict guidelines; used a proprietary computer system developed specially for the library to obtain records of patron's library transactions, fees due, and materials checked in/out or overdue.

1998-2000: LIBRARY PAGE. Westlake Branch Library, Albuquerque, NM.
Shelved materials returned by library patrons, and ensured that all items were placed in the appropriate section; placed materials returned by library patrons on carts, grouping materials together according to section to facilitate efficient shelving; provided limited assistance to customers, helping them to locate materials upon request.

Other experience:
INDUSTRIAL TECHNICIAN, Hydraulic Industrial Resources, Albuquerque, NM (1996-98). Perform various duties throughout the plant which include preparing tool kits for packaging of cut saws; placing labels on hedge trimmers; operating a press machine which places screws inside metal plates for use in omega drills; and positioning jig saws for packaging by a packaging machine.
- Have received extensive training in quality assurance and safety.

PERSONAL

Enjoy researching, creating, and writing documents. Can provide outstanding references on request. Thrive on conquering new challenges.

Exact Name of Person
Title or Position
Name of Company
Address (no., street)
Address (city, state, zip)

PARALEGAL
for a law office
in Oklahoma

Dear Exact Name of Person: (or Dear Sir or Madam if answering a blind ad.)

I would appreciate an opportunity to talk with you soon about how I could contribute to your organization through my experience and education in Paralegal Technology.

As you will see from my resume, since graduating with my Associate of Arts in Paralegal Technology, I have worked for a law firm with 18 attorneys. Although I am excelling in my job, I am relocating soon to the Dallas area with my husband, who recently graduated from dental school. We hope to establish roots in the Dallas area, and I am seeking an employer who could benefit from my diversified experience as a Paralegal. I can provide outstanding personal and professional references.

We will be in the Dallas area frequently in the coming months in order to identify suitable housing options, and I would be pleased to make your acquaintance at a time which is convenient for you.

I hope you will call or write me soon to suggest a time convenient for us to meet and discuss your current and future needs and how I might serve them. Thank you in advance for your time.

Sincerely yours,

Laura S. Nowinski

LAURA S. NOWINSKI

1110½ Hay Street, Fayetteville, NC 28305 • preppub@aol.com • (910) 483-6611

OBJECTIVE

To contribute my exceptional attention-to-detail and fact-finding skills to a law firm that can use an energetic paralegal who understands the importance of being an effective assistant.

EDUCATION

Associate of Arts degree in Paralegal Technology, Tulsa Community College, Tulsa, OK, 2003.

Specialized Courses

Paralegalism	Contract Law & the UCC
Legal Research	Civil Litigation II
Tort Law	Legal Writing
Partnership and Corporate Law	Family Law
Criminal Law	Investigation
Law Office Management	Property/Real Estate Law
Wills, Trusts & Estates	Bankruptcy & Collections
Investigative Photography	Property/Title Searches
Property/Real Estate Closings	

SPECIAL SKILLS

Can contribute in many areas including:

probate matters	conducting investigations
searching public records	preparation of tax forms
library research	bookkeeping
serving and filing legal documents	
providing office management assistance	

EXPERIENCE

PARALEGAL. Winfield, Braxton & Mills, Tulsa, OK (2003-present). Handle a variety of administrative and paralegal duties including researching, filing and serving legal documents, conducting title searches, obtaining character witness statements, making changes to wills, and searching public records.

ADMINISTRATIVE ASSISTANT. Logistics Office, Tulsa, OK (1997-03). Managed the daily operations of a busy logistical support:
* Kept records of financial and counseling transactions.
* Reviewed and organized career literature, information, and resources.
* Performed filing and receptionist duties associated with the retention, maintenance, disposition and control of personnel records.
* Utilized a Windows XP operating systems to process data.
* Received, sorted, and distributed mail.
* Prepared schedules and made arrangements for meetings.
* Prepared and proofread written documents.
* Trained, supervised, and evaluated new assistants.
* Officially commended by the Logistics Division for outstanding devotion to duty and demonstration of technical competence.

Highlights of other experience:
* Established and maintained stock records and other documents such as inventory/ material control, accounting, and supply records; interpreted automated supply documents; and prepared inventory adjustments records as Supply Technician.

COMPUTERS

Proficient with Microsoft Word, Excel, Access, and PowerPoint as well as PageMaker.

PERSONAL

Enjoy problem solving and researching information. Can provide references upon request.

Exact Name of Person
Title or Position
Name of Company
Address (no., street)
Address (city, state, zip)

PARALEGAL & TITLE SEARCHER

for a law firm
in Georgia

Dear Exact Name of Person: (or Dear Sir or Madam if answering a blind ad.)

I would appreciate an opportunity to talk with you soon about how I could contribute to your organization through my outstanding paralegal and supervisory experience, as well as my excellent planning and organizational skills.

As you can see from my resume, I am currently working as a Paralegal & Title Searcher at a busy law firm, researching title documentation while also submitting legal pleadings. During my internship I gained valuable legal procedure experience while assisting my employer in processing a wide range of court documents and preparing cases for trial.

One of my greatest strengths is my ability to handle stressful situations and quickly find the proper solution to the problem. I have built a reputation as a very detail-oriented individual with an eye for finding ways to increase a company's efficiency.

I hope you will welcome my call soon to arrange a brief meeting at your convenience to discuss your current and future needs and how I might serve them. Thank you in advance for your time.

Sincerely,

Sonya Nathaniel

Alternate last paragraph:
I hope you will contact me soon to suggest a time convenient to meet and discuss your current and future needs and how I might serve them. Thank you in advance for your time.

SONYA NATHANIEL

1110½ Hay Street, Fayetteville, NC 28305 • preppub@aol.com • (910) 483-6611

OBJECTIVE

To benefit an organization in need of a hardworking young professional who offers outstanding paralegal and supervisory experience and excellent organizational and planning skills.

COMPUTERS

Am proficient in a wide range of software, including Microsoft Word, Excel, PowerPoint, and QuarkXpress.

EXPERIENCE

PARALEGAL & TITLE SEARCHER. McDaniels & McDaniels, Macon, GA (2002-present). Assist in quickly and accurately researching title documentation involving land, residences, condominiums, and shopping malls.
- Have refined my research and analytical skills.
- Draft legal descriptions to determine history of subdivisions and other legal descriptions.
- File summons, complaints, motions, and other legal pleadings.
- Interpret platted property.

PARALEGAL INTERN. The Law Offices of Ross & Tremble, Macon, GA (1999-02). Gained valuable experience performing a wide range of legal procedures.
- Developed a network of contacts within the judicial and social services system.
- Prepared trial subpoenas and trial notebooks.
- Drafted complaints, summons, and motions.
- Assisted in trial preparation and research.
- Managed legal files and selected documentation.

SALES ASSOCIATE. Chains and Things, Macon, GA (1998-99). Handled a large number of financial transactions daily while also promoting extensive customer service.

FINANCIAL ASSISTANT. Citi Financial, Macon, GA (1995-98). Served as point of contact for organizations within the area to provide information concerning whether there was adequate funding for the hiring of additional personnel.
- Learned the internal workings of a financial institution.
- Updated computer files on a daily basis.
- Trained and supervised a two-person staff.

TELECOMMUNICATOR. Macon's Tele-Services, Macon, GA (1994-95). Answered calls and delivered messages for a large number of professional clients using a computerized telephone switchboard.
- Became known for my congenial personality and ability to cheerfully work under deadlines.
- Managed and updated client files.

EDUCATION

Bachelor of Science in Accounting, Mercer University, Macon, GA, 2002.
Associate of Science degree, Paralegal Studies, Macon State College, Macon, GA, 1999. (ABA-Approved)

SKILLS

Operate a variety of office equipment, including multi-line computerized switchboards, 10-key calculators, and adding machines; can type 45 wpm.

PERSONAL

Am a flexible, versatile professional who enjoys challenges and achieving optimum results. Have consistently received outstanding performance evaluations. References upon request.

Date

Exact Name of Person
Title or Position
Name of Company
Address (number and street)
Address (city, state, and zip)

PARALEGAL INTERN
for law offices
in Indiana

Dear Exact Name of Person: (or Sir or Madam if answering a blind ad.)

With the enclosed resume, I would like to initiate the process of being considered for employment within your organization as a Paralegal.

As you will see from my resume, I have recently earned my Bachelor of Science degree in Psychology from Purdue University, where I worked as a Teaching Assistant in upper-division psychology course while completing my degree.

I have also earned a Paralegal Certificate and successfully completed a one-year comprehensive ABA-approved program with coursework in: Legal Research and Writing, Legal Concepts, Litigation I & II, Contracts, Evidence/Advanced Litigation, Corporate Law, Workers Compensation, Criminal Law, Advanced Legal Research & Writing, and Real Estate. As a Paralegal Intern for the Law Offices of Denise Moniz, I prepared demand letters, reviewed case files and medical records, extracted relevant information, and noted discrepancies.

If you can use a hard worker who could become a valuable part of your organization, I hope you will call to suggest a time when I can make myself available for a personal interview at your convenience. Thank you in advance for your time.

Sincerely,

Laura D. Hawkins

LAURA D. HAWKINS

1110½ Hay Street, Fayetteville, NC 28305   •   preppub@aol.com   •   (910) 483-6611

OBJECTIVE

To contribute my office operations know-how to an organization that could benefit from a detail-oriented professional with outstanding written and oral communication skills and a friendly approach to customer service and client relations.

EDUCATION

Bachelor of Science in Psychology, Purdue University, West Lafayette, IN, 2001.
- Because of my superior communication skills and 3.8 GPA, was selected as a Teaching Assistant in upper-division psychology courses.

Paralegal Certificate, Purdue University, West Lafayette, IN, 2003.
Successfully completed a one-year comprehensive ABA-approved program with coursework such as:

Legal Research and Writing	Legal Concepts
Litigation I & II	Contracts
Evidence/Advanced Litigation	Corporate Law
Workers Compensation	Criminal Law
Advanced Legal Research & Writing	Real Estate

- Honors achieved in majority of classes taken.

EXPERIENCE

PARALEGAL INTERN. Law Offices of Denise Moniz, Lafayette, IN (2004-present).
- Prepare demand letters.
- Review case files and medical records.
- Extract relevant information and noted discrepancies.
- Calculate lost wages, as well as general and special damages.
- Communicate with clients, medical personnel and claims adjusters.

RECEPTIONIST. Carla Logan's Fitness, Lafayette, IN (2001-04). For approximately a year, this job was simultaneous with the job above.
- Responded to members' inquiries and complaints.
- Trained all new receptionists for three clubs.
- Maintained contract files and daily bookkeeping.
- Created Receptionist Manual which was adopted by the corporation and distributed to all its clubs.

CLERICAL ASSISTANT. Lancaster, Inc., Lafayette, IN (1998-01).
- Processed rental/leasing applications and followed through to completion.
- Provided necessary information to clients.

GROUP LEADER. Purdue University, West Lafayette, IN (1996-98). Assisted incoming freshman with transition to university life.

COMPUTER SKILLS

Word Processing: Microsoft Word, PowerPoint & Access
Spreadsheet: Excel
Legal Research: WESTLAW Certificate, Sept. 2003

PERSONAL

Am known for my outgoing personality and ability to communicate and get along with anyone. Believe organization is the key to productivity. A quick learner, rapidly master new concepts.

Exact Name of Person
Title or Position
Name of Company
Address (no., street)
Address (city, state, zip)

PARALEGAL INTERN
seeks full-time
position

Dear Exact Name of Person: (or Dear Sir or Madam if answering a blind ad.)

I would like to talk to you soon about how I could contribute to your organization through my combination of education in criminal justice and paralegal technology as well as secretarial science, and my practical work experience.

If we meet in person, I am confident that you would find me to be an ambitious, conscientious, and dependable professional who could make valuable contributions to your organization. With a reputation as a "computer whiz," I offer an ability to rapidly master new software and operating systems, and I am proficient with the Microsoft Suite including Word, Excel, Access, and PowerPoint.

I hope you will call or write me soon to suggest a time convenient for us to meet and discuss your current and future goals and how I might serve them. Thank you in advance for your time.

Sincerely yours,

Donnetia L. McFadden

DONNETIA L. McFADDEN

1110½ Hay Street, Fayetteville, NC 28305   •   preppub@aol.com   •   (910) 483-6611

OBJECTIVE   To apply my legal knowledge and experience to the field of Law Enforcement or Security.

EDUCATION   **Associate Degree in Paralegal Technology**, Montana State University, Billings, MT, 2003.
Completed one year in the **Criminal Justice** program at Montana State University, Billings, MT, 1999.
Studied **Secretarial Science** at Billings Community College, Billings, MT, 1998.

COMPUTERS   Highly proficient in utilizing computers with software including Word, Excel, Access, PowerPoint.

STRENGTHS   Communicating excellently with others.
Working productively and independently.
Giving and taking directions.
Making quick and sound decisions.

EXPERIENCE   **PARALEGAL INTERN.** State of Montana District Court, Billings, MT (2003-present). Interview incarcerated inmates and serve subpoenas to witnesses.
- Perform administrative functions including collation and copying of trial transcripts, scheduling client appointments, answering the telephone and recording messages, and handling the mail.

NUCLEAR SECURITY OFFICER. Pompey Pilliar Nuclear Power Plant, Billings, MT (2001-02). Processed plant employees into the plant; issue badges and maintained inventory of badges.
- Performed escort duties and patrolled perimeter zones.

PREBOARD SCREENER. Billings International Airport, Billings, MT (2000-01). Viewed contents of carry-on luggage and checked passengers using a handscanner unit for metal readings.
- Confiscated and documented unauthorized weapons as they were detected.
- Ensured the security check point was properly opened and closed.

RECORDS CLERK. Northwestern Credit Union, Billings, MT (1995-99). Received and refilled customer folders, documented outgoing files, sorted and filed correspondence, and related information to the Loan Department.

LIBRARY ASSISTANT. Findlay Middle School, Billings, MT (1994-95). Willfully directed patrons seeking assistance, sorted and shelved library materials, maintained discipline in the library, typed cards, and posted due notices.

PERSONAL   Am a conscientious, honest, career-oriented professional who prides myself on my ability to cooperate and get along with anyone and my dependability.

Date

Exact Name of Person
Title or Position
Name of Company
Address (number and street)
Address (city, state, and zip)

PARALEGAL SPECIALIST
for the Department of
Transportation

Dear Exact Name of Person: (or Sir or Madam if answering a blind ad.)

Can you use a hard-working young professional who has excelled as a paralegal and legal secretary?

In my current job I work with a staff of attorneys, paralegals, and secretaries with the State of Idaho Department of Transportation. Since the department's primary mission is to continue building Idaho's network of roads and superhighways, we deal routinely with contractors who are out in the field valuing real estate that the DOT might want to buy. I use the dictaphone routinely and work with several popular software programs while also functioning as an executive secretary, organizing and scheduling meetings among the contractors and legal staff.

I can provide outstanding personal and professional references from previous employers, who would describe me, I am certain, as a cheerful and adaptable office professional who can be counted on to meet tight deadlines and produce quality work under pressure. You would find me to be an intelligent person who is good at problem solving in office environments.

I hope you will call or write me soon to suggest a time convenient for us to meet and discuss your current and future needs and how I might serve them. Thank you in advance for your time.

Sincerely yours,

Kim Ferguson

KIM FERGUSON

1110½ Hay Street, Fayetteville, NC 28305   •   preppub@aol.com   •   (910) 483-6611

OBJECTIVE

To contribute to an organization that can use a poised young professional who offers specialized training and experience as a paralegal and legal receptionist.

EDUCATION

Associate of Paralegal degree, Boise State University, Boise, ID, 2002.
- Excelled academically with a 3.9 GPA based on a 4.0 scale.

Fields of study included the following:

Civil Litigation	Legal Research I & II
Legal Document Writing	Torts
Real Estate	Criminal Law
Legal Vocabulary	Business Law
Computer Applications	Accounting I, II, and III
Eminent Domain	

EXPERIENCE

PARALEGAL SPECIALIST. State of Idaho Department of Transportation, Boise, ID (2002-present). Earned a reputation as a cheerful worker who readily adapted to new working environments as needed while working within a department which was primarily concerned with the mission of building roads throughout Idaho; interface regularly with contractors who are "in the field" valuing properties that the department might want to purchase in order to continue Idaho's highway transportation system.
- Work with a staff of attorneys, paralegals, and secretaries.
- Routinely utilize software including Microsoft Word and Excel.
- Have developed expertise in the area of preparing legal documents.
- Prepare expert witness contracts as well as discovery requests, orders, and letters.
- For several months, was assigned to operate a busy three-line switchboard and became known for my telephone etiquette.
- Use the dictaphone on a daily basis in the process of transcribing communication of attorneys.
- Function frequently in the capacity of an Executive Secretary as I organize and schedule meetings among attorneys and contractors so they could meet face-to-face over matters of land valuation.

SALES ASSISTANT. Butler's Shoe Store, Boise, ID (2001-02). Became skilled in working with customers in a retail environment while assisting people with shoe selection; was entrusted with the responsibility of opening and closing the store on several occasions.
- Won the respect of management because of my attention to detail when handling financial transactions and accounting for cash.
- Helped the store cement its relationships with previous customers through my warm personality and customer service skills.

WAITRESS/HOSTESS. Popeye's, Boise, ID (1999-01). Was rapidly promoted to greater responsibility related to handling cash and receipts in this popular "fast-food" restaurant.
- Assisted customers with menu selections and seated patrons.

COMPUTERS
- Familiar with Microsoft Word and Excel
- Offer proven ability to rapidly master interoffice software packages
- Experienced in using the Internet

Date

Exact Name of Person
Title or Position
Name of Company
Address (no., street)
Address (city, state, zip)

**PARALEGAL SPECIALIST
& ADMINISTRATOR**

for a legal services
division of the Army

Dear Exact Name of Person: (or Dear Sir or Madam if answering a blind ad.)

I would appreciate an opportunity to talk with you soon about how I could contribute to your organization through my outstanding abilities in training program development and office administration.

Among my greatest strengths are my superior communication, motivational, and managerial skills. I excel in quantifying objectives and standards and created more than 15 separate programs with the trust of my superiors that I would produce outstanding results. My background as a paralegal has allowed me to be effective in establishing legal support operations and legal training programs. In addition to setting up professional development training programs, I also offer experience in conducting the actual training.

I am a highly adaptable and versatile professional offering excellent time management, planning, and organizational skills. As you will see by my enclosed resume, I have additional experience in counseling and interviewing, substance abuse and prevention education, equal opportunity supervision, and public affairs.

I am certain that through the combination of a degree in Business Administration and my versatile experience, I can provide the leadership, talents, and knowledge that will make me valuable to businesses that are in need of proven and tested professionals.

I hope you will call soon to suggest a time convenient for you to meet and discuss your current and future needs and how I might serve them. Thank you in advance for your time.

Sincerely yours,

Jennifer Jefferson

JENNIFER JEFFERSON

1110½ Hay Street, Fayetteville, NC 28305   •   preppub@aol.com   •   (910) 483-6611

OBJECTIVE

To acquire a responsible and challenging management position where my experience and education can be effectively used to meet the goals of a multifaceted corporation.

EDUCATION

Bachelor of Science degree in **Business Administration** with a minor in **Management**, University of Arizona, Ft. Huachuca campus, AZ, 2002.
- Maintained a 3.5 GPA and graduated *magna cum laude*.
- Displayed exceptional time management skills completing degree in three years while working in a demanding full-time government job.

EXPERIENCE

PARALEGAL SPECIALIST & ADMINISTRATOR Legal Services Division, Fort Huachuca, AZ (2001-present). Develop and implement new programs as the principal legal assistant to the chief executive of an office which provided guidance to 40 legal offices in 25 states.
- Maintain a legal assistance program including conducting client interviews, providing tax assistance, and drafting a wide range of legal documents.
- Advise the chief executive on personnel issues relating to promotions, military justice, human relations, and equal opportunity.
- Streamline processing for personnel preparing wills and other legal documents prior to departure to international assignments.
- Developed and manage an annual budget and a supply account with 100% accountability.

CHIEF PARALEGAL SPECIALIST. U.S. Army Judicial Court, Fort Knox, KY (1998-00). Managed administrative support in a legal office; ensured files and records remained current and complete while supervising office personnel.
- Established a legal specialist qualification course and instructed participants.
- Counseled employees considering career decisions, qualifications, goals, and personal objectives.
- Served as Personnel Manager for over 10,000 soldiers for the largest allied forces training exercise.

PARALEGAL. Legal Services Division, Fort Gordon, GA (1996-98). Worked in various areas of the legal system including pre/post-trial, criminal law, trial defense, and as a Legal Clerk.

TRAINING & SPECIAL SKILLS

Selected to attend more than 1,680 hours of specialized training in areas such as advanced leadership, operations management, and personnel supervision; civil affairs and disaster relief operations; worldwide legal management; and procedures for income tax advisors. Completed course work leading to certification in Total Quality management and group facilitator techniques.

COMPUTER SKILLS

Knowledgeable in computer software including Microsoft Word, Excel, Access and Adobe PageMaker; operate a variety of office equipment.

PERSONAL

Familiar with Latin. Will travel/relocate. Have become known as a resourceful problem-solver with outstanding decision-making and strategic management abilities.

LIFE EXPERIENCE

- Strength in planning, implementing, executing and monitoring/follow-up.
- Results oriented; confident in making on-the-spot decisions.
- Capable of managing multiple projects and people.
- Talent for facilitating-consensus building.

Date

Exact Name of Person
Title or Position
Name of Company
Address (number and street)
Address (city, state, and zip)

Dear Exact Name of Person: (or Sir or Madam if answering a blind ad.)

I would appreciate an opportunity to talk with you soon about how I could contribute to your organization through my proven organizational, management, and communication skills.

Before relocating to Dallas with my husband, I demonstrated my versatility and ability to excel in a wide range of jobs in Denver. We are now permanent residents of Dallas, and I am seeking an opportunity to make a significant and long-term contribution to an organization that can use a highly motivated and creative individual.

As you will see from my resume, my work experience includes managing an internship program, authoring proposals for and administering government grants, working in law firms where I performed research and managed a clerical staff, acting as a college instructor, assisting an author in preparing his memoirs, and coordinating volunteer programs.

Holding a B.A. degree in Political Science and having completed nearly two years of graduate-level course work in Public Administration, I offer highly refined written and oral communication skills. I also offer the proven ability to step into an unknown situation and quickly "get on my feet" through my strong analytical and problem-solving skills.

If you can use a highly motivated self starter with unlimited personal initiative and a high energy level, I would enjoy talking with you in person. I hope you will welcome my call soon to arrange a brief meeting to discuss your current and future needs and how I might serve them. I can provide outstanding personal and professional references.

Sincerely,

Arlene C. Michaels

Alternate last paragraph:
I hope you will call or write me soon to suggest a time convenient for us to meet and discuss your current and future needs and how I might serve them. Thank you in advance for your time.

ARLENE C. MICHAELS

1110½ Hay Street, Fayetteville, NC 28305 • preppub@aol.com • (910) 483-6611

OBJECTIVE

To contribute to an organization that can use a talented communicator with experience in instructing, counseling, and training others along with a proven ability to transform concepts into well-organized programs.

EDUCATION

Completed 1-1/2 years of graduate course work toward a **Master's degree in Public Administration,** University of Colorado at Denver.
Bachelor of Arts in Political Science, University of Colorado at Denver, 2003.
• Maintained a 3.9 GPA while working full-time to finance my education.

EXPERIENCE

PROGRAM COORDINATOR. Denver Bible College, Denver, CO (2003-present). Organized two volunteer groups and provide them with leadership and guidance.
• Supervise and train teachers and staff for a church vacation Bible school with children attending two consecutive summers.
• Operate a family support group providing information/support for military wives whose husbands were away frequently.

COLLEGE INSTRUCTOR. Metropolitan State College of Denver, Colorado (2001-03). Refined my public speaking skills while teaching Paralegal Technology and American Government; prepared lesson plans.
• Was commended for my ability to motivate students, to communicate concepts, and to provide student feedback/evaluations tactfully.

COUNSELOR/LEGAL ADVOCATE. My Sisters' House, Denver, CO (1997-01). Provided advice and assistance to battered women: advised them of their legal rights, helped them prepare documents to be used in court, and accompanied them to court.
• Wrote a grant proposal which resulted in a HUD grant for the shelter.
• Was Assistant Instructor for a self-help class which taught women their legal rights.
• Monitored legislation and was able to contribute to the development of anti-stalking legislation in one of the first states to do so.
• Was commended for my skill in clarifying complex issues while working closely with law enforcement, legal, and military personnel.

INTERN. The Denver Council, Denver, CO (1995-96). As an intern specializing in community development, prepared block grants for a six-county region and administered the HUD grant funding the intern program. Researched material and prepared speeches for the executive director; drafted proposals for the funding committee.

LEGAL RESEARCHER. Gregg & Pittman, LLP, Denver, CO (1992-95). Assisted the managing partner while preparing/researching legal documents and maintaining master calendar/dockets. Established and maintained a network of contacts throughout the city.

RESEARCH ASSISTANT. Andrew Phillips, Attorney-at-Law, Denver, CO (1991-92). Performed research and functioned as the "right arm" for a prestigious Lawyer preparing his documents for domestic violence cases.

Highlights of earlier experience: Advanced from a clerical position to take charge of an eight-person department for a 120-employee law firm.

PERSONAL

Highly motivated individual with initiative. Permanent resident of Denver.

Date

Exact Name of Person
Exact Title
Exact Name of Company
Address
City, State, Zip

**RECEPTIONIST &
ADMINISTRATIVE
ASSISTANT**
for an attorney
city service in
Houston, TX

Dear Exact Name of Person: (or Dear Sir or Madam if answering a blind ad):

With the enclosed resume, I would like to make you aware of my experience in legal environments which I could put to work for your company.

As you will see from my resume, I was recently employed with the Attorney City Services as a Receptionist/Administrative Assistant. I was fully responsible for programming the telephone system, answering 16 incoming lines, while managing the library and inputting daily incoming checks. I provided computer technical support, established a spreadsheet system to keep track of people attending an annual fundraiser, provided clients with information and legal referral resources and conducted a preliminary assessment of new cases.

In a previous position as a Receptionist for the Department of Immigration, I processed data into the donor database, answered and routed six incoming telephone lines. I copied, prepared, and sent mailings. I also helped to organize legal seminars, updated law books, and performed bookkeeping duties by preparing weekly deposits and inputting incoming checks into the database.

If you can use an articulate, poised young professional whose abilities have been proven in a number of challenging positions, I hope you will welcome my call soon when I try to arrange a brief meeting to discuss your goals and how my background might serve your needs. I can provide outstanding references at the appropriate time.

Sincerely,

Allen G. Gentry

Alternate Last Paragraph:
I hope you will write or call me soon to suggest a time when we might meet to discuss your needs and goals and how my background might serve them. I can provide outstanding references at the appropriate time.

ALLEN G. GENTRY

1110½ Hay Street, Fayetteville, NC 28305   •   preppub@aol.com   •   (910) 483-6611

JOB OBJECTIVE   I would like to be considered for your position as a Legal Assistant.

EDUCATION   Completed two years of college studies, North Harris College
Houston, TX
From: 8/00
To: 12/02

Graduated in the top 10% of my class, Tourneau Academy High School
Houston, TX
From: 8/96
To: 5/00

EMPLOYMENT HISTORY

Receptionist/Administrative Assistant
Attorney City Services
Houston, TX
From: 11/02
To: present
My duties at the Attorney City Services included being fully responsible for programming the telephone system, answering 16 incoming lines, managing the library, and inputting daily incoming checks. Provided computer technical support. Established a spreadsheet system to keep track of people attending an annual fundraiser. Provided clients with information and legal referral resources. Conducted a preliminary assessment of new cases.

Receptionist
Department of Immigration
Houston, TX
From: 3/01
To: 11/02
My duties at Department of Immigration included processing data into the donor database; answering and routing six incoming telephone lines; copying, preparing, and sending mailings; helping in the organization of legal seminars; updating law books; and doing some bookkeeping by preparing weekly deposits and inputting incoming checks into the database.

Clerk
Phillips, Anderson & Mayes
Houston, TX
From: 7/00
To: 3/01
Entered data on prospective clients into the database, made copies, and processed mail.

SPECIAL SKILLS   Bilingual in German and English.
Am computer literate with experience in Microsoft Word, Excel, PowerPoint, and QuarkXpress software as well as a working knowledge of LANs, Internet/WWW, CD-ROM, and online tools such as Lexis/Nexus.
Type approximately 65 wpm.

Date

Exact Name of Person
Title or Position
Name of Company
Address (number and street)
Address (city, state, and zip)

RECOVERY CLERK
for the Department
of Defense

Dear Exact Name of Person: (or Sir or Madam if answering a blind ad.)

With the enclosed resume, I would like to acquaint you with my background as an office clerk, secretary, and receptionist while also making you aware of the strong organizational, interpersonal, and communication skills I could offer your organization. Now living in the Washington, DC area, I am seeking employment with an organization that can use a hard-working young professional with a proven ability to make significant contributions to efficiency and profitability.

As you will see from my resume, I offer more than ten years of office experience, and I have demonstrated my ability to excel in various environments including the real estate and legal fields. A versatile and adaptable individual with a cheerful personality, I can assure you that my outstanding customer service and time management skills would be assets to any organization.

Fluent in Spanish, I have earned a reputation as a skilled communicator with a talent for dealing effectively with people. I believe my hard-working nature and ability to work with little or no supervision have been the keys to my success.

If you can use a motivated professional with strong office and computer operations skills, I hope you will contact me to suggest a time when we can discuss your present and future needs, and how I might meet them. I can provide outstanding personal and professional references, and I thank you in advance for your time and consideration.

Sincerely,

Kathy Deroscher

KATHY DEROSCHER

1110½ Hay Street, Fayetteville, NC 28305 • preppub@aol.com • (910) 483-6611

OBJECTIVE

To benefit an organization that can use an experienced secretary, office clerk, or receptionist with exceptional organizational, communication and interpersonal skills.

COMPUTERS

Proficient with Microsoft Word, Excel, Access, PowerPoint and Windows XP.

EXPERIENCE

RECOVERY CLERK. Department of Defense, Finance Department, Washington, DC (2004-present). Demonstrate excellent organizational and time management skills. Effectively handle the collection of money owed the government while keeping all files up to date with no backlog.

- Contributed significantly to the unit's profitability by establishing and maintaining excellent check recovery figures.
- Write demands on carriers to ensure the recovery of government money and prepared weekly and monthly reports and written letters of acceptance/denial.
- Inventory office supplies and maintain appropriate stock levels.

RECEPTIONIST. Office Depot Corporate Office, Washington, DC (2002-04). Performed a variety of secretarial and clerical office tasks on a volunteer basis in order to refine my knowledge of business and office practices.

- Operated a multi-line phone system, answering and directing phone calls and taking messages.
- Typed business letters and other correspondence.
- Handled scheduling of appointments and contacted clients.
- Tracked inventory and maintained appropriate stock levels of all office supplies.

Excelled in promotion with Systel, Incorporated, located in downtown Washington, DC (1996-02).
1999-02: HEAD SECRETARY. As Head Secretary, managed the production of other office workers and secretarial staff.

- Communicated with clients and agents, scheduling and maintaining the appointment calendar for a busy real estate office.
- Wrote and typed newspaper advertisements, letters, and memos.
- Handled incoming and outgoing correspondence, dispersing mail to agents.
- Familiarized myself with local real estate market in order to better serve customers and agents.
- Made travel arrangements, such as hotel and airline reservations, for the office.

1996-99: RECEPTIONIST. Performed general office duties for a busy realty office; developed excellent telephone and customer service skills.

- Operated a multi-line phone system, answering and directing calls and taking messages.
- Served as liaison between the agency and the customer, answering customer inquiries for information on specific properties and requesting listing information from clients; photocopied and filed letters and other documents.

APPRENTICE. Washington Technical Institute, Washington, DC (1994-96). Worked a secretarial apprenticeship while studying at the school for secretaries. Learned basic skills of letter writing, shorthand, proper telephone etiquette, written and verbal communication, and presenting a professional appearance.

PERSONAL

Excellent personal and professional references are available upon request.

Date

Exact Name of Person
Title or Position
Name of Company
Address (no., street)
Address (city, state, zip)

RESEARCH ASSISTANT
at Norfolk State
University

Dear Exact Name of Person: (or Dear Sir or Madam if answering a blind ad.)

Can you use a well-rounded and enthusiastic young professional who offers certification as a paralegal?

As you will see from my resume, I currently attend Longwood College in Farmville, VA where I am completing the Paralegal Studies program. Previously I received my B.A. in History with a concentration in Legal Studies at the Norfolk State University. I was one of very few undergraduate students given the opportunity to conduct an independent research project.

Through an internship with Leonard, Rollins & Wayne, LLP, and my research assistantship with the university's History Department, I gained extensive experience in research, analysis, and preparing concise written reports.

I was chosen to supply my research skills and background in History for a six-month project with the Historical Archives Museum. My assistance to the curator's branch of the museum gave me the chance to locate, analyze, and present materials gathered from various sources which were used to prepare a special exhibit on women's political activism, legal status, and rights.

I feel that my unique mixture of education in Legal Studies and History, my practical experiences in business management and office administration, and outstanding communication, research, and customer service skills combine to make me a professional with a great deal to offer. I hope you will welcome my call soon to arrange a brief meeting at your convenience to discuss your current and future needs and how I might serve them. Thank you in advance for your time.

Sincerely yours,

Charlotte Stubbs

Alternate last paragraph:
I hope you will call or write soon to suggest a time convenient for us to meet and discuss your current and future needs and how I might serve them. Thank you in advance for your time.

CHARLOTTE STUBBS

1110½ Hay Street, Fayetteville, NC 28305   •   preppub@aol.com   •   (910) 483-6611

OBJECTIVE

To benefit an organization seeking an adaptable, energetic, creative young professional who offers proven sales, public relations, and customer service abilities, along with exceptionally strong research, analytical, problem-solving, and communication skills.

EDUCATION

Earned **B.A. in History** with a concentration in American History and with additional course work in Legal Studies, the Norfolk State University, Norfolk, VA, 2000.
- Completed extensive computer science course work based on Windows XP system.
- During my junior and senior years of college, worked 30 hours weekly for a Virginia Law firm; was rapidly promoted from Receptionist to Office Manager to supervise 15 people.

Completed the **Paralegal Studies Program**, Longwood College, Farmville, VA; will receive certification as a Paralegal, 2004.
- Currently maintain a 3.4 GPA in specialized course work such as:
  American Jurisprudence   Estates, Trusts, and Probate
  Legal Research and Writing   Litigation, Pleadings, and Arbitration
- Earned a Certificate of Distinction for "perfect performance" in course work and projects.

EXPERIENCE

Was selected for prestigious internships as a student at Norfolk State:
RESEARCH ASSISTANT. History Department, NSU (2004-present). Polished my talents for research and writing while helping faculty members on research projects on the subjects of fugitive slave laws, early American legal issues, and the Bill of Rights.
- Selected as one of very few undergraduate students to conduct independent research projects, edited articles for publication in law journals and legal case books.
- Conducted the research and authored a speech on ideas of justice and freedom of religion, which was presented at the university's celebration of the Bill of Rights.

INVESTIGATIVE ASSISTANT. Leonard, Rollins, & Wayne, Norfolk, VA (2002-04). Assisted 10 attorneys by screening/interviewing clients in the office and correctional facilities; was commended for exceptional customer service and public relations skills.
- Researched materials in a legal library; was praised for high productivity.
- Was handpicked to help the Chief Investigator with outside investigations.

Polished my time management skills combining school, work, and extracurricular activities:
RESEARCH ASSISTANT. Historical Archives Museum, Farmville, VA (1999-02). Worked independently in the curation branch while collecting, analyzing, and preparing materials for exhibits emphasizing legal status, rights, and political activism.

Highlights of other experience:
OFFICE MANAGER and BOOKKEEPER. For a multi-unit restaurant, supervised 65 employees while taking care of payroll, accounts receivable/payable, budgeting, bank transactions, and daily and monthly sales reports; trained managers on bookkeeping/financial systems and gave the restaurant a "high-visibility" profile through my extensive civic work.
MEMBERSHIP DIRECTOR. As Membership Director for a health club, was consistently at least 105% above quota in every performance category measured.
SALES ASSOCIATE. In a retail clothing operation, reduced inventory losses 11.5%.

PERSONAL

Offer general office skills including using Microsoft Word, Excel and Access as well as a 10-key adding machines and multiline phones; type 50 wpm. Enjoy music and water activities.

CAREER CHANGE

Date

Exact Name of Person
Exact Title
Exact Name of Company
Address
City, State, Zip

**TITLE SEARCH FIRM
GENERAL MANAGER**

is selectively exploring
other opportunities
outside the legal field.
What she does not say
in this cover letter is
that she is tired of her
supervisory
responsibilities and
wishes to work more
independently in a
challenging customer
service role.

Dear Exact Name of Person: (or Dear Sir or Madam if answering a blind ad):

With the enclosed resume, I would like to make you aware of my strong background in leading, training, and motivating others and to acquaint you with my reputation as an outgoing, detail-oriented professional whose exceptional communication and interpersonal skills could benefit your company.

While earning my Associate's degree in Paralegal Technology, I was also afforded the opportunity to explore my interest in the French language, and I completed additional coursework in that language. I also have a working knowledge of French language and culture, gained during the six years that I lived in that country. I have traveled extensively throughout the United States, Canada, and France.

As you will see from my resume, I am excelling as the General Manager of Van Robinson's Insurance & Title Agency. At Van Robinson's, I oversee all human resources for the company to include interviewing, hiring, and training all employees. I have supervised many paralegals and office assistants, conducting title searches for local law firms and attorneys.

Although I enjoy the legal field and have excelled in all aspects of my job, I am seeking to transition my skills into an environment where I will be more involved in customer service. The exceptional communication skills and natural leadership that allowed me to succeed thus far will also make me a valuable addition to the company's team of customer service professionals.

If you can use a self-motivated, enthusiastic individual whose decision-making skills and ability to deal effectively with others have been proven in challenging environments, I hope you will write or call me soon to suggest a time when we might meet to discuss your needs and goals and how my background might serve them. I can provide outstanding references at the appropriate time.

Sincerely,

Martha L. Searle

MARTHA L. SEARLE

1110½ Hay Street, Fayetteville, NC 28305   •   preppub@aol.com   •   (910) 483-6611

OBJECTIVE

To benefit an organization that can use an articulate professional with an outgoing personality, exceptional organizational skills, and strong attention to detail gained through a background in customer service, training, and management.

EDUCATION

Associate of Applied Science degree in Paralegal Technology, Truckee Meadows Community College, Reno, NV, 1999; graduated with a 4.0 cumulative GPA.
Completed additional coursework in French.

COMPUTERS

Proficient with software including Word, Access, Excel, and PowerPoint.

EXPERIENCE

GENERAL MANAGER. Van Robinson's Insurance & Title Agency, Reno, NV (1999-present). After beginning as a Paralegal with Jackson & Stevens Attorneys-at-Law, became the Lead Paralegal and General Manager of this firm which provides title search services to attorneys in Reno.

- Interview, hire, and supervise paralegals and office professionals while establishing and managing multiple offices.
- An acknowledged expert in searching titles, instruct paralegal staff in the proper methods for conducting accurate title searches.
- Known for my outgoing personality, personally oversaw all marketing efforts, presenting the company's services to local attorneys and law firms.
- Learned to adapt and interact effectively with a wide range of personalities, from builders, to real estate agents, to attorneys.
- Honed my ability to make sound judgments, negotiate contracts, and commit to decisions under tight deadlines and in stressful situations.
- Personally performed a large number of title searches, in addition to monitoring the performance of my staff in an industry in which no mistakes could be tolerated.
- In 2004, was recognized by the Reno Legal Association with a luncheon in my honor for my efforts in training paralegals in the community.

LICENSES

Hold NV Title Insurance License.
Licensed Notary Public for the state of Nevada.

AFFILIATIONS

Member, Reno Area Chamber of Commerce
Member, National Association of Business Women
Volunteer, American Red Cross
Member, First Baptist Church of Reno

TRAVEL

Traveled extensively throughout the United States as well as in France and Canada.

LANGUAGES

Have a working knowledge of both written and spoken French gained during my time living in that country. Completed several courses in French and have some knowledge and a great interest in that language; have a personal goal to become fluent in French.

PERSONAL

Known as a highly outgoing, personable, caring, and social individual. Am willing to travel and relocate to meet the needs of my employer. Excellent personal and professional references are available upon request.

CAREER CHANGE

Date

Exact Name of Person
Title or Position
Name of Company
Address (no., street)
Address (city, state, zip)

WRIT OF EXECUTIONS CLERK

for the police department in Charleston, SC has relocated to Tempe, AZ, with her husband and is seeking similar work

Dear Exact Name of Person: (or Dear Sir or Madam if answering a blind ad.)

I would appreciate an opportunity to talk with you soon about how I could contribute to your organization through my versatile skills related to legal data processing, finance and collections, as well as public relations and customer service.

As you will see from my resume, I was promoted in a strong track record of performance with the Charleston County Police Department. I began as a Switchboard Operator, promoted to handle legal word processing, and then selected by the sheriff for the position of the Writ of Executions Clerk. However, my husband's new job will soon be taking us to Tempe, and we are excited about making Tempe our new home. I am eager to find an employer who can make use of my considerable skills and abilities.

As you will see from my resume, I excelled most recently as a Writ of Executions Clerk and in that job I processed more than 300 new executions and tax warrants monthly. I excelled in collections, and I collected more than $200,000 in an 14-month period. I am skilled in composing and typing most types of legal documents including Notices of Hearing, Reports of Sale, and Orders, and I have planned and organized the public auctions of levied personal and real properties.

If you feel you could use my versatile background, outstanding character, and dedicated nature somewhere in your organization, please call or write me and I will make myself available at your convenience for a personal interview. I would enjoy the opportunity to meet you to see if my knowledge and skills could be of value to you. I am known for my superior problem-solving ability and for my knack for taking abstract concepts and transferring them into documents or forms which can be used to enhance efficiency. I can provide outstanding references at your request.

Sincerely yours,

Carla V. Simmons

Alternate last paragraph:
I hope you will welcome my call soon to arrange a brief meeting at your convenience to discuss your current and future needs and how I might serve them. Thank you in advance for your time.

CARLA V. SIMMONS

1110½ Hay Street, Fayetteville, NC 28305 • preppub@aol.com • (910) 483-6611

OBJECTIVE
To benefit an organization that can use a dedicated young professional with expertise in operating telecommunications equipment along with experience in preparing a wide range of legal documents while performing liaison with attorneys, private investigation services, and law enforcement agencies.

EDUCATION
Associate of Science degree in **Criminal Justice**, Trident Technical College, Charleston, SC, 2000. Recipient of a four-year scholarship. Completed credits in the following courses:

secretarial sciences	health sciences
computer programming	Microsoft Office Suite software
algebra/advanced algebra	English composition and literature
accounting	pre-calculus

Completed extensive training sponsored by the South Carolina Department of Justice, SBI Division of Criminal Investigation.
Obtained Writs of Execution Certification, Institute of Government, Charleston, SC 2001.

EXPERIENCE
Excelled in the following track record of promotion to increasing responsibilities in the Charleston County Police Department, Charleston, SC; can provide outstanding personal and professional references from the sheriff and many other officials:
WRIT OF EXECUTIONS CLERK. (2004-present). Have excelled in a job which involves handling extensive legal paperwork as well as financial collections; processed and collected Civil Writs of Execution and State and County Tax Warrants.
- Process 300 new executions and tax warrants monthly; collected $200,000 in an 14-month period after calculating monies owed (collected more monies than any predecessor).
- Plan and organize public auctions of levied personal and real properties, and then supervise the conduct of sales by deputies.
- Perform background checks on judgment debtors to assist deputies in locating them and their properties; verify property ownership for deputies.
- Assign specific executions to specific deputies for collection.
- Handle data entry of executions and tax warrants into the county's mainframe computer system. Compose and type sheriff's legal documents including Notices of Hearing, Reports of Sale, and Orders; Am skilled in performing title searches and performing criminal and background checks.
- Supervise the process of conducting inventories of businesses and personal estates which the sheriff closed under order of seizure.
- Advise 25 deputies of legal protocol in serving criminal and civil papers.

LEGAL CLERK/DATA ENTRY SPECIALIST. (2001-04). Performed data entry related to most legal processes handled by the police office including civil and criminal summons, criminal warrants, subpoenas, and notices.
- Operated a two-way radio base unit to assist deputies.
- Graciously assisted the public; answered telephone inquiries.
- Became skilled in using the Clerk of Court computers and the county's mainframe system.
- On my own initiative, played a valuable role in assisting the county's data processing department in modifying our tracking system program.

PERSONAL
Am an outstanding problem-solver with an ability to take abstract concepts and transfer them into documents or forms which can be used to increase efficiency. Am accustomed to handling information which requires discretion and confidentiality. References upon request.

In this section, you will find resumes and cover letters of judges and attorneys. You will notice that the format for the resumes in this section do not differ from the format of resumes in the previous section. We have created a separate section for attorneys and judges just for ease of reference.

A word about follow-up letters...
An especially effective tool in a job hunt is a follow-up letter. Employers are constantly seeking to discern who *really* wants the job from among those whom they interview, so you can help the employer choose you by sending a follow-up letter expressing your strong interest in the position. A follow-up letter often gives you a chance to say things that you didn't say in the interview, and a follow-up letter often gives you an opportunity to emphasize some skill or personal quality that you know is of importance to the employer. An example of a follow-up letter is on page 16.

Date

Exact Name of Person
Exact Title
Exact Name of Company
Address
City, State, Zip

**ASSISTANT TO THE
DISTRICT ATTORNEY**

is selectively
exploring other
opportunities. Notice
that this is a "generic"
cover letter which can
be sent to any firm or
public organization

Dear Exact Name of Person: (or Dear Sir or Madam if answering a blind ad):

With the enclosed resume, I would like to initiate the process of confidentially exploring opportunities within your firm. I am writing to you because I am aware of your fine reputation, and I feel that my personal qualities and professional strengths could make me a valuable asset to your firm as an attorney.

As you will see from my enclosed resume, I earned a Juris Doctor degree from Drexel University and was admitted to the Pennsylvania State Bar in May of 2002. I hold a Bachelor of English degree from LaSalle University and graduated *summa cum laude* with a GPA Overall: 3.78/4.0.

Currently employed by the Office of the District Attorney, I serve as a liaison for the Office of District Court Judges. I represent the State of Pennsylvania in the criminal prosecution of felonies and misdemeanor appeals via jury trials, motions, pleas and hearings as well as provide legal research for Senior Assistants. As an Assistant for the District Court I have prosecuted extensive misdemeanor dockets via bench trials and pleas, and I have served as a liaison with the Office of District Court Judges.

If you can use a highly professional attorney who offers superior writing, research, and verbal communication skills, I hope you will contact me to suggest a time when we might meet to discuss your needs. Thank you in advance for your time and professional courtesies.

Sincerely,

Jenny L. McCoy

JENNY L. McCOY

1110½ Hay Street, Fayetteville, NC 28305 • preppub@aol.com • (910) 483-6611

CERTIFICATION

Admitted to the Pennsylvania State Bar, May 2002.

LEGAL EDUCATION

Drexel University School of Law, Philadelphia, Pennsylvania.
Juris Doctor, *summa cum laude* (December 2002).
GPA overall: 3.4/4.0, Top 20%.

Honors & Activities: Kevin Moniz Scholarship; Negotiation Competition; Law Fellows; Masters Swimming; Women's Law Student Organization.

UNDERGRADUATE EDUCATION

LaSalle University, Philadelphia, Pennsylvania
Bachelor of Arts degree in English, *Summa cum laude* (1999).
GPA Overall: 3.78/4.0, Inducted to Alpha Theta Alpha (1998).

EXPERIENCE

OFFICE OF THE DISTRICT ATTORNEY. Philadelphia, PA (2003-present). Represent the State of Pennsylvania in the criminal prosecution of felonies and misdemeanor appeals via jury trials, motions, pleas and hearings while also providing legal research for Senior Assistants. As an **Assistant (District Court),** prosecute misdemeanor dockets via bench trials and pleas; coordinated court schedule and serve as a liaison.

MAXWELL & HARDING, ATTORNEYS AT LAW. Associate, Philadelphia, PA (2002-03). Drafted complaints and motions; interviewed and represented clients at mediation and arbitration. Assisted senior litigators at trial and with legal research.

Other experience, including externship and internship:
Extern: **THE HONORABLE PATRICK K. BROWN, JUDGE OF CIRCUIT COURT.** Judicial Circuit of Pennsylvania. *(Judicial Clerkship Program),* Philadelphia, PA (2001-02). Prepared bench memos and observed trials and courtroom proceedings.

Intern: **OFFICE OF THE GENERAL SOLICITOR.** *(Third Year Practice Certified),* Philadelphia, PA (Summer 2001). Interviewed and represented criminal defendants at various stages of the legal process.

Legal Research Associate: **SENATOR CAROL BARNES OFFICE.** Pennsylvania State Senate. Philadelphia, PA (Summer 2000). Examined feasibility of possible revisions to the Pennsylvania State Administrative Procedure Act.

Legislative Aide: **SENATOR WILLIAM T. VASENKO.** Pennsylvania State Senate. Philadelphia, PA (Spring 1999). Assisted with co-sponsorship legislation, answered constituent inquiries.

Intern (Session Assistant): Philadelphia, PA (April 1999-October 1999). Prepared daily Senate calendar; monitored Senate floor action.

Intern: **PENNSYLVANIA STATE ATTORNEY GENERAL'S OFFICE.** Philadelphia, PA (Nov 1998-May 1999). Resolved consumer complaints with merchants.

PERSONAL

Outstanding personal and professional references on request.

Date

Exact Name of Person
Title or Position
Name of Company
Address (no., street)
Address (city, state, zip)

ASSOCIATE

for a small law office
in Massachusetts is
selectively exploring
other opportunities

Dear Exact Name of Person: (or Dear Sir or Madam if answering a blind ad.)

I would appreciate an opportunity to talk with you soon about how I could contribute to your organization as an attorney.

Currently an Associate with the Law Office of Matthew Scott, I work in a high-volume real estate practice. My responsibilities include numerous loan closings, deed preparation, and title searches. I have also been involved in litigation work which includes DWI defense, domestic law, and personal injury.

As an Assistant District Attorney for the Bossier County District Attorney's Office, I gained extensive negotiating and communication skills in the courtroom. I prosecuted traffic violators and criminal misdemeanors in district court for almost two years while I simultaneously managed very large caseloads in district court. With six months experience in juvenile court, I handled several probable cause hearings seeking to try serious offenders as adults. With six months experience in superior court exposed to felony and misdemeanor appeal jury trials, I worked closely with victims and witnesses in very serious cases. I was appointed to courthouse FOCUS groups to help improve efficiency within the various departments of the courthouse.

You would find me to be a person known for my capacity for hard work and long hours. I am a highly adaptable professional who offers exceptionally research skills along with the proven ability to master difficult cases and persuasively argue them to judges and juries.

I hope you will welcome my call soon to arrange a brief meeting at your convenience to discuss your current and future needs and how I might serve them. Thank you in advance for your time.

Sincerely yours,

Daryl M. Gibbes

Alternate last paragraph:
I hope you will call or write me soon to suggest a time convenient for us to meet and discuss your current and future needs and how I might serve them. Thank you in advance for your time.

DARYL M. GIBBES

1110½ Hay Street, Fayetteville, NC 28305   •   preppub@aol.com   •   (910) 483-6611

OBJECTIVE

I want to contribute to an organization that can use an articulate young attorney with an reputation for outstanding analytical and problem-solving skills.

EDUCATION

Juris Doctor degree, Boston School of Law, Boston, MA, December 2001.

Honors and Activities

Dean's List (four semesters)
Volunteer Intern, Worcester County D.A.'s Office, Worcester, MA (Spring 2001)
Volunteer Law Clerk, Massachusetts State Legal Services - indigent work (1999-00)
Worcester YMCA County Special Olympics, volunteer swimming instructor (Spring 1999)

Bachelor of Arts degree in Political Science, Clark University, Worcester, MA, December 1998.
GPA: 3.8

Honors and Activities

Cum Laude; Dean's List (every semester)
Cambridge Community Boy's Club (1997-98)
Disc Jockey, college radio station WKID (1997)
Intramural golf champion (1996)
Outward Bound Massachusetts (Summer 1996)

EXPERIENCE

ASSOCIATE. Law Office of Matthew Scott, Worcester, MA (2004-present). Have gained hands-on experience in a high-volume real estate practice. Handle loan closings, deed preparation, and title searches. Litigation work includes DWI defense, domestic law, and personal injury.

ASSISTANT DISTRICT ATTORNEY. Bossier County District Attorney's Office, Worcester, MA (2001-2004). Gained extensive negotiating and communication skills in the courtroom. Prosecuted traffic violations and criminal misdemeanors in district court for almost two years. Managed very large caseloads in district court.
- Six months experience in juvenile court included several probable cause hearings seeking to try serious offenders as adults.
- Six months experience in superior court included felony and misdemeanor appeal jury trials. Worked closely with victims and witnesses in very serious cases.
- Appointed to courthouse FOCUS group to help improve efficiency within the various departments of courthouse.

INTERN. Harrisburg County District Attorney's Office, Cambridge, MA (Spring 2000). Took advantage of my third-year practice certification and tried over thirty cases in district court as a law student. Interviewed victims and witnesses in preparation for trial. Full-time volunteer and financed my summer working in a restaurant during evenings and weekends.

SUMMER LAW CLERK. Delaney, Smith & Bryant, Cambridge, MA (Spring 1999). Prepared business-related legal memoranda for attorneys. Honed research and writing skills. Became proficient in Microsoft Word, Westlaw, and Lexis.

PERSONAL

Enjoy golf, fly-fishing, backpacking, and guitar. Founding member and president of The Crouch Organization, a tax-exempt organization whose purpose is to aid Haitian orphanages and universities. Member of St. Luke Catholic Church, Worcester, MA. Proud of my accomplishments as President of both my high school's Student Council and Drama Club.

Exact Name of Person
Title or Position
Name of Company
Address (no., street)
Address (city, state, zip)

ASSOCIATE
ATTORNEY

for a company that
emphasizes insurance
defense

Dear Exact Name of Person: (or Dear Sir or Madam if answering a blind ad.)

I would appreciate an opportunity to talk with you soon about how I could contribute to your organization as an attorney.

As you will see from my enclosed resume, I have a Juris Doctor degree from the University of Akron in Ohio and a Bachelor of Arts degree in Political Science and English. I am also a member of the Ohio Bar Association and the American Bar Association.

As an Associate Attorney for the Green, Bratwurst, & Cummings Law Firm in Akron, OH, I have gained extensive Civil litigation experience with an emphasis on insurance defense. On numerous occasions I have appeared in Small Claims, District and Superior Courts, conducted depositions of witnesses, and drafted pleadings and briefs. In a previous position as an Assistant District Attorney for the District Court of the Midwest Region, I have extensive District Court experience prosecuting traffic violations and other general misdemeanors as well as Jury trial experience in Superior Court prosecuting misdemeanor appeals and felonies. I am responsible for child support prosecution.

You would find me to be a person known for my capacity for hard work and long hours. I am a highly adaptable professional who offers exceptionally research skills along with the proven ability to master difficult cases and persuasively argue them to judges and juries.

I hope you will welcome my call soon to arrange a brief meeting at your convenience to discuss your current and future needs and how I might serve them. Thank you in advance for your time.

Sincerely yours,

David G. Locklear

Alternate last paragraph:
I hope you will call or write me soon to suggest a time convenient for us to meet and discuss your current and future needs and how I might serve them. Thank you in advance for your time.

DAVID G. LOCKLEAR

1110½ Hay Street, Fayetteville, NC 28305　•　preppub@aol.com　•　(910) 483-6611

OBJECTIVE　　I want to contribute to an organization that can use a talented prosecutor and negotiator.

EDUCATION　　**Juris Doctor, The University of Akron School of Law,** Akron, OH, May 2001
OH Bar License, 2001

Cornell University, Ithaca, NY, May 1999
B.A. Political Science and English
G.P.A. 3.606 Magna Cum Laude Rank 166/1487

HONORS AND　　*Post-Graduate:*　　Ohio Bar Association
ACTIVITIES　　　　　　　　　　　American Bar Association
　　　　　　　　　　　　　　　　　Findlay County Lawyer Association
　　　　　　　　　　　　　　　　　Oberlin County Legal Association
　　　　　　　　　　　　　　　　　YMCA Basketball Coach
　　　　　　　　　　　　　　　　　Teacher of Corporate Law, Lorain County Community College

　　　　　　　　　　Law School:　　2000-2001 Dean's List
　　　　　　　　　　　　　　　　　Prisoners' Rights Project
　　　　　　　　　　　　　　　　　Moot Court Competition
　　　　　　　　　　　　　　　　　Staff Writer, Environmental Law Project Newsletter
　　　　　　　　　　　　　　　　　Member, National Lawyer's Guild
　　　　　　　　　　　　　　　　　Volunteer, Habitat for Humanity

　　　　　　　　　　Undergraduate:　　1996-1998 Dean's List With Distinction
　　　　　　　　　　　　　　　　　Community Service Coordinator, Kappa Psi Fraternity
　　　　　　　　　　　　　　　　　National Conservation Organization
　　　　　　　　　　　　　　　　　Freshman Representative, Cornell Student Government

EXPERIENCE　　**ASSOCIATE ATTORNEY.** Green, Bratwurst & Cummings, LLP, Akron, OH. (2004-present). Civil litigation experience with emphasis on insurance defense. Appear in Small Claims, District and Superior Courts. Conduct depositions of witnesses. Drafted pleadings and briefs.

ASSISTANT DISTRICT ATTORNEY. District Court for Midwest Region, Akron, OH (2001-04). Extensive District Court experience prosecuting traffic violations and other general misdemeanors. Jury trial experience in Superior Court prosecuting misdemeanor appeals and felonies. Responsible for child support prosecution.

CONGRESSIONAL INTERN. Department of Justice, Ithaca, NY (2000-01). Worked with Majority Counsel during drafting process. Compiled campaign data and prepared constitutional analysis of proposed legislation. Lobbied on behalf of campaign reform.

SUMMER LAW CLERK. Bryant, Delaney & Smith, Ithaca, NY (1999). Researched and prepared memoranda involving employment discrimination, insurance, banking, corporate, and contract law. Constructed motions, affidavits, and deeds which involved title searches. Attended numerous depositions and trials and assisted in loan closings. Conducted extensive interviews with clients both in person and via telephone.

PERSONAL　　Outstanding personal and professional reputation. Excellent references on request.

Exact Name of Person
Exact Title
Exact Name of Company
Address
City, State, Zip

ASSOCIATE ATTORNEY
for a litigation firm

Dear Exact Name of Person: (or Dear Sir or Madam if answering a blind ad):

With the enclosed resume, I would like to initiate the process of confidentially exploring opportunities within your firm. I am writing to you because I am aware of your fine reputation, and I feel that my personal qualities and professional strengths could make me a valuable asset to your firm.

As you will see, I am currently excelling as a litigation attorney with a busy Hamilton firm, where I have worked on complex cases that included insurance defense litigation, plaintiff's personal injury actions, landlord/tenant litigation, collection matters, and representation of small business owners. I am building a reputation as a skilled orator who excels in all facets of case preparation and research.

While earning my J.D., I distinguished myself in both moot court competitions and on trial teams. I was named Best Oralist in the Sanford Law School Court Competition. In the Regional Competition, I competed against law schools including Colgate University, Hofstra University, Cornell University and State University of New York College. I also won first place on the National Trial Team in Washington, D.C.

While I am highly regarded by my present employer and can provide outstanding references at the appropriate time, I have decided to permanently relocate to establish my career. I am asking that you treat my interest in your firm in the strictest confidence until after we have had the chance to meet in person.

If you can use a highly professional young attorney who offers superior writing, research, and verbal communication skills, I hope you will contact me to suggest a time when we might meet to discuss your needs. Thank you in advance for your time and professional courtesies.

Sincerely,

Michelle K. Roberts

MICHELLE K. ROBERTS

1110½ Hay Street, Fayetteville, NC 28305   •   preppub@aol.com   •   (910) 483-6611

OBJECTIVE   To contribute to an organization that can use an experienced young attorney who offers a background of excellence in various types of litigation and a reputation as a superior orator with strong legal research and writing skills.

EDUCATION   Received my **Juris Doctor (JD)** from Sanford Law School, Hempstead, NY, 2002.
- Won a spot on the National Trial Team; Quarterfinalist on the Regional Trial Team.
- Was named Best Oralist in the Sanford Law School Court Competition.
- Named to the National Court Team; was a Finalist in the Regional Competition; and was named Best Oralist in the Regional Competition in which I competed against law schools including **Colgate University, Hofstra University, Cornell University** and **State University of New York College.**

Earned **Bachelor of Arts degree in English, magna cum laude,** Syracuse University, Syracuse, NY, 1999.

EXPERIENCE   **ASSOCIATE ATTORNEY.** Mitchell & Taylor Law Firm, Hamilton, NY (2004-present). As a litigation attorney, have gained expertise in various types of litigation.
- Review and organize voluminous documents and records, analyzing this information to prepare complex legal strategies and arguments for insurance defense litigation.
- Demonstrate my skill at rhetoric while presenting personal injury actions on behalf of the plaintiff.
- Handle contract disputes and other types of legal cases for small business owners.
- Represent landlords and real estate companies in landlord/tenant litigation.
- Prepare and present litigation on collection matters.

ASSOCIATE ATTORNEY. Sterling & Sterling, LLP, Syracuse, NY (2003-04). Prepared and answered discovery; reviewed and organized voluminous documents and records in complex civil cases; and provided critique and review of management contracts and partnership agreements; was involved in nearly every aspect of trial preparation.
- Learned to skillfully maximize settlements of complex civil cases.
- Was praised by clients for my "impressive proficiency and attention to detail in legal arguments" as well as for my "grace and true professionalism."
- Skilled in techniques of drafting discovery and in preparation for complex civil trials.
- Learned the intricacies of contract interpretation and partnership law.

Other experience:
LAW CLERK. The Law Firm of Glazier & Britton, Syracuse, NY (Jan 03-Mar 03). Was commended for my impressive abilities related to performing legal research, drafting briefs, and preparing memoranda of law while clerking for this firm.
LAW CLERK. Lafayette, LLP, Syracuse, NY (January 02-August 02). Improved my legal research and writing skills while excelling as a law clerk.
INTERN. Ithaca County District Attorney's Office, Syracuse, NY (2000-01). Organized case files and updated pattern jury and instructions.

AFFILIATIONS   Order of the Barristers, New York Bar Association, Bar No. 00000; Bar Member No. 00000
New York Academy of Trial Lawyers, Association of Trial Lawyers of America (ATLA)
American Bar Association (ABA), Junior League of Ithaca and Oakdale Counties

PERSONAL   Have traveled extensively throughout Europe. Excellent personal and professional references are available upon request.

CAREER CHANGE

Date

Exact Name of Person
Title or Position
Name of Company
Address (no., street)
Address (city, state, zip)

ATTORNEY
for the Department
of Defense is
preparing to leave
the military justice
system and enter
the civilian legal
world.

Dear Exact Name of Person: (or Dear Sir or Madam if answering a blind ad.)

I would appreciate an opportunity to talk with you soon about how I could contribute to your organization as an attorney.

As you will see from my resume, I am currently a Recovery Judge Advocate in which I assert, negotiate, and settle government claims under the provisions of the Federal Claims Act and the Medical Care Recovery Act. I prepare Rule Four and Trial Memorandum of Law for contracts appealed to the ASBCA. In a previous position as an attorney for the U.S. Army Legal Services Division, I was responsible for providing legal advice to commanders and soldiers in Iraq in the areas of international law, contract law, and military justice.

You would find me to be a highly adaptable professional who offers exceptionally research skills along with the proven ability to master difficult cases and persuasively argue them to judges and juries. I won a very prestigious medal (the "Bronze Star") for my extraordinary contributions during the war in the Middle East; the citation accompanying the "Bronze Star" medal lauded my skill in handling "some of the most complicated cases that arose during the war."

Although I was strongly encouraged to remain in military service and assured of continued rapid advancement, I decided to resign my commission as an officer and enter the civilian work force. I offer an exceptionally strong knowledge of labor law as well as an appetite to become involved in practicing any other types of law which you handle.

I hope you will welcome my call soon to arrange a brief meeting at your convenience to discuss your current and future needs and how I might serve them. Thank you in advance for your time.

Sincerely yours,

Richard W. Allen

Alternate last paragraph:
I hope you will call or write me soon to suggest a time convenient for us to meet and discuss your current and future needs and how I might serve them. Thank you in advance for your time.

RICHARD W. ALLEN

1110½ Hay Street, Fayetteville, NC 28305   •   preppub@aol.com   •   (910) 483-6611

OBJECTIVE

To contribute to an organization that can use my outstanding communication skills and expertise as an attorney.

EXPERIENCE

ATTORNEY (LABOR), GS-13. Department of Defense, Office of the Staff Judge Advocate, Washington, DC (2003-present). Primary legal advisor and trial lawyer for the installation command group on all issues related to federal sector labor relations, employee discipline and performance based actions, workers' compensation claims, unemployment compensation claims, and equal employment opportunity complaints.
- As an **ADJUNCT FACULTY MEMBER**. Georgetown University, Washington, DC, provide instruction in criminal law, constitutional law, evidence, and business law.

TRIAL COUNSEL, CAPTAIN. Department of Justice, Washington, DC (2001-03). Primary legal advisor and trial lawyer for Jasper Medical Center. Prosecuted over 40 felony cases including murder, drug distribution, rape, larceny, forgery, and fraud cases.

STAFF JUDGE ADVOCATE, CAPTAIN. U.S. Army, Supply Division, Iraq (2000-01). As primary legal advisor for a Supply Division comprised of 7,000 soldiers, provided legal advice to the brigade commander on international/operational law and contract law issues. Provided legal assistance to soldiers on domestic relations, debtor/creditor, and landlord/tenant legal issues. Throughout all phases of the ground offensive and gave on-the-spot legal advice to said commander on a host of international law issues.

CLAIMS JUDGE ADVOCATE, CAPTAIN. U.S. Army, Office of the Staff Judge Advocate, Fort Campbell, KY (1999-00). Served as the primary legal advisor on medical-legal issues to the medical staff and command.
- Interpreted and applied state tort law and the Federal Tort Claims Act.
- Investigated potentially compensable medical malpractice claims and negotiated with civilian attorneys for the settlement of said claims.

LEGAL CLERK/ATTORNEY. Matthew Taylor, Attorneys at Law, Lexington, KY (1998-99). Conducted legal research on a variety of legal issues for a civil litigation law firm.
- Wrote legal memoranda, motions, pleadings, and appellate briefs on cases dealing with medical malpractice suits and other general tort law issues. Assisted the firm's senior partner in court during a medical malpractice case in a Kentucky Common Pleas Court.

LICENSES

Member, Kentucky State Bar (1998)
Member, United States District Court Kentucky
Member, United States Court of Military Review and Court of Military Appeals

EDUCATION

Juris Doctor, 1998.
University of Kentucky School of Law, Lexington, Kentucky
- Member, National Trial Team; Recipient of the Distinguished Achievement Award in Trial Advocacy by the International Academy of Trial Lawyers
Bachelor of Arts, Journalism, 1996.
University of Kentucky, Lexington, Kentucky.
Graduated Magna Cum Laude, Distinguished Military Graduate

ASSOCIATIONS

Kentucky Bar Association, American Bar Association

Date

Exact Name of Person
Exact Title
Exact Name of Company
Address
City, State, Zip

Dear Exact Name of Person: (or Dear Sir or Madam if answering a blind ad):

   With the enclosed resume, I would like to initiate the process of confidentially exploring opportunities within your firm. I am writing to you because I am aware of your fine reputation, and I feel that my personal qualities and professional strengths could make me a valuable asset to your firm as an attorney.

   As you will see from my enclosed resume, I earned a Juris Doctor degree in Law from the University of New Hampshire and a Bachelor of Science degree in Business Administration with a concentration in Finance from Dartmouth College. I am affiliated with the following organizations: Commonwealth of New Hampshire Bar, American Bar Association, New Hampshire Bar Association and the Manchester Bar Association.

   Currently employed with Attorney James R. Donaldson as an Associate in his Law Office, I perform duties which involve title searching, legal research, public records research, drafting legal documents, interviewing clients and witnesses as well as assembling loan packages and loan closings. In a previous position as a Congressional Intern for Congressman Carl Salisbury, I researched important issues while making contact with constituents relative to their concerns. I assisted in the general operation of the office and performed in all areas where needed.

   If you can use a highly professional young attorney who offers superior writing, research, and verbal communication skills, I hope you will contact me to suggest a time when we might meet to discuss your needs. Thank you in advance for your time and professional courtesies.

                                        Sincerely,

                                        Roger F. Cumberland

ROGER F. CUMBERLAND

1110½ Hay Street, Fayetteville, NC 28305 • preppub@aol.com • (910) 483-6611

OBJECTIVE   To contribute to a law firm that can use a talented young attorney with top-notch analytical and communication skills.

EXPERIENCE   **ATTORNEY**
04/02-present   James R. Donaldson
                   4171 St. Phillips Street
                   Manchester, NH 17131

                   Associate in the Law Offices of James R. Donaldson. Major duties consist of title searching, legal research, public records research, drafting legal documents, interviewing clients and witnesses, as well as assembling loan packages and loan closings.

12/01-04/02   **LAW CLERK**
                   James R. Donaldson
                   4171 St. Phillips Street
                   Manchester, NH 17131

                   Was offered a senior position with this firm after excelling as a Law Clerk.

06/00-11/01   **CONGRESSIONAL INTERN**
                   Congressman Carl Salisbury
                   The Mosley House Office Building
                   Hanover, NH 17134

                   Researched issues important to constituents while making contact with constituents relative to their concerns, assisting in the general operation of the office and performing in all areas where needed.

EDUCATION   University of New Hampshire School of Law
                   Durham, NH
                   J.D. – May 2000

                   Dartmouth College
                   Hanover, NH
                   B.B.A., Finance – May 1997

MEMBERSHIPS   Commonwealth of New Hampshire Bar
                   American Bar Association
                   New Hampshire Bar Association
                   Manchester Bar Association
                   Registered Representative (Securities)– Connecticut, Maine, and New York

PERSONAL   Excellent references available on request.

Exact Name of Person
Title or Position
Name of Company
Address (number and street)
Address (city, state, and zip)

Dear Exact Name of Person: (or Sir or Madam if answering a blind ad.)

With the enclosed resume, I would like to make you aware of my desire to practice law for a public defender's office.

As you will see from my resume, I am excelling in a law firm which practices immigration law while also preserving the constitutional rights of inmates. Although I feel fulfilled in this position and am held in high regard by my peers, I feel that I could make significant contributions to a public defender's office.

My commitment to making a difference in the community is solid, and I have volunteered my time generously in order to provide free expertise to the legal departments and clinics of the city of Baltimore. As a volunteer, I have played a major role in directing and referring the victims of criminal acts to the appropriate governmental resources and agencies. As a volunteer, I have organized judicial and social clinics, and I have prepared the transition of young offenders between the correctional centers and their families.

I can provide outstanding personal and professional references at the appropriate time, and I would greatly appreciate an opportunity to talk with you in person about current or future opportunities which might arise in the public defender's office. Thank you in advance for your time.

Very respectfully yours,

Phyllis A. Danford

PHYLLIS A. DANFORD

1110½ Hay Street, Fayetteville, NC 28305 • preppub@aol.com • (910) 483-6611

OBJECTIVE

I want to contribute to an organization that can use an outstanding communicator with an ability to a public defender's office.

EXPERIENCE

ATTORNEY. Smith and Danford, Baltimore, MD (2002-present). As an attorney in a 10-attorney firm, practice immigration law for refugees, international students, investors, and exporters. In order to grant and preserve the constitutional rights of inmates, we have pioneered and established a number of administrative procedures into the Baltimore County detention system such as:
- parole hearings
- temporary leave hearings
- transfer hearings
- illegal detention procedures (Habeas corpus and conditional release)
- humanitarian procedures (medical and family motions)
- survey and revision procedures to verify sentencing period time

Highlights of special projects and consulting work:

2004: Info-Tech, Inc. Act as a Registered Agent for this software company, handling all legal aspects of opening and operating the company.

2003: *District Court of Baltimore.* For The Honorable Madam Justice Hannah P. Besselman, created a jurisprudential card-index system into penal, criminal, and constitutional law for the Honorable Judge.

2002: *The Federal Credit Bureau.* Acted as a financial and legal verifier which included investigating and verifying the credit and solvency of debtors, and verifying the financial status of creditors.

2002: *The Department of Labor.* Revised the constitutionality of the laws and bylaws concerning the acceptance of refugees.

PUBLICATIONS

Created a legal document for Professor Marco Symington of the Law Faculty, University of Maryland. Gave an opinion on national and international legalities. Created informative pamphlets on racial discrimination at work.

VOLUNTEER EXPERIENCE

Have offered time for social and community work to the legal departments and clinics of the city of Baltimore:
- Directed and referred the victims of criminal acts to the appropriate governmental resources and agencies.
- Organized judicial and social clinics. Prepared the transition of the young offenders between the correctional centers and their families.

EDUCATION

Juris Doctor degree in Civil Law, University of Maryland, Baltimore County, MD, 2002.
Bachelor of Arts degree in Political Science, Western Maryland College, Westminister, MD, 1999.
Associate of Arts (Sociology), LeMoyne College, Syracuse, New York, 1997.

HONORS & AWARDS

The Phipps International Law Competition, 1999, Westminister, Maryland.
The Maryland National Debate Competition, 1998, Representative for Baltimore.
The Maryland Symposium 1997, Representative for the Baltimore, Maryland.

LANGUAGES

Fluently speak and write in German and English; am in the process of learning Hellenic.

COMMUNITY

Am an active member of the NAACP and actively participate in church activities.

Date

Exact Name of Person
Exact Title
Exact Name of Company
Address
City, State, Zip

ATTORNEY
for a law firm
that emphasizes
product liability

Dear Exact Name of Person: (or Dear Sir or Madam if answering a blind ad):

With the enclosed resume, I would like to initiate the process of confidentially exploring opportunities within your firm.

As you will see from my enclosed resume, I earned a Juris Doctor degree in Law from the University of New Orleans and a Bachelor of Arts degree from Mississippi Valley State University. I graduated in the top 10% of my class and received the Phillip E. Baker Scholarship for winning 2nd place in the Freshman Moot Court Competition. Currently I am a member of the Louisiana Young Lawyers Association, the Bayou State Order of Barristers and the National Order of Barristers.

Currently employed with Claiborne, Donaldson & Fritz Law Firm in New Orleans, I am involved in insurance defense with an emphasis on product liability. The cases I handle involve product liability, chemical exposure (toxic torts), auto accidents, premises liability, worker's compensation, construction law, and other areas.

In previous position, I was involved in insurance defense with an emphasis on aviation, medical malpractice, and other areas.

If you can use a professional attorney who offers an outstanding professional reputation, I hope you will contact me to suggest a time when we might meet to discuss your needs. Thank you in advance for your professional courtesies.

Sincerely,

Vincent D. Howser, Jr.

VINCENT D. HOWSER, JR.

1110½ Hay Street, Fayetteville, NC 28305 • preppub@aol.com • (910) 483-6611

OBJECTIVE
To contribute to an organization that can use an award-winning public speaker who offers a proven ability to communicate and persuade.

EDUCATION & HONORS

University of New Orleans (J.D., *cum laude* 1995).
Top 10%; Phillip E. Baker Scholarship
2nd place; Freshman Moot Court Competition--1st quarter
1st place; Regional Moot Court Competition
1st place; Louisiana Young Lawyers Association State Moot Court Competition
The Bayou State Order of Barristers; National Order of Barristers.

Mississippi Valley State University, (B.A., *cum laude* 1992).
Four years on Debate Team winning numerous awards at various tournaments throughout the country, ranked 8th in nation in senior year. Dean's List.
Mississippi Valley State Honorary Forensic Fraternity.

PROFESSIONAL EXPERIENCE as an ATTORNEY

Claiborne, Donaldson, & Fritz, New Orleans, LA (2003-present). Am involved in insurance defense with an emphasis on product liability.
- **Cases involve:**

Product liability	Chemical exposure (toxic torts)
Prescription drugs	Auto accidents
Premises liability	Worker's compensation
Construction law	Labor relations
Domestic relations	Corporate law
Collections	Consumer protection.

- **Representative clients for whom I work:**

General Electric	Cummings Electric
Atlas Van Line	Chevrolet Autos

- Involved in 11 jury trials and seven appellate court appearances.

Meredith Bozeman, Attorney-at-Law, New Orleans, LA (2001-03). Was involved in insurance defense with some emphasis on aviation.
- **Cases involved:**

Defense of civil rights actions	Construction law
Professional malpractice (accountant, medical, podiatry)	
Auto accidents	Worker's compensation.

- **Representative clients for whom I worked:**

Allstate Insurance Group	Nextel Communications
Geico Insurance	Prudential, Inc.

- Involved in four jury trials and two appellate court appearances.

Davis & Davis Law Firm, Itta Bena, MS (1998-00). Plaintiff personal injury involving product liability, auto accidents, premises liability, some medical malpractice. Handled nine jury trials.

Fischer & McClain, Attorneys at Law, Itta Bena, MS (1997-98). Plaintiff personal injury specializing in medical malpractice. Handled two jury trials.

Date

Exact Name of Person
Exact Title
Exact Name of Company
Address
City, State, Zip

Dear Exact Name of Person (or Dear Sir or Madam if answering a blind ad):

   With the enclosed resume, I would like to make you aware of my interest in exploring employment opportunities with your organization and introduce you to my background.

   As you will see from the enclosed resume, I am currently working as a Senior Attorney for Bevill Medical Center in Anchorage. At this major medical center, I was specially selected as an attorney to provide guidance to other attorneys and senior military executives on areas of law including these: medical malpractice, military justice, employee and labor relations law, fiscal issues, international law, human rights, operational law, court martials, and rules of engagement. I serve as Trial Counsel in all court-martial cases, as the government's representative at all administrative elimination boards, as the trusted counsel for senior military executives, and provide legal advice on the organization's international operations. I also provide all organizations relocating on official military business with legal briefs. I recently received the highest evaluations of my performance and was described as "a brilliant attorney with foresight and vision."

   A skilled communicator, I have published legal guides, authored special operating procedures, and developed legal opinions which have impacted Special Forces activities worldwide. I earned a Juris Doctor degree from the University of Alaska and have received numerous awards for my excellent writing and research skills. I hold a Bachelor of Science degree in Criminal Justice Administration.

   If my background and skills interest you, I hope you will contact me to suggest a time when we could meet in person to discuss your needs. I can provide outstanding references. Thank you in advance for your time.

                                                                  Yours sincerely,

                                                                  Thomas McKnight

THOMAS McKNIGHT

1110½ Hay Street, Fayetteville, NC 28305 • preppub@aol.com • (910) 483-6611

OBJECTIVE

To benefit an organization that can use an experienced executive who offers a background as an attorney along with strong analytical, problem-solving, and strategic thinking skills.

EDUCATION

Received **Juris Doctor**, University of Alaska, Anchorage, AK, 2003. Completed this degree in my spare time while excelling in my full-time job.
- Received the American Jurisprudence Award for writing and research.
- Member, Law Review; published an article on arbitrating security disputes published in the University of Alaska Law Journal.

Earned **Bachelor of Science degree in Criminal Justice Administration,** University of Alaska, Anchorage, AK, 1999.

EXPERIENCE

ATTORNEY. Bevill Medical Center, Anchorage, AK (2003-present). At this major medical center, was specially selected as an attorney to provide guidance to other attorneys and to senior military executives on areas of law including these:

medical malpractice	military justice	employee and labor relations law
fiscal issues	international law	human rights
operational law	court martials	rules of engagement

- Serve as Trial Counsel in all court-martial cases; also serve as the government's representative at all administrative elimination boards.
- Serve as the trusted counsel for senior military executives, and provide legal advice on the organization's operations in Central and South America. Provide all organizations relocating on official military business with legal briefs.
- Provide legal advice pertaining to the conduct of 25 major missions, numerous investigations, and dozens of direct action and special reconnaissance operations.
- Received the highest evaluations of my performance and was described as "a brilliant attorney with foresight and vision."

POLICE DEPARTMENT DISPATCHER & COMMUNICATIONS OPERATOR. Anchorage Police Department, Anchorage, AK (1995-02). Established an excellent reputation within the Anchorage community and participated in many emergency situations.
- Processed emergency and non-emergency information to officers.
- Was promoted to train new dispatchers; monitored the activities of more than 30 officers per shift while also monitoring and operating seven police channels using CAD (Computer Aided Dispatch) system.
- Dispatched vehicle operators to military flightline and various other places on and off the base. Provided customer service by phone and in person.
- On my own initiative, created a filing system which greatly improved efficiency.
- Issued military licenses; handled and relayed secure information. Was responsible for maintenance of two-way radios. Input data, created spreadsheets, and developed presentations using Word, Excel, and PowerPoint.
- Responsible for employees' work schedules, lunch breaks, and annual leave.

Other experience: Became a part of the work force in Alaska by becoming a temporary worker with Tempo Temporary Service.

COMPUTERS

Proficient in using computers with MS Word, Excel, PowerPoint, and other software.

PERSONAL

Outstanding references on request. Thrive on solving problems through people.

Date

Exact Name of Person
Title or Position
Name of Company
Address (no., street)
Address (city, state, zip)

ATTORNEY
seeks first full-time position

Dear Exact Name of Person: (or Dear Sir or Madam if answering a blind ad.)

I would appreciate an opportunity to talk with you soon about how I could contribute to your organization as an attorney.

As you will see from my enclosed resume, I earned a Juris Doctor degree in Law and a Bachelor of Arts degree in History. I completed law school at night while excelling in very responsible jobs which required me to supervise other professionals gathering, analyzing, and preparing reports related to highly sensitive and top secret events worldwide. I have become known as an outstanding writer and public speaker and have taken the bar exam and am awaiting results.

As a Supervisor and Cryptologic Technician for the United States Federal Trade Commission, I supervised up to 10 people involved in data collection operations in support of national cryptologic efforts. I have gained skills as an analyst and transcriber while analyzing complex technical data. I have prepared concise and insightful reports under tight deadlines which contained analyses and recommendations which were reviewed and considered at high government levels.

You would find me to be a dynamic communicator who is known for my capacity for hard work and long hours. I am a highly adaptable professional who offers exceptionally research skills along with the proven ability to master difficult cases and persuasively argue them to judges and juries.

I hope you will welcome my call soon to arrange a brief meeting at your convenience to discuss your current and future needs and how I might serve them. Thank you in advance for your time.

Sincerely yours,

Frank D. Sowder

Alternate last paragraph:
I hope you will call or write me soon to suggest a time convenient for us to meet and discuss your current and future needs and how I might serve them. Thank you in advance for your time.

FRANK D. SOWDER

1110½ Hay Street, Fayetteville, NC 28305   •   preppub@aol.com   •   (910) 483-6611

OBJECTIVE
To contribute to an organization that can use a legally-trained young professional with skills related to data collection and analysis, experience in training and supervising other professionals, and a proven ability to handle multiple challenging assignments simultaneously.

EDUCATION
Earned **Juris Doctor degree in Law**, Butler University School of Law, Indianapolis, IN, 2004.
- Completed law school at night while excelling in very responsible jobs which required me to supervise other professionals gathering, analyzing, and preparing reports related to highly sensitive and top secret events worldwide.
- Became known as an outstanding writer and public speaker.
- Have taken the bar exam and am awaiting results.

Received **Bachelor of Arts in History**, Ivey Tech State College-Central Indiana, Indianapolis, IN, 1997.
- Completed my undergraduate degree while serving on active duty in the military.

CIVILIAN EXPERIENCE
SUPERVISOR and **ANALYST**. United States Federal Trade Commission, Indianapolis, IN (2000-present). Supervise employees involved in data collection operations in support of national cryptologic efforts.
- Gained skills as an analyst and transcriber while analyzing complex technical data.
- Prepare concise and insightful reports under tight deadlines which contained analyses and recommendations which were reviewed and considered at high government levels.
- While managing others, am known for my belief in "leadership by example" and was respected for my high productivity; personally contributed to 41% of the section's output.
- Refined my ability to manage time and people working in a perpetually time-sensitive environment; learned how to achieve high overall productivity while developing an internal organizational climate known for responsiveness to employee needs and problems. Received an official commendation for exceptional performance.

MILITARY EXPERIENCE
CRYPTOLOGIC TECHNICIAN. U.S. Naval Weapons Station, Jackson, MS (1998-00). Used my bilingual English/Spanish skills to analyze large volumes of complex data and produce, under tight deadlines, written reports which presented information used by top Navy officials and high-ranking officials to make decisions related to national security.

INVENTORY CONTROLLER/PROCUREMENT MANAGER. U.S. Naval Procurement Port, Jacksonville, FL (1997-98). Became skilled in most aspects of inventory control and procurement while managing the ordering, receipt, and distribution of aviation parts used for the maintenance and repair of a fleet of 60 airplanes.
- Refined my problem-solving skills in the process of learning the "shortcuts" involved in obtaining needed parts outside normal supply channels when urgent needs required creative solutions.

COMPUTER SKILLS
Have a working knowledge of the following computer software programs:

| Microsoft Word | Excel | Access |
| PowerPoint | FrontPage | PageMaker |

PERSONAL
Can provide excellent references upon request. Am willing to relocate.

Exact Name of Person
Exact Title
Exact Name of Company
Address
City, State, Zip

ATTORNEY
in her first job
after law school

Dear Exact Name of Person (or Dear Sir or Madam if answering a blind ad):

With the enclosed resume, I would like to make you aware of my interest in exploring employment opportunities with your firm. Although I can provide outstanding references at the appropriate time, I would appreciate your holding my interest in confidence until we talk.

A member of the South Carolina State Bar and the American Bar Association, I am also a member of the South Carolina Bar Association. In my current position, I am practicing law in a firm which specializes in real estate law, and I have become very knowledgeable of contract and business law. Although I am held in the highest regard by the firm's senior attorney and its clients, I am selectively approaching other firms which might be seeking a highly motivated young attorney known for meticulous attention to detail as well as an ability to handle multiple tasks.

Although my current position is my first full-time job as an attorney since being admitted to the bar, I worked part-time as a Legal Assistant during law school and gained exposure to family law, employment law, traffic law, and personal injury law. Through volunteering for two years during law school as a Guardian Ad Litem, I became skilled in researching matters related to child abuse and neglect. During college, I spent three summers as an Intern in the Office of the Governor in Columbia, SC, where I learned a great deal about the legislative process and the workings of state government. I also spent a summer abroad in London, England.

With an outstanding personal and professional reputation, I am confident that I could become a valuable asset to a firm which wishes to maximize growth and profitability. I am known for my ability to establish strong working relationships with individuals and organizations, and I would enjoy an opportunity to meet with you personally to discuss your firm's current or future needs for a hard-working and versatile young attorney.

Yours sincerely,

Elizabeth Turner

ELIZABETH TURNER

1110½ Hay Street, Fayetteville, NC 28305 • preppub@aol.com • (910) 483-6611

OBJECTIVE   I want to contribute to an organization that can use a dynamic and articulate young attorney who offers strong analytical and research skills along with a proven ability to deal effectively with clients.

MEMBERSHIPS   Admitted to the South Carolina State Bar, 2004; Admitted to the American Bar Association, 2004; Member, South Carolina Academy of Trial Lawyers; Member, SC Bar Association

EDUCATION   **Juris Doctorate,** University of South Carolina, School of Law, Columbia, SC, 2003.
- Member, ABA Law Student Division
- Member, Women in Law
- Member, SC Bar Association, Student Division

Bachelor of Arts degree, Criminal Law, University of South Carolina, Columbia SC, 2000. Partially financed my college education through two prestigious scholarships which I was awarded: the Carolinas Scholarship and the Aaron Wright Scholarship.

Study Abroad: Earned college credits from the South Carolina State University School of Law through the Summer Study Abroad Program, London, England, 2002.

EXPERIENCE   **ATTORNEY.** John O. Harrison, Attorney at Law, Columbia, SC (2004-present). In my first full-time job as an attorney since receiving my J.D. degree in 2003, practice law in a firm which specializes in real estate and contract law. Am involved in representing clients involved in the purchase and sale of property.
- Prepare paperwork related to the sale and refinance of property and negotiate sales contracts for commercial and residential property. Expertly search title loans.
- Am skilled in preparing the full range of documents pertaining to the sale of personal and business assets. Have earned respect for my meticulous attention to detail.
- Am skilled at working with clients at all economic levels, from the financially sophisticated to those with limited knowledge of legal or real estate issues.

LEGAL ASSISTANT. David Nelson, Attorney at Law, Columbia, SC (2003-04). After law school, worked part-time for six months while studying for the bar exam. Joined a new firm which was just starting up, and made significant contributions to overall efficiency.
- Researched and drafted complaints in contract law. Learned about construction law.
- Researched family law and became familiar with Department of Social Services issues.
- Researched employment law and researched personal injury issues. Interviewed clients in order to prepare motions and interrogations. Assisted with traffic law clients.
- Established the firm's filing system and created internal office procedures "from scratch." Played a key role in marketing the firm's services through preparing mass mailings.

Other experience:
GUARDIAN AD LITEM. Richland County, SC (2001-03). As a volunteer for two years while in law school, investigated reports of child abuse and neglect and drafted court documents.
INTERN, OFFICE OF THE GOVERNOR. Columbia, SC (1997-00). During the tenure of Governor Smith, worked for three summers; gained insights into the legislative process and state bureaucracy. Drafted letters to citizens for the governor's signature, resolved citizen problems, and assisted employees working full-time in the Correspondence Unit.

PERSONAL   Outstanding communicator who enjoys sharing my knowledge with others. Can provide excellent references. Offer strong computer skills which include experience with Word, Soft Pro, Works, Corel.

Date

Exact Name of Person
Exact Title
Exact Name of Company
Address
City, State, Zip

ATTORNEY

seeking to transition
from family law to civil
litigation. This young
attorney does not
wish to specialize in
family law, so she is
selectively exploring
opportunities in firms
which practice a
broader base of
contract law.

Dear Exact Name of Person (or Dear Sir or Madam if answering a blind ad):

With the enclosed resume, I would like to make you aware of my interest in exploring employment opportunities with your firm. Although I can provide outstanding references at the appropriate time, I would appreciate your holding my interest in your firm in confidence until we talk.

A member of the Oregon State Bar and the National Bar Association, I currently serve as the Young Lawyers Representative. In my current position, I practice law in a firm which specializes in family law, and I serve as the firm's Child Support Enforcement Attorney. In addition to representing a diverse range of clients in district court, I manage 26 child support workers who handle more than 18,000 cases and collect more than $1 million monthly in child support through a contract which contributes $180,000 annually to the firm. I have established warm working relationships with attorneys, public and private agencies, public officials, and law enforcement officials throughout the state, and I have earned a reputation as an aggressive, outspoken, persuasive, and respected communicator.

In a prior internship with the Portland District Attorney's Office, I gained exposure to criminal, traffic, and juvenile law. In a separate internship with Legal Services of Oregon, I was involved in providing legal services to the indigent while representing clients in district court on matters related to family law, consumer law, estate planning, and public benefits.

With an outstanding personal and professional reputation, I am confident that I could become a valuable asset to a firm which wishes to maximize growth and profitability. Although I am excelling in my current position and am regarded as an expert in family law, I would like to be involved in a broader range of civil litigation. I would enjoy an opportunity to meet with you personally to discuss your firm's current or future needs for a hardworking and versatile young attorney with a proven talent for handling multiple responsibilities and complex tasks.

Yours sincerely,

Rebecca Woodruff

REBECCA WOODRUFF

1110½ Hay Street, Fayetteville, NC 28305 • preppub@aol.com • (910) 483-6611

OBJECTIVE

I want to contribute to an organization that can use a dynamic and articulate young attorney who offers strong management abilities along with outstanding communication skills and the "power of persuasion."

MEMBERSHIPS

The National Bar Association, Family Law Division
The Oregon Bar Association, Young Lawyers Representative
The Oregon Academy of Trial Lawyers, Family Law Division

HONORS

Recipient of Oregon Academy of Trial Lawyers Student Advocacy Award, 2003-04
Listed in "Who's Who Among American Law Students," 2002-03
Listed in the National Dean's List Book

EDUCATION

Juris Doctorate, Portland State University, Portland, OR, 2004.
• Member, Oregon Bar Association, Student Division
Bachelor of Arts degree, Major in Pre-Law Government with a minor in History, Portland State University, Portland, OR, 2001.
• Member, Beta Kappa Chi Legal Fraternity

EXPERIENCE

ATTORNEY. Walker & Walker, Attorneys at Law, Portland, OR (2004-present). In my first full-time job as an attorney since receiving my J.D. degree in 2004, practice law in a firm which specializes in family law. Have been promoted to Child Support Enforcement Attorney. Manage 26 child support workers who handle more than 18,000 child support cases; child support workers are involved in collecting $1 million monthly in child support through a contract which contributes $180,000 annually in revenue for the law firm.
• Have demonstrated my ability to manage a team of professionals who play a significant role in bettering the lives of Portland's children.
• Represent clients in district court on matters related to family law and social security benefits.
• Have created legal forms for the firm's social security matters.
• Have become skilled at handling a large volume of cases while efficiently monitoring the caseload management of multiple professionals. Have also become skilled at representing diverse clients from different social and economic backgrounds. Have established warm working relationships with attorneys, public and private agencies, public officials, and law enforcement officials throughout the state.

INTERN, DISTRICT ATTORNEY'S OFFICE. Office of the District Attorney, Portland, OR (2004). In this spring internship, was able to practice law in district court under the Third Year Supervision Rule. Gained exposure to criminal, traffic, and juvenile law.

INTERN & SUMMER ASSOCIATE. Legal Services of Oregon, Portland, OR (2003). Was involved in providing legal services to the indigent while representing clients in district court on matters related to family law, consumer law, estate planning, and public benefits.
• Gained knowledge of law affecting social security benefits, public benefits, employment law, and small claims matters. Increased the productivity of the Estate Planning Department. Boosted the number of clients interviewed and cases handled, and created legal forms for domestic matters.

PERSONAL

Can provide excellent references. Strong computer skills and experience with Word.

CAREER CHANGE

Date

Exact Name of Person
Title or Position
Name of Company
Address (no., street)
Address (city, state, zip)

DISTRICT COURT JUDGE

for a Missouri-based judicial court is seeking to leave "the bench" and enter private practice

Dear Exact Name of Person: (or Dear Sir or Madam if answering a blind ad.)

I would appreciate an opportunity to talk with you soon about how I could contribute to your organization as an attorney.

Currently as a District Court Judge for Warrensburg, Lees Summit and Joplin Counties in the state of Missouri, I preside over the District Court for the 13th Judicial District and handle administrative matters as Acting Chief District Court Judge. I advise defendants at felony first appearances and set bond and accept misdemeanor and felony pleas in cases where the court has felony jurisdiction. As I preside over criminal trials as well as traffic court and criminal juvenile proceedings, I also direct civil court activities on matters up to $10,000 as well as magistrate appeals and family court issues. As you know, in our state district court judges are elected, and I have decided not to seek re-election so that I can enter private practice with an outstanding law firm.

In a previous position as an Assistant District Attorney for Joplin County, I prosecuted felonies and misdemeanors including juvenile and domestic criminal matters in the 13th Prosecutorial District. I also conducted bond hearings, interviewed witnesses, and advised law enforcement personnel.

As you will see from my resume, I hold a Juris Doctor (JD) from the University of Missouri-Columbia School of Law where I achieved honors which included recognition in "Who's Who Among Law Students" and the Student Bar Association Service Award. I served as vice president of the Student Bar Association and was on the Disciplinary Committee. With a Bachelor of Science degree in Business Administration with a concentration in Finance, I graduated *magna cum laude*.

I am approaching only a select number of firms, and I hope you will contact me if you have an interest in discussing how my experience and talents could be put to work for you. Thank you in advance for your time.

Sincerely yours,

Peggy S. Robeson

PEGGY S. ROBESON

1110½ Hay Street, Fayetteville, NC 28305   •   preppub@aol.com   •   (910) 483-6611

OBJECTIVE

To contribute through my extensive experience as a judge and attorney known for possessing a strong interest in public service and a record of community involvement.

EDUCATION

Juris Doctor (JD), University of Missouri-Columbia School of Law, Columbia, MO, 1989.
- Achieved honors which included recognition in "Who's Who Among Law Students" and earned the Student Bar Association Service Award.
- Served as vice president of the Student Bar Association and was on the Disciplinary Committee; was a member of Sigma Gamma Mu Law Fraternity.

Bachelor of Science, Business Administration (concentration in Finance), Rockhurst College, Kansas City, MO, 1986.
- Graduated *magna cum laude*; named to the Dean's List.
- Held membership in Alpha Kappa Alpha Honor Society.

Have completed numerous judicial continuing education sponsored by the National College of District Attorneys Trial Advocacy Course, St. Louis, MO. Complete yearly courses sponsored by the MO Association of District Court Judges and MO Western State School of Law.

BAR ADMISSION

Admitted to the Missouri Bar, September 1989

EXPERIENCE

DISTRICT COURT JUDGE. Warrensburg, Lees Summit and Joplin Counties, Missouri (2000-present). Preside over District Court for the Thirteenth Judicial District and handle administrative matters as Acting Chief District Court Judge.
- Advise defendants at felony first appearances and set bond.
- Accept misdemeanor and felony pleas in cases where the court has felony jurisdiction.
- Preside over criminal trials as well as traffic court and criminal juvenile proceedings.
- Direct civil court activities on matters up to $10,000 as well as magistrate appeals and family court issues.

ASSISTANT DISTRICT ATTORNEY. Joplin County, Joplin, IL (1995-00). Prosecuted felonies and misdemeanors including juvenile and domestic criminal matters in the 13th Prosecutorial District. Handled such actions as conducting bond hearings, interviewing witnesses, and advising law enforcement personnel.

LAW CLERK and **STAFF ATTORNEY.** Richard Fields, Attorney at Law, Columbia, MO (1990-95). Argued motions and obtained depositions as well as preparing pleadings, motions, and briefs while gaining criminal, probate, and appellate experience.
- Received concentrated experience in the litigation of general liability actions encompassing district court trials, superior court jury trials, and small claims cases.

AFFILIATIONS

Hold membership and serve on community boards and committees including the following:

National Council of Juvenile and Family Court Judges	Missouri Bar Association
Warrensburg County Lawyers Association	NAACP
13th Judicial District Bar Association	

MO Cooperative Extension Service – Advisory Council /Committee on Juvenile Studies
Department of Social Services Child Protection Team Advisory Council (Lees Summit County)
MO Association of District Court Judges (Juvenile Justice Committee)

PERSONAL

Have earned awards for community service with the United Way and Habitat for Humanity organizations. Excellent references available upon request.

Date

Exact Name of Person
Exact Title
Exact Name of Company
Address
City, State, Zip

Dear Exact Name of Person (or Dear Sir or Madam if answering a blind ad):

With the enclosed resume, I would like to make you aware of an experienced attorney who is excelling as a U.S. Army officer working in the field of environmental law.

As you will see from my resume, after building a reputation as an exceptionally articulate and persuasive young attorney in versatile areas of military law, I was selected to receive training and move into this highly specialized field. As an advisor on federal and state environmental laws, construction, and land use issues, I represent the Ft. Eustis, VA military installation before agencies which include the Department of Agriculture.

Among my current projects is one in which four acres of contaminated land owned by the U.S. Army is to be disposed of and turned over to the City of Newport News. Another case with the Department of Agriculture is currently being negotiated to reduce fines on multiple environmental safety violations. Another current project involves coordinating with the General Electric Business Center and contractors on an Environmental Impact Statement concerning an 11,000 acre section which was purchased by the Army with plans to use it as a training area.

Licensed to practice law in three states, I earned my J.D. degree from Virginia Commonwealth University Law School in Richmond and my bachelor's degree in International Relations from Champlain College. My training has included attendance at the ten-week Judge Advocate General Corps course in military law as well as other programs focusing on environmental, fiscal, and criminal law as well as an ethics course.

Although I was strongly encouraged to remain in military service and assured of continued rapid advancement in rank, I decided to leave the military and enter private practice. If you can use an outstanding attorney with high degrees of enthusiasm, energy, and drive, I hope you will contact me soon to suggest a time we might meet to discuss how I could contribute to your organization. I can provide excellent professional and personal references at the appropriate time. Thank you for your time and consideration.

Sincerely,

Amber D. Jenkins

AMBER D. JENKINS

1110½ Hay Street, Fayetteville, NC 28305   •   preppub@aol.com   •   (910) 483-6611

OBJECTIVE

To contribute through exceptional analytical and research skills as well as a reputation as a persuasive, articulate, intelligent attorney with specialized expertise in environmental law.

EDUCATION & TRAINING

Juris Doctor degree, Virginia Commonwealth University School of Law, Richmond, VA, 1988.
Bachelor of Arts degree in **International Relations**, Champlain College, Burlington, VT, 1985.
Completed the ten-week Judge Advocate General's Corps course in military law, as well as other military programs in environmental law, ethics, fiscal law, and criminal law.

EXPERIENCE

Hold the rank of Captain and have gained versatile experience in legal assistance, torts, criminal law, administrative, and environmental law, U.S. Army:
ENVIRONMENTAL LAW ATTORNEY. Ft. Eustis, VA (2000-present). As a specialist in environmental law, am the advisor on federal and state environmental laws, construction, and land use issues which impact this military installation.

- Represent this military installation before the Department of Agriculture (DoA) and the Virginia Department of Environment and Natural Resources (VADENR).
- Am representing Ft. Eustis in numerous cases which include: negotiating before the DoA a fine for violations of the Safe Water Drinking Act and a conditional settlement with the state VADENR for hazardous waste violations.
- Am handling a project during which four acres of contaminated land owned by the U.S. Army are to be disposed of and turned over to the City of Newport News.
- Established a satellite office and integrated my activities into the client operations of the General Electric Business Center in order to gain understanding of the pollution control and prevention programs, natural resource management, and infrastructure.
- Initiated a program for tracking compliance with the resource conservation to place an emphasis on laws concerning hazardous waste.

ADMINISTRATIVE LAW ATTORNEY. Ft. Carson, CO (1995-00). Officially evaluated as "a leader others look to for guidance," provided legal advice on administrative and regulatory issue to all organizations, units, and staff sections on the 150,000-acre installation with the heaviest training density in the Army. Became recognized as the subject matter expert on fundraising, private organizations, commercial solicitation, and government housing issues.

LEGAL CENTER MANAGER. Richmond, VA (1992-95). Officially evaluated as "truly spectacular" in a demanding job usually held by a higher ranking officer, was cited for my maturity, good judgment, and superb leadership of a legal center which serviced 16,000 people. Provided advice and services on family law, consumer law, estate planning, military administrative law, personal finances, and civil law issues.

TRIAL COUNSEL. Burlington County Court House, Burlington, VT (1990-92). Cited as "particularly persuasive in oral arguments and presenting the government's case in sentencing," represented the United States in difficult and complex courts-martial cases such as those involving sexual assault, child abuse, and drug distribution.

LEGAL ASSISTANCE ATTORNEY. Cox, Miller & Ridell, Richmond, VA (1988-89). Quickly became known for my ability to handle stress and change in a busy center which provided legal counseling, representation, and guidance.

PERSONAL

Am known for my sound judgment, keen insight and analytical skills, and common sense.

Date

Exact Name of Person
Title or Position
Name of Company
Address (no., street)
Address (city, state, zip)

FEDERAL PROSECUTOR
for a magistrate court

Dear Exact Name of Person: (or Dear Sir or Madam if answering a blind ad.)

I would appreciate an opportunity to talk with you soon about how I could contribute to your organization as an attorney.

From the enclosed resume you will see that I hold a J.D. degree as well as a B.A. degree in Political Science. In the process of becoming an attorney, I excelled in a semester internship with the U.S. Attorney's Office and I also excelled as a Teaching Assistant and Head Teaching Assistant at the Emory University School of Law over two summers. I was named "Outstanding Teaching Assistant" while teaching Property, Contracts, Legal Research, and Writing. I taught Torts, Civil Procedure, and Writing at Emory the following summer.

Since graduating with my J.D. degree, I have served my country as a Captain in the U.S. Army and have excelled as a U.S. Magistrate Court Prosecutor, Legal Assistance Attorney, and Group Judge Advocate during the war in the Middle East. In addition to prosecuting criminal cases, I have managed a large number of civil cases and have helped soldiers with legal problems involving contract law, landlord/tenant law, consumer protection law, domestic law, and wills and estate law. I successfully argued a client consumer protection case in state court, and I once negotiated a large settlement for a client from the Pitney Bowes Corporation.

You would find me to be a dynamic communicator who is known for my capacity for hard work and long hours. I am an articulate professional who offers exceptional research skills along with the proven ability to master difficult cases and persuasively argue them to judges and juries. I hope you will welcome my call soon to arrange a brief meeting at your convenience to discuss your current and future needs and how I might serve them. Thank you in advance for your time.

Sincerely yours,

David C. Culbreath

Alternate last paragraph:
I hope you will call or write me soon to suggest a time convenient for us to meet and discuss your current and future needs and how I might serve them. Thank you in advance for your time.

DAVID C. CULBREATH

1110½ Hay Street, Fayetteville, NC 28305   •   preppub@aol.com   •   (910) 483-6611

OBJECTIVE   I want to contribute to an organization that can use an astute young attorney with exceptional analytical and research skills along with the proven ability to persuasively communicate complex concepts to judges and juries.

MEMBERSHIP   Member of the Oklahoma Bar and the Pennsylvania Bar.

EDUCATION   Earned **Juris Doctor degree**, Mansfield University School of Law, Mansfield, PA, 1998.
- Was selected as Head Teaching Assistant, Mansfield University School of Law, Summer 1996: tutored students in Torts, Civil Procedure, Writing, Property, Contracts, and Legal Research.
- Was president of a prominent law student association, 1996-98.
- Excelled in a semester internship with the U.S. Attorney's Office, 1997.

Received **Bachelor of Arts degree**, Rhode Island College, Providence, RI, 1992.
- Majored in Political Science.

EXPERIENCE   **FEDERAL PROSECUTOR**. U.S. Army, Ft. Sill, OK (2003-present). While working at this military installation, prosecute in U.S. Magistrate Court all individuals who commit misdemeanor criminal offenses on the Ft. Sill base. Prosecute all misdemeanor motor vehicle and wildlife violations committed on those military bases.
- Direct the operation of the U.S. Magistrate Program at Ft. Sill.
- Was described in writing as a "tireless worker" while excelling as a Special Assistant to the U.S. Attorney; rapidly mastered the rules of the Magistrate Court system as well as the intricacies of the Federal Rules of Evidence and Federal Rules of Criminal Procedure.
- Draft felony indictments, present them to Grand Juries, and negotiate plea agreements.
- Won the confidence of the Federal Magistrate while prosecuting a heavy caseload of hundreds of cases monthly.
- Was officially praised for "exceptional talent as a litigator" on a performance evaluation.
- Learned the importance of getting involved early with police and investigators during cases.

INSTRUCTOR (PART-TIME). Cameron University, Lawton, OK (2003-present). At nights and on weekends, have instructed classes in Business Law, Criminal Law, Constitutional Law, and American Government.

COMMAND JUDGE ADVOCATE. Department of Justice, Mansfield, PA (2000-03). Served as the sole legal advisor to 25 executives while providing a wide range of legal services to 250 people; was awarded the highly prestigious "Legal Services Award" for my "superb handling of some of the most complicated cases."
- Conducted classes on criminal law, legal assistance, wills, powers of attorney, and consumer protection law.

LEGAL ASSISTANCE ATTORNEY. Bailey, Clark & Taylor, Mansfield, PA (1998-00). Assisted the Pitney Bowes Corporation with varying legal problems involving contracts, landlord-tenant law, property law, and wills and estates.
- Successfully argued a consumer protection case in State Court.
- Excelled in managing large numbers of civil cases.
- Negotiated a settlement for a client from the Pitney Bowes Corporation.

CAREER CHANGE

Date

Exact Name of Person
Exact Title
Exact Name of Company
Address
City, State, Zip

GENERAL PRACTICE ATTORNEY

who is self-employed in Dayton, OH is seeking to join a larger practice

Dear Exact Name of Person: (or Dear Sir or Madam if answering a blind ad):

With the enclosed resume, I would like to initiate the process of confidentially exploring opportunities within your firm. I am writing to you because I am aware of your fine reputation, and I feel that my personal qualities and professional strengths could make me a valuable asset to your firm as an attorney.

Since graduating from law school, I have been self-employed as a General Practice Attorney in Dayton, where I handle plaintiff cases involving personal injury, product liability, auto accidents, premises liability. I specialize in medical malpractice suits and have argued in multiple successful jury trials. Although I have excelled as an entrepreneur, I am exploring opportunities to serve as corporate counsel for a company which seeks highly effective in-house counsel.

If you can use a highly professional young attorney who offers superior writing, research, and verbal communication skills, I hope you will contact me to suggest a time when we might meet to discuss your needs. Thank you in advance for your time and professional courtesies.

Sincerely,

John W. Hopkins

JOHN W. HOPKINS

1110½ Hay Street, Fayetteville, NC 28305   •   preppub@aol.com   •   (910) 483-6611

OBJECTIVE

To obtain a position in the field of law, either in the practice of law, paralegal education, or any law-related occupation.

EDUCATION

Juris Doctor degree, Ohio University, Athens, OH, 1993.
Bachelor of Arts degree in Sociology, Cleveland State University, Cleveland, OH, 1990.

EXPERIENCE

GENERAL PRACTICE ATTORNEY. Self- Employed, Dayton, OH (1993-present). Plaintiff personal injury including products liability, auto accidents, premises liability, specializing in medical malpractice. Multiple jury trials.
Honors, Activities, and Memberships:
Current member, Ohio Bar.
Executive Director, Ohio State Lawyers Association, Dayton Chapter

INSTRUCTOR & DEPARTMENT CHAIRPERSON. The Law School and the Paralegal Department, Sinclair College, Dayton, OH (1995-present). As an Adjunct Professor in my spare time, perform department head duties and teach classes in all major areas of law, with a majority of classes being in these areas:

real estate	wills and trusts
estates	contracts

Honors and Activities:
Past chairperson, Leadership Development Committee, Sinclair College, Dayton, OH.
Current Chairperson, Student Affairs Committee, Sinclair College, Dayton, OH.
Current Secretary, Governing Committee, Sinclair College, Dayton, OH.
Advisor, Alpha Kappa Alpha Honor Society, Sinclair College, Dayton, OH.
Advisor, Paralegal Club, Sinclair College, Dayton, OH.

LOCAL HONORS & APPOINTMENTS

2001: Appointed to the Board of Directors of the Dayton Regional Hospital System. Play a key role in administering a multimillion-dollar budget, and was a major force in the expansion of the hospital into a major regional medical center.
2002: Elected as a member of the Board of Directors of the Dayton School System; have been a leading force for change.
2002: Recognized as Coach of the Year, YMCA, for my efforts in coaching Little League teams.

PERSONAL

Outstanding reputation. Offer a reputation as a person of integrity and vision. Am known for my ability to think strategically and solve problems resourcefully.

Date

Exact Name of Person
Title or Position
Name of Company
Address (no., street)
Address (city, state, zip)

LAW CLERK

for a law office that
specializes in criminal and
matrimonial law

Dear Exact Name of Person: (or Dear Sir or Madam if answering a blind ad.)

With the enclosed resume, I would like to acquaint you with my background as a newly minted attorney and express my interest in exploring employment opportunities with your firm. A recent graduate of Oregon Law School, I have relocated to the Eugene area. I am sending my resume to you on the advice of Mr. Peter White. My undergraduate degree is in accounting, and I am particularly interested in a position with your firm.

My ultimate goal is to obtain my CPA, so that I can combine my accounting and law degrees. I have already started this process by supplementing my accounting background with numerous business courses at law school, including tax, corporate tax, counseling and planning for small corporations, trusts and estates, and bankruptcy.

I am confident that my employment experiences, together with my education make me a qualified and capable addition to your firm. I would welcome the opportunity to discuss the possibility of pursuing a position with your firm. I look forward to hearing from you in the near future.

Sincerely,

Wanda M. Ackerman

WANDA M. ACKERMAN

1110½ Hay Street, Fayetteville, NC 28305   •   preppub@aol.com   •   (910) 483-6611

EDUCATION

J.D., December 2004
University of Oregon, Eugene, OR
- Eric Kirkland Moot Court Competition, Fall 2002
- Senior Prize Trials Competition, Fall 2003, Spring 2004

B.B.A., *cum laude,* December 2001
Portland State University, Portland, OR
- Accounting Major/Philosophy Minor
- Academic Honors List
- Presidential Scholar (High Honors) List
- Selected for *Who's Who in American Universities and Colleges*

EXPERIENCE

Law Clerk
Allard, Kerr & McDaniels, LLP, Eugene, OR   Fall, 2003
Research and preparations for hearings and trials. Memorandum and motion drafting, as well as assisting with client interviews. Emphasis on criminal and matrimonial law.

Law Clerk
Lane County District Attorney's Office, Eugene, OR   Summer, 2003
Extensive use of research and writing skills in preparing memorandums of law and motion drafting. Participated in town court misdemeanor plea bargaining and prosecutions.

Legal and Corporate Finance Assistant
Scarborough, Zack, Wrey, Eugene, OR   Spring, 2002
Wrote formation, employment, and related business and transactional agreements for Partnerships, Limited Partnerships, and Corporate entities. Duties also included business analysis and working with Microsoft Excel spreadsheets.

Legal Office Assistant
Zackary & Taylor, Portland, OR   Summer, 2001
Examined wills and client files for various documentation. Assisted in establishing a branch office for the firm.

Legal Intern
Oregon State Department of Law, Portland, OR   Fall, 2000
Dispute resolution and mediation of cases between businesses and the public, emphasis on automobile warranties, private contractors, mail fraud, unfair business practices, etc. Compiled data on individuals and businesses for commencement of potential class-action, public interest lawsuits.

Office Assistant
Bradley, Galloway & O'Connell, LLP, Portland, OR   Summer, 1997
Compiled financial statements, worksheets, and payroll ledgers for clients. Also handled data transfer, typed tax returns, and archived client files.

ACTIVITIES

Oregon Law School Tennis Club, 1999-02
Accounting Tutor, 1996-1999
Public Affairs Committee (1995-1997), Portland State University
Tour Guide, Admissions Office, Portland State University

CAREER CHANGE

Date

Exact Name of Person
Exact Title
Exact Name of Company
Address
City, State, Zip

**PROMINENT
ATTORNEY**

with an
outstanding track
record of
accomplishments
is seeking to
make a career
change into
municipal
government as a
City Manager.

Dear Exact Name of Person: (or Dear Sir or Madam if answering a blind ad):

With the enclosed resume, I would like to initiate the process of responding to your advertisement for a City Manager for Martin, Tennessee.

As you will see from my enclosed resume, I earned a Juris Doctor degree in Law from the University of Tennessee at Martin where I was elected President of the student body (Bar Association). Previously I earned a Bachelor's degree in General Education with a specialty in Business Management and excelled in extensive training as a professional pilot in the U.S. Air Force, named as a Distinguished Graduate.

Expertise as an attorney

In my current position as an Attorney for Librand & McNally Law Firm, I act as a Managing Partner, handling civil and criminal litigation in federal and state courts. As Retained Counsel for the Martin Housing Developments for 15 years, I have developed expert knowledge related to public housing. As a trusted counselor/advisor, I represent individuals and corporate clients before governmental agencies.

Extensive leadership in state and local government

I believe strongly in contributing to the community in which I live, and I have served with distinction as Chairman for the Bradford County Republican Party. In that capacity I have served as the party's "chief executive officer" and am responsible for recruiting, training, and supervising volunteers in those 57 precincts. As a member of the Board of Directors of the Bradford County Department of Social Services for five years, I have provided advice to the Executive Director pertaining to the policies, procedures, administration, and operation of $140 million in county-wide programs funded by federal, state, and local governments. Also active in state government, I have been appointed by Governor Tinsdel to serve as a member of the Board of Trustees which oversees a $15 billion retirement system in our state.

I am confident that I could serve with distinction as City Manager of Martin, and I hope you will give me an opportunity to talk with you and show you in person that I am the highly qualified visionary you are seeking to lead our great city into the next decade.

Sincerely,

Charles B. Jarvis

CHARLES B. JARVIS

1110½ Hay Street, Fayetteville, NC 28305 • preppub@aol.com • (910) 483-6611

OBJECTIVE

I want to contribute to the political process and enhance the effectiveness of government through the leadership ability I have demonstrated in both the public and private sector, the reputation for unquestioned integrity which I have earned, and my ability to solve problems creatively using strong analytical, communication, and consensus-building skills.

EDUCATION

Juris Doctor (J.D.) degree in Law, The University of Tennessee at Martin, 1990.
 • Elected President of the student body (Bar Association), 1990.
Bachelor's degree in General Education with specialty in Business Management, University of Tennessee at Martin, 1983.
 • Lettered in tennis on the varsity team.

EXPERIENCE

ATTORNEY. Librand & McNally Law Firm, Martin, TN (1990-present). As a Managing Partner in law firm, handle civil and criminal litigation in federal and state courts; as Retained Counsel for the Martin Housing Developments for 15 years, have developed expert knowledge related to public housing; and as a trusted counselor/advisor, represent individuals and corporate clients before governmental agencies.
 • Have argued cases before the U.S. District Court of Appeals, The Tennessee Supreme Court, the Tennessee Court of Appeals, as well as lower federal and state courts.

MILITARY PILOT. U.S. Naval Station, Flight Squadron, Millington, TN (1983-87). Was rapidly promoted to Captain (a promotion I declined in order to enter University of Tennessee School of Law). Served as combat pilot; flew combat missions.

POLITICAL LEADERSHIP

CHAIRMAN, BRADFORD COUNTY DEMOCRATIC PARTY. Bradford County, TN (2000-present). Have loyally served as the party's "chief executive officer" overseeing activities of 57 precincts, all with their own leadership; am responsible for recruiting, training, and supervising volunteers in those precincts.
 • As co-chairman of Vision 2004 Committee, led a successful non-partisan effort to bring a new coliseum to Bradford County for the benefit of the Mid-South in Tennessee; on March 7, 2003, the county commissioners approved financing for the project.
 • Through aggressive voter registration and education campaigns implemented in the 57 precincts, voter registration in the Democratic Party increased by 20% in two years.
 • Chaired the successful presidential campaign in Bradford County, and worked with party leaders statewide.

LOCAL GOVERNMENT LEADERSHIP

MEMBER, BOARD OF DIRECTORS. Bradford County Department of Social Services, Gallatin, TN (1997-03). For five years, provided advice to the Executive Director of the Department of Social Services pertaining to the policies, procedures, administration, and operation of $140 million in county-wide programs funded by federal, state, and local governments.

STATE GOVERNMENT LEADERSHIP

MEMBER, BOARD OF TRUSTEES (appointed by Governor Tinsdel). Tennessee Retirement Systems, Martin, TN (1998-present). Along with other trustees, manage assets in excess of $15 billion which constitute the retirement systems for educators and state employees, judicial officials, as well as state and local government employees.
 • Play a key role in directing operations of a major governmental agency.

PERSONAL

Believe my breadth of knowledge about Tennessee's citizens and governmental affairs could be of great service to the community where I live and have reared my family.

Date

Exact Name of Person
Title or Position
Name of Company
Address (no., street)
Address (city, state, zip)

PROSECUTOR
for a public
defender's office

Dear Exact Name of Person: (or Dear Sir or Madam if answering a blind ad.)

With the enclosed resume, I would like to make you aware of my interest in the position as Police Attorney.

In my current position as Prosecutor with the State of Utah's Public Defender's Office, I have handled more than 400 felony cases, and I have worked closely with jailers and bailiffs in Salt Lake City. I am well acquainted with the need for police officers to thoroughly understand the Rules of Evidence so that their actions as police officers do not expose the city to litigation. While working as Senior Criminal Prosecutor, I actually wrote the Rules of Engagement for the Army while stationed in Stuttgart, Germany.

My police law experience includes my work in Salt Lake City, where I served as Assistant Attorney General. In that capacity I traveled extensively throughout Utah while prosecuting capital cases for the death penalty. Throughout my military career, I worked frequently as a Magistrate gaining experience in a variety of communities.

I offer the city of Austin a unique combination of experience and knowledge related to police and criminal, and I believe I could make significant contributions to the city in that role. I would enjoy an opportunity to discuss the job with those individuals seeking to identify the most capable and qualified individual for the job.

Yours sincerely,

Brent R. Rhodes

BRENT R. RHODES

1110½ Hay Street, Fayetteville, NC 28305   •   preppub@aol.com   •   (910) 483-6611

SUMMARY

Sixteen years of experience as Criminal Trial Litigator, Procurement Counsel, General Counsel, and College Professor. Expertise in municipal law, litigation, contract law, and police law.

EDUCATION

Juris Doctor degree from the University of Utah-School of Law, Salt Lake City, UT, 1990. Earned a **Bachelor of Science degree in Political Science with a minor in Sociology** from St. Edwards University, Austin, TX, 1987.

EXPERIENCE

PROSECUTOR. The State of Utah's Public Defender's Office, Salt Lake City, UT (2003-present). Was recruited for this position by Andy Thomas; have handled more than 250 felony cases of all levels.

MUNICIPAL CONTRACT ATTORNEY. Salt Lake Municipal Court, Salt Lake City, UT (2001-03). Was handpicked by the Attorney General for this job because of my extensive contracting experience and knowledge of contract law. Utilized my knowledge of the Freedom of Information and Open Government Acts while handling open government requests.
* Became skilled in municipal law while drafting all contracts for the City Attorney.

ASSISTANT ATTORNEY GENERAL. Attorney General's Office, Salt Lake City, UT (1999-01). Traveled extensively Utah while prosecuting capital cases for the death penalty. Prosecuted successfully over a dozen capital cases for the Capital Murder Team in close liaison with local District Attorneys, Prosecution Assistant Division.

Highlights of military experience:
LEGAL ADVISOR AND SENIOR ARMY COUNSEL. Fort Carson, CO (1996-99). Represented the Legal Services Division and advised a 4-star general on these areas:

international law	international agreements	contracts
treaties	government information practices	ethics
litigation	federal administrative regulations	labor law
environmental law	employment law	claims

PROFESSOR OF LAW. Fort Sill, OK (1994-96). Taught international, criminal, contract, and administrative law.

SENIOR CRIMINAL PROSECUTOR. Stuttgart, Germany (1993-94). Settled claims when people sued the U.S. Government; handled more than 100 felony cases including three murder cases. Supervised 10 attorneys, three paralegals, and secretarial support.

CHIEF OF LEGAL AID OFFICE. Camp Casey & DMZ of South Korea (1991-93). Supervised four attorneys and three paralegals while advising clients in and out of court in areas including administrative as well as these other areas:

domestic relations	child support	real property
probate	bankruptcies	collections
consumer protection	estates	business transactions
employment law	employee benefits	family law

CRIMINAL DEFENSE COUNSEL. Ft. Benning, GA (1990-91). Handled over 150 felony cases including a capital murder case; represented individual clients in personnel proceedings.

PERSONAL

Skilled at knowing when to litigate and when to settle. Professional references on request.

Real-Resumes Series edited by Anne McKinney **153**

Date

Exact Name of Person
Title or Position
Name of Company
Address (no., street)
Address (city, state, zip)

RECOVERY JUDGE ADVOCATE

for the U.S. Army
in Georgia

Dear Exact Name of Person: (or Dear Sir or Madam if answering a blind ad.)

I would appreciate an opportunity to talk with you soon about how I could contribute to your organization as an attorney.

As you will see from my resume, I am currently a Recovery Judge Advocate and, in that position, I assert, negotiate, and settle government claims under the provisions of the Federal Claims Act and the Medical Care Recovery Act. I prepare Rule Four and Trial Memorandum of Law for contracts appealed to the ASBCA. In a previous position as an attorney for the U.S. Army Legal Services Division, I was responsible for providing legal advice to commanders and soldiers assigned to the National Logistic Support Command in Iraq in the areas of international law, contract law, and military justice.

You would find me to be a dynamic communicator who is known for my capacity for hard work and long hours. I am a highly adaptable professional who offers exceptionally research skills along with the proven ability to master difficult cases and persuasively argue them to judges and juries.

Although I was aggressively recruited to remain in military service and assured of continued rapid advancement in rank and responsibility, I decided to leave the military and pursue a career as an attorney in private practice.

I hope you will welcome my call soon to arrange a brief meeting at your convenience to discuss your current and future needs and how I might serve them. Thank you in advance for your time.

Sincerely yours,

Richard W. Allen, Jr.

Alternate last paragraph:
I hope you will call or write me soon to suggest a time convenient for us to meet and discuss your current and future needs and how I might serve them. Thank you in advance for your time.

RICHARD W. ALLEN, JR.

1110½ Hay Street, Fayetteville, NC 28305   •   preppub@aol.com   •   (910) 483-6611

OBJECTIVE

I want to contribute to an organization that can use an articulate communicator with outstanding interpersonal, analytical, and problem-solving skills.

EDUCATION

DePaul University School of Law
61 52nd Street, Chicago, Illinois 55555
J.D., December 1998.
Activities:
Moot Court
Kappa Alpha Psi Fraternity
Student Bar Association

DePaul University
1171 Becton Avenue, Chicago, Illinois 55555
B.S.B.A, December 1995, Major: Accounting
Activities: Alpha Lambda Nu Social Fraternity

TRAINING

Department of Justice
Judicial Findings Course
March 2000 – June 2000

EXPERIENCE

RECOVERY JUDGE ADVOCATE. U.S. Army Trial Judiciary Court, Fort Benning, GA
2003–present
Asserted, negotiated, and settled government claims under the provisions of the Federal Claims Act and the Medical Care Recovery Act. Prepared Rule Four and Trial Memorandum of Law for contracts appealed to the ASBCA.

ATTORNEY. U.S. Army Legal Services Division - Iraq
2002-03
Responsible for providing legal advice to commanders and soldiers assigned to the National Logistic Support Command - Iraq in the areas of international law, contract law, and military justice.

CLAIMS ATTORNEY. Fort Campbell, KY
2001-02
Investigated and adjudicated claims under the Federal Tort Claims Act. Prepared Litigation Reports and appointed to a Foreign Claims Commission for the investigation, negotiation, and settlement of claims under the Foreign Claims Act.

LEGAL ASSISTANCE ATTORNEY. Fort Carson, CO
1998-01
Represented clients on matters ranging from consumer affairs, divorce, child custody and support, paternity, insurance, taxation, and bankruptcy.

LICENSES

Member of the Colorado, Kentucky, and Georgia State Bar Associations

COMPUTERS

Proficient with Westlaw and with Microsoft Word, Access, Excel, and PowerPoint.

PERSONAL

Outstanding personal and professional references upon request.

Date

Exact Name of Person
Exact Title
Exact Name of Company
Address
City, State, Zip

Dear Exact Name of Person: (or Dear Sir or Madam if answering a blind ad):

With the enclosed resume, I would like to make you aware of my interest in exploring employment opportunities with your organization.

As you will see from my resume, I am currently completing my Juris Doctor at State University of New York School of Law, where I have been selected to one of three prestigious positions as a New York's Scholar by the Property Law Department. I previously earned a Bachelor of Science in Business Administration from the Ashland University, and I have been active in civic and college activities throughout my academic career.

Currently I am excelling as a Research & Administrative Assistant to Professor Elijah Williamson assisting with the editing, proofreading, and research necessary to prepare the latest revision to New York's Real Estate, the standard text on this subject, for its upcoming publication. In addition to researching real estate case law to ensure that all current citations are correct, I am also tasked with analyzing the supplement to the current edition in order to integrate that material into the appropriate sections of the main body of text in the revision.

Prior to entering law school, I served as Community Director of the Make-A-Wish Foundation, coordinating marketing, promotions, and planning of various fundraising events. I served as the Chairperson for the annual Make-A-Wish Foundation's Auction, coordinating with the management of local restaurants to secure their participation in the event and soliciting donations from corporate sponsors throughout the area, as well as recruiting and supervising volunteers.

If you can use an articulate, poised young attorney whose abilities have been proven in a number of challenging positions, I hope you will welcome my call soon when I try to arrange a brief meeting to discuss your goals and how my background might serve your needs. I can provide outstanding references at the appropriate time.

Sincerely,

Carletta McNally

CARLETTA McNALLY

1110½ Hay Street, Fayetteville, NC 28305 • preppub@aol.com • (910) 483-6611

OBJECTIVE

To benefit an organization that can use an articulate young professional with exceptional communication and organizational skills who offers a strong background in a variety of supervisory, administrative, and clerical roles in legal research and nonprofit environments.

EDUCATION

Earned a **Juris Doctor (JD)**, State University of New York (SUNY), Buffalo, NY, 2004.
- Selected by Professor Elijah Williamson as one of Buffalo's Scholars for Property Law.
- Was a semi-finalist from 30 teams entered in the Client Counseling Competition.
- Received the Property I Book Award for the highest grade in the class.

Received **Bachelor of Science** degree in **Business Administration**, Ashland University, Ashland, NY, 1995.
- Elected Advisor of the Ashland Student Alumni Association.
- Recognized as one of the Ashland University's Academic Achievers; served on the Ashland University Student/Trustee Liaison Committee.
- President of Ashland's Law Club for future lawyers.

EXPERIENCE

RESEARCH & ADMINISTRATIVE ASSISTANT. New York's Real Estate Law, Professor Elijah Williamson, State University of New York School of Law, Buffalo, NY (2004-present). Perform research, clerical, and administrative duties for the Property Law Department of State University of New York School of Law.
- Assist with editing and proofreading tasks involved in preparing the latest revision to New York's Real Estate Law, the standard text on the subject.
- Read and analyze information in the supplement to the current edition, in order to integrate that material appropriately into the main body of the text in the revised edition.
- Research real estate case law to ensure that all citations are listed accurately and correctly illustrate the point of law examined in that section of the text.

LAW STUDENT. State University of New York School, Buffalo, NY (2001-04). Pursued a rigorous Juris Doctor degree program full-time.

COMMUNITY DIRECTOR. American Heart Association, Buffalo, NY (1998-01). Was responsible for events planning; recruitment, training, and supervision of volunteers; and other administrative tasks for this busy nonprofit organization, the local focus of which is funding the Neo-Natal Intensive Care Unit at St. Francis Xavier Hospital.
- Served as Chairperson for the annual American Heart Association's Auction, coordinating with local restaurants to secure their participation; managed 25 volunteers.
- Oversaw all marketing for the event, soliciting donations from corporate sponsors such as Kellogg's, Verizon Wireless and local legal organizations. Organized the American Heart Association, assisting in recruitment, training, and supervision of 40 volunteers.

COMMUNITY DIRECTOR. Make-A-Wish Foundation, Ashland, NY (1995-98). Through my exceptional planning, organizational, and communication skills, made significant contributions working as a volunteer for numerous local charities; this later led to a position in nonprofit management.
- Provided clerical and administrative support as an office volunteer for the Ashland Urgent Care Center, which offers medical services to the needy. Even as a member of the Make-A-Wish Foundation, volunteered my time with other charitable organizations.

PERSONAL

Known as a dedicated, self-motivated professional with strong communication and problem-solving skills. Excellent personal and professional references are available upon request.

Exact Name of Person
Title or Position
Name of Company
Address (no., street)
Address (city, state, zip)

**RESEARCH SPECIAL
ASSISTANT**
for a local
mayor's office

Dear Exact Name of Person: (or Dear Sir or Madam if answering a blind ad.)

With the enclosed resume, I would like to make you aware of my interest in exploring employment opportunities with your organization.

In my most recent position, I was a Research Special Assistant for the Mayor's Office of West Long Beach, NJ. My responsibilities including investigating, researching, and recommending to the Mayor the merit of Executive Clemency petitions to include: absolute, conditional, and simple pardons and removal of convicted felons from civil disabilities. In another position as a Legal Clerk for the Clerk of Court Office, I was sworn in as an Assistant Commonwealth Attorney/Assistant City Attorney under Third Year Practice Rule. I participated in bond hearings, sentencing hearings, and other criminal law motions. I also researched and drafted legal memoranda, briefs, and trial-level pleadings.

As you will see from my resume, I earned a Juris Doctor degree from Monmouth University in West Long Beach, NJ. I was selected to be the President of the Pre-Law Society and member of the Student Council.

If you can use an articulate, poised young professional whose abilities have been proven in a number of challenging positions, I hope you will welcome my call soon when I try to arrange a brief meeting to discuss your goals and how my background might serve your needs. I can provide outstanding references at the appropriate time.

Sincerely yours,

Linda M. Brogan

Alternate last paragraph:
I hope you will call or write soon to suggest a time convenient for us to meet and discuss your current and future needs and how I might serve them. Thank you in advance for your time.

LINDA M. BROGAN

1110½ Hay Street, Fayetteville, NC 28305   •   preppub@aol.com   •   (910) 483-6611

MEMBER	New Jersey State Bar
EDUCATION	**Juris Doctor Degree,** Monmouth School of Law, West Long Beach, New Jersey, May 1998 **Activities:** Herkimer National Moot Court Team Law Admissions Student Recruitment Assistant The Law Student Association, Secretary Justice, Monmouth Honor Council Awarded the Public Administration Fund Scholarship **Bachelor of Science, Public Administration,** Montclair State University, NJ, 1995 **Activities:** Pre-Law Society, President; Student Council Member **Honors:** Graduated *cum laude*, Dean's List four of five semesters
EXPERIENCE	**Research Special Assistant,** Mayor's Office of West Long Beach, West Long Beach, NJ, 2003-04. • Investigated, researched, and recommended to the Governor the merit of Executive Clemency petitions to include: absolute, conditional, and simple pardons and removal of convicted felons' civil disabilities. • Recommended, researched, and investigated nominees for gubernatorial appointment to study committees, commissions, and boards throughout the Mayor's Office & Board of Commissioners. • Provided legal advice to all study committees where the Secretary of the Board of Commissioners was the chair. • Participated in all hearings for notaries. **Legal Clerk,** Clerk of Court Office, West Long Beach, NJ, 2001-02 • Sworn in as Assistant Commonwealth Attorney/Assistant City Attorney under Third Year Practice Rule. • Prosecuted criminal cases in Circuit, General District, Traffic, and Juvenile and Domestic Relations Court. • Participated in bond hearings, sentencing hearings, and other criminal law motions. • Researched and drafted legal memoranda, briefs, and trial-level pleadings. • Assisted in advising the administration on municipal and state law. • Represented the city in civil actions such as temporary restraining orders and warrants. **Summer Associate,** Roxanne Phillips-Dryer Thomas, Montclair, NJ, Summer 2000 • Researched and drafted legal memoranda, pleadings, and orders; conducted initial client interviews; performed title searches; assisted in cases in the following areas: family law, probate, and personal injury. **Administrative Intern,** Montclair Chamber of Commerce, Montclair, NJ, 1998-99 • **Assisted with litigation involving annexation and immunity:** researched and drafted answers to interrogatories, analyzed and responded to requests for production of documents, assisted in preparing trial exhibits, attended court proceedings. • **Prepared reports and policies in the following areas:** educational assistance, employee smoking, police hiring/recruitment, city council manual, and horticulture. • **Participated in special projects involving:** public safety officers, volunteer fire fighters and sensitivity training programs.

Date

Exact Name of Person
Title or Position
Name of Company
Address (no., street)
Address (city, state, and zip)

SENIOR ATTORNEY
for a law firm in
Washington, DC

Dear Exact Name of Person: (or Dear Sir or Madam if answering a blind ad.)

I would appreciate an opportunity to talk with you soon about how I could contribute to your organization through my diverse background in social services administration, judicial administration and international law, as well as senior management.

Currently a Senior Attorney with the Law Offices of Mansfield & Phillips, I work with the Children and Families Program specializing in cases related to child abuse and neglect. In my previous position, I served as Assistant State Attorney for the Fairfield County District Court.

In a previous job, I worked in Biddeford, Maine with the Department of Health and Human Services as its Director. In that job I managed a multimillion-dollar budget, increasing the advisory staff to cover community issues and policies, created new programs which strengthened citizen involvement in foster parent and senior citizen programs, and established a program which reduced fraud in social services programs. That job as Director of the Department of Health & Human Services allowed me to excel in a top-level city management role as I made major contributions in the areas of organizational development, budgeting and fiscal management, intergovernmental affairs, and labor relations.

I can assure you that you would find me to be an individual known for absolute integrity as well as common sense and creativity. I can provide outstanding personal and professional references at the appropriate time. Throughout my career, I have excelled in managing both human and financial resources while supervising hundreds of people and flawlessly accounting for multimillion-dollar assets, both financial and material.

If my considerable knowledge and talents could be of value to you, I hope you will contact me to suggest a time when we might meet in person to discuss your needs and how I might serve them. Thank you in advance for your time.

Yours sincerely,

Richard McDaniels

RICHARD McDANIELS

1110½ Hay Street, Fayetteville, NC 28305 • preppub@aol.com • (910) 483-6611

OBJECTIVE   To contribute to an organization that can use an experienced attorney and administrator who offers a reputation as an outstanding advocate and team builder with exceptionally strong communication and negotiating skills along with an ability to implement new programs, galvanize public opinion, and shape public policy.

EDUCATION   Graduated with **Juris Doctor, cum laude,** Fairfield University, Fairfield, CT, 1998.
- Received the prestigious J.P. Award for Administrative Law and Property.

B.S. degree in Social Studies Education, Connecticut State University, OH, 1985.

AFFILIATIONS   Member, Connecticut Bar; Maine Bar

EXPERIENCE   **SENIOR ATTORNEY.** Mansfield & Phillips, LLP, Washington, DC (2004-present). Act as a Senior Attorney in defending a variety of cases related to child abuse and neglect; am frequently involved in terminating parental rights.
- Advise the Program Administrator on case law pertaining to child abuse and neglect.
- Developed a procedure for getting children into long-term placement which has greatly improved the safety and well-being of many young people.

ATTORNEY/LEGAL ADVISOR. Department of Justice, Washington, DC (2003-04). As a Civil Affairs Direct Support Team Leader, participated in several overseas peace operations and acted as an International Law Specialist while planning, supervising, and synchronizing civil-military operations.
- Received special recognition for my legal advice which aids in solving national/international conflicts. In a formal written evaluation, was commended for "flawlessly coordinated operation teams on the most difficult and complex challenges and missions."

ASSISTANT STATE ATTORNEY & JUVENILE ATTORNEY. Fairfield County District Court, Fairfield, CT (2000-03). Was specially recruited by the District Attorney for this position; practiced juvenile/felony law in Fairfield as well as New Haven, Connecticut.
- As Staff Attorney for Intake, advised police officers on whether or not they had enough evidence to build cases.
- Conducted investigations into a wide range of matters related to juvenile justice.

LAW CLERK & RESEARCH ASSISTANT. Paulson & Miller, Fairfield, CT (1998-00). After graduating from law school, worked in these areas of research: Worker's Compensation and Social Security. Criminal Appeals. Bankruptcy, Family Law, and Debt.

DIRECTOR. Department of Health and Human Services, Biddeford, ME (1994-95). Provided oversight to all programs of Biddeford County while making significant contributions in fiscal management, budgeting and intergovernmental affairs, and labor relations.
- Managed the administration of protective services programs and provided oversight for protective investigations, foster care, and adoption programs. Established a Success Fraud Program which greatly reduced the abuse of food stamps and other services.

STAFF ASSISTANT. Department of the Interior, Biddeford, ME (1991-93). Scheduled and arranged speaking engagements for statewide campaign.

PERSONAL   Offer exceptionally strong skills in leadership and team building. Am known for my ability to provide insight and strategic direction during crises and in the midst of serious problems.

CAREER CHANGE

Date

Exact Name of Person
Title or Position
Name of Company
Address (no., street)
Address (city, state, zip)

SERVICE INTERVIEW ANALYST

for a financing company will soon be receiving his J.D. degree

Dear Exact Name of Person: (or Dear Sir or Madam if answering a blind ad.)

I would appreciate an opportunity to talk with you soon about how I could contribute to your organization as an attorney.

From the enclosed resume, you will see that I am currently completing the Juris Doctor of Law and will graduate soon. During my undergraduate career, I gained a reputation as an articulate student leader and was involved in extracurricular activities which included acting as Editor of the Faulkner Student Newspaper, Vice President of the student dorm, and Senator of student government.

As a Service Interview Analyst for DiTech 2000, I am responsible for interviewing clients and distinguishing their financial needs through CBI/TRW, equity computation, and lending institution programs. As a part-time Entertainer's Agent for Ocala Entertainment, I established employment prospects, created/negotiated agreement contracts, powers-of-attorney, and contract disputes while also advising clients of career choices, obligations, and opportunities.

You would find me to be a dynamic communicator who is known for my capacity for hard work and long hours. I am a highly adaptable professional who offers exceptionally research skills along with the proven ability to master difficult problems with effective solutions.

I hope you will welcome my call soon to arrange a brief meeting at your convenience to discuss your current and future needs and how I might serve them. Thank you in advance for your time.

Sincerely yours,

Phillip S. Collier

Alternate last paragraph:
I hope you will call or write me soon to suggest a time convenient for us to meet and discuss your current and future needs and how I might serve them. Thank you in advance for your time.

PHILLIP S. COLLIER

1110½ Hay Street, Fayetteville, NC 28305 • preppub@aol.com • (910) 483-6611

OBJECTIVE

I am seeking to contribute to an organization that can use an astute negotiator and problem solver who offers outstanding communication and analytical skills.

EDUCATION

Juris Doctor of Law degree for Business, Industry and Government, Troy State University, degree anticipated in 2005.

Bachelor of Science degree in English Grammar with a minor in Speech Communication, Faulkner University, Montgomery, AL, 2002.
- Extracurricular activities included: Faulkner Student Newspaper, vice-president of student dorm, senator of student government.

EXPERIENCE

SERVICE INTERVIEW ANALYST. DiTech 2000, Montgomery, AL (2003-present). Responsible for interviewing clients and distinguishing their financial needs through CBI/TRW, equity computation, and lending institution programs. Also responsible for training and supervision of new employees.

PART-TIME ENTERTAINERS AGENT. Ocala Entertainment, Inc., Montgomery, AL (1999-03). Established employment prospects, created/negotiated agreement contracts, power-of-attorney, and contract disputes. Also advised clients of career choices, obligations and opportunities.

MANAGER. Best Buy, Montgomery, AL (1996-99). Assigned to retail store carrying stereo, television, computers, calculators and electronic software, with the following duties: In charge of training for three sales clerks. Responsible for markdowns, replenishing stock, taking inventory, making schedules, completing daily reports via computer. As display coordinator, prepared case, window and counter displays.

PART TIME SALES CLERK. Sears, Montgomery, AL (1995-96). Trained on CRT for selling transactions, inventory inquires and shipment of merchandise from and to other company stores.

SUBSTITUTE ENGLISH, GRAMMAR AND BUSINESS ENGLISH TEACHER. Radcliffe High School, Montgomery, AL (1994-95). Fulfilled teacher's lesson plans and assisted students with understanding materials. Corrected and graded papers when instructed to do so.

HONORS

Member, National Association of Businessmen, Montgomery, AL.

PERSONAL

Outstanding personal and professional references upon request.

Date

Exact Name of Person
Title or Position
Name of Company
Address (no., street)
Address (city, state, zip)

**SHAREHOLDER &
ASSOCIATE ATTORNEY**

for attorneys-at-law
in Beaufort,
South Carolina

Dear Exact Name of Person: (or Dear Sir or Madam if answering a blind ad.)

I am writing to express my interest in a position with your firm as I am a trusts and estates attorney currently practicing in Beaufort, SC.

I offer a combination of federal tax training and practical work experience that would allow me to produce high-quality estate planning documents and generate fees immediately. I hold a Masters of Law in taxation degree and a Juris Doctor degree from Charleston Southern University as well as two business degrees from the University of South Carolina. While my required course of study at Charleston Southern University covered all areas of taxation, my elective course of study focused on corporate taxation and transfer taxation.

I have significant work experience gained from building my own estate planning and estate administration practice. I have drafted all types of estate planning documents from simple wills to generation skipping trusts, prepared death tax returns, and handled a variety of business transactions. I have also drafted a number of premarital agreements, worked closely with the executive director of the local community foundation on charitable giving issues, and lectured at continuing education seminars for the regional chapter of certified public accountants. I know how to develop clients and service them promptly, efficiently, and effectively. I expect most of my high net worth clients to follow me if I relocate.

I am enclosing my resume for your review and, if your firm has an opening, I would be happy to meet with you at your convenience to discuss my interest and qualifications. I can provide excellent personal and professional references upon request. I have not yet terminated my present position and would appreciate your keeping my interest confidential. Thank you in advance for your time.

Yours truly,

Timothy O. Caulder

TIMOTHY O. CAULDER

1110½ Hay Street, Fayetteville, NC 28305 • preppub@aol.com • (910) 483-6611

EDUCATION

LLM in Taxation, May 1995
Charleston Southern University School of Law, Ladson, SC
- Curriculum emphasis on corporate taxation, taxation of property transactions, timing issues in income taxation, taxation of deferred compensation, advanced corporate taxation, taxation of S corporations, tax procedure and research, and estate and gift taxation

Juris Doctor, May 1993
Charleston Southern University School of Law, Ladson, SC
- Charleston Southern Law Faculty Scholar
- American Jurisprudence Award in Legal Research and Writing
- American Jurisprudence Award in Constitutional Law
- Scholarship List
- Elective curriculum emphasis on commercial law

Master of Business Administration, May 1990
University of South Carolina, Beaufort, SC
- Harold Banks Scholar

Bachelor of Arts in Economics, May 1988
University of South Carolina, Beaufort, SC

EXPERIENCE

SHAREHOLDER and **ASSOCIATE ATTORNEY.** Sabari & Chase, Attorneys at Law, Beaufort, SC (1998-present). Prepare simple wills, credit shelter trusts, generation skipping trusts, life insurance trusts, split dollar insurance plans, family limited partnerships, and other estate planning documents for clients seeking to minimize transfer taxes.
- Administer estates, including preparation of federal and state death tax returns.
- Form limited liability companies and corporations for business owners.
- Prepare stock redemption and cross-purchase agreements for business owners.
- Prepare and close asset purchase agreements for closely held corporations.
- Prepare premarital agreements.
- Lecture at seminars for the regional chapter of certified public accountants.

ASSOCIATE ATTORNEY. Melissa C. Collins, LLP, Beaufort, SC (1996-98). Represented mortgage companies and other financial institutions in state foreclosure proceedings and consumer bankruptcy cases.
- Supervised closing of a large number of residential and commercial real estate transactions.
- Secured approval of firm as qualified outside counsel for the Federal Deposit Insurance Corporation.
- Prepared manuscript for seminar on creditors' rights for a local credit union.

ASSOCIATE ATTORNEY. George Edwards & Associates, Ladson, SC (1993-96). Represented insurance companies and employers in worker's compensation proceedings before the South Carolina Industrial Commission.
- Prepared record on appeal to the South Carolina Court of Appeals.
- Prepared petition for discretionary review to the South Carolina Supreme Court.
- Prepared drafts of manuscripts on workers' compensation topics for presentation at continuing legal education seminars.

Date

Exact Name of Person
Title or Position
Name of Company
Address (no., street)
Address (city, state, zip)

Dear Exact Name of Person: (or Dear Sir or Madam if answering a blind ad.)

I would appreciate an opportunity to talk with you soon about how I could contribute to your organization through my proven abilities as a trial attorney and my experience related to criminal, insurance, consumer, contract, and international law.

After receiving my J.D. degree, I entered the U.S. Army and became chief of a legal assistance office serving more than 15,000 military professionals and their families. In that job I also became skilled in techniques related to mediation and arbitration as I resolved many cases without litigation. Promoted ahead of schedule to captain, I was commended for exceptional management skills and was cited as the driving force behind this legal office's being singled out as one of the best by the Army Chief of Staff.

In a subsequent job providing expert legal advice to military executives, I prepared a briefing regarding Rules of Engagement and the Posse Comitatus Act related to drug interdiction along the Mexican border. In that job I reviewed and conducted personnel investigations, and I became familiar with the Army claims systems while investigating and reviewing cases which involved the Federal Tort Claims Act.

Most recently as a Trial Defense Attorney, I have handled a heavy and varied work load as one of four defense attorneys in a highly regarded law firm serving the Little Rock community. Because of our small legal staff, I have conducted all legal research for my cases and drafted all requests, responses, agreements, briefs, and motions while gaining experience with cases that involved issues ranging from domestic violence and rape, to armed robbery and fraud, to personnel matters. I recently received a prestigious award from the city for extraordinary accomplishments as a trial attorney.

I can provide excellent personal and professional references which would attest to my reputation for integrity, congenial personality, and dedication to excellence. I am certain I could add value to your organization as I have to the other organizations I have worked for. I hope you will welcome my call soon to arrange a brief meeting at your convenience to discuss your needs and goals and how I might serve them. Thank you in advance for your time.

Sincerely yours,

Thaddeus Allendale

THADDEUS ALLENDALE

1110½ Hay Street, Fayetteville, NC 28305   •   preppub@aol.com   •   (910) 483-6611

OBJECTIVE   To contribute to an organization that can use a dedicated young attorney with trial experience who offers excellent decision-making, negotiating, research, and investigative skills as well as experience related to criminal, insurance, consumer, contract, and international law.

MEMBERSHIPS   The State Bar of Arkansas, The Tennessee Bar, The Kentucky Bar
The Court for the Middle District of Arkansas, The Army Court of Military Review
The American Bar Association; President of the Little Rock Arkansas Chapter

EDUCATION   Earned a **Juris Doctor degree**, University of Arkansas School of Law, Little Rock, AR 1994; moot court competition participant
Received **Bachelor of Arts degree in Political Science**, Harding University, Searcy, AR, 1991. Named to Dean's List
Completed the three-month Judge Advocate (JAG) School, the Kentucky Attorney General's Course for military attorneys, and the Criminal Trial Advocacy Course.

EXPERIENCE   **TRIAL DEFENSE ATTORNEY.** Hutchinson & Ross, Attorneys-at-Law, Little Rock, AR (2003-present). Handle a heavy and varied work load as one of four defense attorneys in a highly regarded firm serving the Little Rock community; have received local, state, and national recognition for my performance as a trial attorney.
* Defend clients charged with federal felonies, misdemeanors, and state charges, and provide legal counsel to clients facing marital disputes.
* Present pretrial motions, negotiate plea agreements, conduct voir dire of juries, provide opening statements, conduct direct examination of defense witnesses and cross examine prosecution witnesses, make and respond to objections or motions, give closing arguments, and prepare and present sentencing cases.
* Utilize and train other attorneys to use the firm's legal research computerized system.

COUNSELOR/ADMINISTRATIVE LAW ATTORNEY. Lance Fischer & Associates, Little Rock, AR (2002-03). While providing written legal research and opinions to a commanding general and other business executives, wrote articles and edited monthly "preventive law" newsletters distributed throughout Arkansas's fourth largest community, Little Rock.
* Presented briefings to executives regarding Rules of Engagement, the Posse Comitatus Act, and drug interdiction activities along the Mexican and Canadian border involving military personnel as well as the Drug Enforcement Agency and Federal Border Patrol.
* Became very familiar with the National Legal Claims systems and its handling of personal injury claims while investigating numerous cases and reviewing the legal sufficiency of cases which involved the Federal Tort Claims Act and personnel matters.

CHIEF, LEGAL ASSISTANCE OFFICE. U.S. Army, Ft. Gordon, GA (1995-02). Supervised caseloads of attorneys and legal specialists while managing a law office serving more than 15,000 military professionals and their families. Became skilled in techniques of arbitration and mediation while resolving many cases without litigation in law that involved consumer credit, the Fair Debt Collection Practices Act, and the Lemon Law.

LAW CLERK. The Law Offices of Brigham & Franklin, Little Rock, AR (1992-94). Provided research in a case which resulted in the largest plaintiff's verdict in AR.

PERSONAL   Skilled with Microsoft Word, Excel and PowerPoint as well as WESTLAW & LEXIS.

You may already realize that applying for a federal government position requires some patience and persistence in order to complete rather tedious forms and get them in on time. Depending on what type of federal job you are seeking, you may need to prepare an application such as the SF 171 or OF 612, or you may need to use a Federal Resume, sometimes called a "Resumix," to apply for a federal job. But that may not be the only paperwork you need.

Many Position Vacancy Announcements or job bulletins for a specific job also tell you that, in order to be considered for the job you want, you must also demonstrate certain knowledge, skills, or abilities. In other words, you need to also submit written narrative statements which microscopically focus on your particular knowledge, skill, or ability in a certain area. The next few pages are filled with examples of excellent KSAs. If you wish to see many other examples of KSAs, you may look for another book published by PREP: "Real KSAs--Knowledge, Skills & Abilities--for Government Jobs."

Although you will be able to use the Federal Resume you prepare in order to apply for all sorts of jobs in the federal government, the KSAs you write are particular to a specific job and you may be able to use the KSAs you write only one time. If you get into the Civil Service system, however, you will discover that many KSAs tend to appear on lots of different job announcement bulletins. For example, "Ability to communicate orally and in writing" is a frequently requested KSA. This means that you would be able to use and re-use this KSA for any job bulletin which requests you to give evidence of your ability in this area.

What does "Screen Out" mean? If you see that a KSA is requested and the words "Screen out" are mentioned beside the KSA, this means that this KSA is of vital importance in "getting you in the door." If the individuals who review your application feel that your screen-out KSA does not establish your strengths in this area, you will not be considered as a candidate for the job. You need to make sure that any screen-out KSA is especially well-written and comprehensive.

How long can a KSA be? A job vacancy announcement bulletin may specify a length for the KSAs it requests. Sometimes KSAs can be 1-2 pages long each, but sometimes you are asked to submit several KSAs within a maximum of two pages. Remember that the purpose of a KSA is to microscopically examine your level of competence in a specific area, so you need to be extremely detailed and comprehensive. Give examples and details wherever possible. For example, your written communication skills might appear more credible if you provide the details of the kinds of reports and paperwork you prepared.

KSAs are extremely important in "getting you in the door" for a federal government job. If you are working under a tight deadline in preparing your paperwork for a federal government position, don't spend all your time preparing the Federal Resume if you also have KSAs to do. Create "blockbuster" KSAs as well!

EXAMPLE OF A RESUMIX OR FEDERAL RESUME

MEGAN STEWART

1110 1/2 Hay Street, Fayetteville, NC 28305
Home: (000) 000-0000; work: (000) 000-0000
E-mail: preppub@aol.com
SSN: 000-00-0000

Position, Title, Series, Grade: GS-00-00
Announcement Number: 0000-00-0000

**ENVIRONMENTAL
LAW ATTORNEY**

utilizes this "resumix"
to apply for a federal
government job

EDUCATION

Juris Doctor degree, Georgetown University School of Law, Washington, DC, 1992.
Bachelor of Arts degree in International Relations, Ocean County College, Toms River, NJ, 1989.

TRAINING

Have completed military training programs for legal professionals which have included the following:
Environmental Law Course – environmental law and updates, 1998
Ethics Course – laws and policy governing ethics, 1997
Fiscal Law Course – laws governing federal expenditures, 1996
Criminal Law Course – rules of evidence and case law, 1996

LAW LICENSE

Licensed to practice law in New Jersey since 1992.

COMPUTERS

Offer skills in automated legal research utilizing Lexis.

EXPERIENCE

Advanced to Captain while serving in the U.S. Army:
ENVIRONMENTAL LAW ATTORNEY. HHC, 187th Legal Services Division, Ft. Dix, NJ 11525 (2004-present). Annual salary: CPT. Supervisor: LTC James Clamore, (111) 111-1111. As a specialist in environmental law, am the advisor on federal and state environmental laws, construction, and land use issues which impact this military post with a million dollar annual budget.

- Am involved in negotiations with the Environmental Protection Agency on multiple violations of the Safe Water Drinking Act.
- Represent Ft. Dix in current negotiations of a conditional settlement in a case before the state's Department of Environment and Natural Resources (NJDENR): am working within the guidelines of military limitations on not paying environmental fines or using appropriated funds for environmental projects without congressional approval.
- Am working on a project related to four acres of contaminated land owned by the U.S. Army which are to be disposed of.
- Established a satellite office and integrated my activities into the operations of my client – the Public Works Business Center (PWBC) – in order to gain the strongest understanding of the technology and science of the infrastructure, pollution control and prevention programs, and natural resource management activities.
- Taught National Environmental Policy Act (NEPA) procedures to the PWBC's resident specialist in order to encourage him to use their checklist and take advantage of the expertise of other specialists such as the Air Emissions Program Manager and Endangered Species Wildlife Biologist.
- Initiated a program for tracking compliance involving resource

conservation and placing special emphasis on laws concerning hazardous waste: created sample documents required by law and posted them on a website for the benefit of units which needed to track their compliance with the laws.

- Work closely with the O'Keefe National Wildlife Reserve to increase land for training while also recovering and protecting the habitat of five endangered species.
- Advise a number of committees which include: Environmental Quality Control, Qualified Recycling Program, Integrated Natural Resources Management Plan Steering, and Installation Environment and Facilities Maintenance Working Group.

ADMINISTRATIVE LAW ATTORNEY. ARCOM, 3-139th Regiment, Fort Carson, CO 87955 (2001-04). Annual salary: CPT (O3). Supervisor: LTC Lindsey Jenkins, (222) 222-2222. Officially evaluated as "a leader others look to for guidance," provided legal advice on administrative and regulatory issues to all organizations, units, and staff sections.

- Earned respect for my ability to provide timely, accurate guidance on even the most difficult legal questions while preparing legal opinions and advising managers and investigating officers on legal issues for this community of 32,000.
- Wrote preventive law articles for the post newspaper.
- Singled out as a leader among captains, was cited for setting the pace for the administrative division during a period of severe personnel shortages.

LEGAL CENTER MANAGER and **CHIEF OF LEGAL ASSISTANCE AND CLAIMS.** Department of Defense, 5495 Lee Avenue, Washington, DC 11028-5545 (1996-01). Salary: CPT (O3). Supervisor: MAJ Mark C. Vance, (333) 333-3333. Officially evaluated as "truly spectacular" in a demanding field grade position, was cited for my maturity, good judgment and superb leadership of a legal center which served a community of military, family members, civilians, and retirees.

- Supervised three judge advocates while advising executives, supervising a tax assistance office, and administering a preventive law program.
- Provided advice and services on family law, consumer law, estate planning, military administrative law, personal finances, and civil law issues.
- Was credited as the key player in the center's recognition with a Chief of Staff Award.
- Provided oversight for the most successful tax assistance office in the region which serviced clients and generated refunds for its clients during the fiscal year.

Other experience:

TRIAL COUNSEL. The District Municipal Court of Toms River, 7957 Allendale Drive, Toms River, NJ 11655 (1996-99). Salary: 30,000. Supervisor: Neil Pershing, (444) 444-4444. Cited as "particularly persuasive in oral arguments and presenting the government's case in sentencing," represented the U.S. in difficult and complex courts-martial cases such as cases of sexual assault, child sexual abuse, and drug distribution.

- Sought out for my guidance on tough issues, was also effective in developing and teaching classes on sexual harassment, Law of War, substance abuse, and military justice.

ATTORNEY. Pettiford, Shockley & Associates, 206 Saxony Avenue, Toms River, NJ 11645 (1992-96). Salary: 28,000. Supervisor: Robert Tyler, (555) 555-5555. Quickly became known for my ability to handle stress and change in a busy center which provided legal counseling, representation, and guidance.

- Handled activities which ranged from preparing court documents and correspondence to educating clients on how to use nonlegal alternatives.
- Wrote articles for the base newspaper; taught classes to soldiers; executed wills and powers of attorney while helping personnel prepare for overseas assignments.

PERSONAL   Am known for sound judgment, keen insight and analytical skills, and vision.

EXAMPLE OF A KSA

ROSS A. CHELSEA

SSN: 000-00-0000

CRIMINAL INVESTIGATOR, GS-00-13 ANNOUNCEMENT #XYZ123

Knowledge of law enforcement concepts, principles, and practices.

CRIMINAL ATTORNEY uses this two-page KSA as part of his application for a federal government job. KSA stands for "Knowledge, Skills, and Abilities."

In my current position as a Criminal Attorney for the Las Cruces Police Department, Protective Services Division, GS-11 (2002-present), my knowledge of law enforcement concepts, principles, and practices is exhibited while planning, organizing, and conducting criminal and non-criminal investigations, and performing mobile and stationary surveillance to observe the activities of individuals involved in the investigation. When sufficient evidence is obtained to justify such action, I prepare requests for and obtain search warrants. Process crime scenes to obtain such physical evidence as latent fingerprints, hair and skin samples, fibers, etc. Operate concealed cameras, audio and videocassette recorders, directional microphones, and other technical investigative aids. Conduct and document interviews with victims, witnesses, and suspects, using learned interrogative techniques to obtain corroborative statements to support the physical evidence.

Most recently, I was assigned to an internal investigation with the Washington Headquarters Services. The position involved investigating fraudulent or inappropriate use of government property by federal employees. Under the auspices of the Washington Headquarters Services, I conducted a week-long surveillance of the suspect, during which time I observed him misusing his government vehicle on numerous occasions, to include allowing non-government personnel the use of the vehicle. In addition, there was some evidence involving contracting fraud, specifically fraudulent payments to government officials by another government employee. This aspect of the investigation is still ongoing.

In April of 2002, a case involving theft of government property involving a number of Hispanic artifacts was turned over to the National Security Agency for investigation. The thefts had occurred in 1998, at which time the International Affairs Division reported the matter to the Las Cruces Police Department. The LCPD took no action, as the case involved Federal government property, and thus was under the jurisdiction of the LCPD. Because the value of the stolen property was only $10,500, the case was assigned a low priority by the LCPD. As a result, almost no action had been taken until the case was turned over to the National Security Agency and assigned to me. The investigation called for a detailed internal audit of the museum's accounting and inventory records. After careful examination of the NSA's invoices, bills of lading, shipping manifests, and payment records, I was able to positively identify the 10 pieces that had been stolen and confirm the dates that they were received. Despite the four-year time lag between the commission of the crime and the start of the investigation, my efforts resulted in recovery of all the stolen artifacts and the identification and apprehension of a suspect, who was charged with felony theft of government property.

I also conducted an internal investigation in a 2000 case involving suspicious payments to a long-term government contractor that was deferred to the NSA by the LCPD Investigator, who had no investigator on-site. I was assigned to the case, which involved a comprehensive and detailed audit of accounting files for the office of the

Representative Department. I reviewed all LCPD contracts, invoices, work orders, payment requests, and authorizations, reconciling all figures to ensure that actual payment amounts matched the figures agreed to in the contract, and that all work which had been paid for was actually performed. As a result of this investigation, it was determined that there were no irregularities in LCPD payments to the contractor. No charges were brought in the matter.

In 1995, I was assigned to an investigation for the Washington Headquarters Services office related to possible fraudulent acquisition of surplus government property. The investigation centered on recent transfers of government surplus communications equipment and vehicles, including dump trucks, heavy construction equipment, boats, light trucks, etc. by the Department of Transportation. After conducting a thorough audit of all accounting paperwork for both agencies, I was able to prepare a complete list of items received from government surplus in order to determine whether or not these items had been obtained under false pretenses. These items were supposedly requisitioned for use by the requesting agencies, but on investigation, I determined that the property was being sold, given to, or used improperly for the benefit of private individuals or companies. As a result of my audit, one investigation was closed and the property in question was seized by the government. Due to the extent of the property fraudulently obtained, other related investigations are still ongoing.

Earlier as Lead Detective/ Police Officer (1990-93), I supervised four or more Investigative Police Officers per assigned shift, overseeing their performance in the full range of law enforcement duties, including but not limited to conducting initial and follow-up investigations, processing crime scenes to obtain physical evidence, and processing search and arrest warrants. Served as a uniformed police officer and leader/trainer in the Protective Services Division, ensuring the safety and protecting the civil rights of individuals while they were on controlled property that was owned or under the control of one of its tenant agencies. Maintained order, preserved the peace, and protected all controlled property. Conducted initial and follow-up investigations of reported thefts, burglaries, assaults, and threats, as well as instances of vandalism and narcotics violations. Interviewed victims, witnesses, and suspects during the investigative process.

Education and Training Related to the KSA:
Juris Doctor (J.D.) degree from New Mexico State University, Las Cruces, NM, 1993. Bachelor of Science in Criminal Justice, with concentrations in Sociology and Correctional Administration, minor in International Studies, New Mexico State University, Las Cruces, NM, 1990.

Completed numerous additional training and development courses at the New Mexico Police Academy in Albuquerque, NM, which included:
- Advanced Physical Security Training Course, 80 hours, 2001
- Data Recovery and Analysis Training Course, 40 hours, 2001
- Financial Investigations Practical Skills Training Course, 40 hours, 2000
- Criminal Intelligence Analyst Training Course, 80 hours, 1999
- Personnel Security Adjudication Training Course, 40 hours, 1999
- Basic Criminal Investigation Course, 320 hours, 1998
- Basic Police Course, 320 hours, 1998

Completed supervisory training courses sponsored by the Las Cruces Police Department, Las Cruces, NM, including:
- Supervising: A Guide for All Levels, 8 hours, 2000
- Constructive Discipline for Supervisors, 6 hours, 2000
- Basic Supervision Course, 6 hours, 2000

EXAMPLE OF A KSA

ROSS A. CHELSEA

SSN: 000-00-0000

CRIMINAL INVESTIGATOR, GS-13 ANNOUNCEMENT #XYZ123

Knowledge of the Principles of Conducting Investigations.

ATTORNEY
will use these KSAs
in order to apply for
a federal
government
position.

In my current position as a Special Attorney for the Criminal Investigation Section of the Las Cruces Police Department, Protective Services Division, GS-11 (2002-present), I plan, organize, and conduct criminal and non-criminal investigations, performing mobile and stationary surveillance to observe the activities of individuals involved in the investigation. When sufficient evidence is obtained to justify such action, prepare requests for and obtain search warrants. Process crime scenes to obtain such physical evidence as latent fingerprints, hair and skin samples, fibers, etc. Operate concealed cameras, audio and videocassette recorders, directional microphones, and other technical investigative aids. Conduct and document interviews with victims, witnesses, and suspects, using learned interrogative techniques to obtain corroborative statements to support the physical evidence.

Most recently, I was assigned to an internal investigation involving fraudulent or inappropriate used of government property by a federal employee. Under the auspices of the Washington Headquarters Services office, I conducted a week-long surveillance of the suspect, during which time I observed him misusing his government vehicle on numerous occasions, to include allowing non-government personnel to use the vehicle. In addition, there was some evidence involving contracting fraud, specifically fraudulent payments to government officials by another government employee. This aspect of the investigation is still ongoing.

In April of 2002, a case involving theft of government property, specifically a number of Hispanic artifacts was turned over to the National Security Agency for investigation. The thefts had occurred in 1998, at which time the International Affairs Division reported to the Las Cruces Police Department. The Las Cruces police took no action, as the case involved Federal government property, and thus was under the jurisdiction of the LCPD. Because the value of the stolen property was only $10,500, the case was assigned a low priority by the LCPD. As a result, almost no action had been taken until the case was turned over to the National Security Agency and assigned to me. The investigation called for a detailed internal audit of the museum's accounting and inventory records. After careful examination of the NSA's invoices, bills of lading, shipping manifests, and payment records, I was able to positively identify the 10 pieces that had been stolen and confirm the dates that they were received. Despite the four-year time lag between the commission of the crime and the start of the investigation, my efforts resulted in recovery of all the stolen artifacts and the identification and apprehension of a suspect, who was charged with felony theft of government property.

I conducted an internal investigation in a 2000 case involving suspicious payments to a long-term government contractor that was referred to the NSA by the LCPD Investigator, who had no investigator on-site. I was assigned to the case, which involved performing a comprehensive and detailed audit of accounting files for the office of the NSA Customer Representative Department. I reviewed contracts, work orders, payment requests, and authorizations, reconciling all figures to ensure that actual payment amounts matched the figures agreed to in the contract, and that all work which had been paid for was actually performed. As a result of this three-week investigation, it was determined that there were no irregularities in the payments to this contractor, and no charges were brought in the matter.

In 1995, I was assigned to an investigation for the Washington Headquarters Services office related to possible fraudulent acquisition of surplus government property. The investigation centered on recent transfers of government surplus communications equipment and vehicles, including dump trucks, heavy construction equipment, boats and light trucks by the Department of Transportation. After conducting a thorough audit of all accounting paperwork for both agencies, I was able to prepare a complete list of items received from government surplus in order to determine whether or not these items had been obtained under false pretenses. These items were supposedly requisitioned for use by the requesting agencies, but on investigation. I determined that the property was being sold, given to, or used improperly for the benefit of private individuals or companies. As a result of my audit, one investigation was closed and the property in question was seized by the government. Due to the extent of the property fraudulently obtained, other related investigations are still ongoing.

ATTORNEY
will use these KSAs in order to apply for a federal government position.

Earlier as Lead Detective/Police Officer (1990-93), I supervised four or more Investigative Police Officers per assigned shift, overseeing their performance of the full range of law enforcement duties, including but not limited to conducting initial and follow-up investigations, processing crime scenes to obtain physical evidence, and processing search and arrest warrants. Served as a uniformed Police Officer and leader/trainer in the Federal Protective Services Division, ensuring the safety and protecting the civil rights of individuals while they were on Federal property that was owned or under the control of one of its tenant agencies. Maintained order, preserved the peace, and protected all Federally owned or controlled property. Conducted initial and follow-up investigations of reported thefts, burglaries, assaults, and threats, as well as instances of vandalism and narcotics violations. Interviewed victims, witnesses, and suspects during the investigative process.

Education and Training Related to the KSA:
Juris Doctor (J.D.) degree from New Mexico State University, Las Cruces, NM, 1993. Bachelor of Science in Criminal Justice, with concentrations in Sociology and Correctional Administration, minor in International Studies, New Mexico State University, Las Cruces, NM, 1990.

Completed numerous additional training and development courses at the New Mexico Police Academy in Albuquerque, NM, which included:
- Advanced Physical Security Training Course, 80 hours, 2001
- Data Recovery and Analysis Training Course, 40 hours, 2001
- Financial Investigations Practical Skills Training Course, 40 hours, 2000
- Criminal Intelligence Analyst Training Course, 80 hours, 1999
- Personnel Security Adjudication Training Course, 40 hours, 1999
- Basic Criminal Investigation Course, 320 hours, 1998
- Basic Police Course, 320 hours, 1998

MORE EXAMPLES OF KSAs

MELANIE T. EUBANKS

SSN: 000-00-0000

LEGAL ASSISTANT, GS-09 ANNOUNCEMENT #XYZ123

KSA #1: Skill in interpersonal relations.

In my most recent position as Legal Assistant within the Department of Defense, I demonstrated my skill in interpersonal relations on a daily basis while interacting on a personal and professional level with attorneys of diverse specialties. I dealt with a heavy volume of office traffic, tactfully and diplomatically fielding questions and complaints from civilian and military attorneys, subcontractors, military personnel, and office visitors both in person and over the telephone and radio. I performed liaison between attorneys and engineers, relaying important information or taking messages if I could not resolve a problem or answer an inquiry. Frequently received calls from attorneys who were angry or upset due to problems or other delays; handled these calls expertly, using tact and diplomacy to defuse the situation, then presenting the attorneys' concerns to the appropriate person in order to efficiently resolve the conflict. Answered multi-line phones in a courteous and professional manner, routing incoming calls to the appropriate person, taking telephone messages, and providing callers with information over the phone.

In earlier positions as Secretary to the Chiefs of the Plans and Operations Division and of the Logistics Communication Division, I interacted daily with a large number of people, both on the phone and in person. I recorded telephone messages and answered multi-line phones, effectively communicating with callers in order to ascertain the purpose of their call. Responded to caller inquiries, furnishing information and resolving their problems when possible and directing calls to the supervisor or appropriate personnel when I was unable to assist them. Maintained lines of communication and developed strong working relationships with higher, lateral, and subordinate counterparts at military headquarters in order to facilitate the exchange of information concerning each division's affairs.

Education and Training Related to This KSA:

In addition to the Certificates I received from Central Florida Community College and the Bethune-Cookman College, the following courses have been helpful in refining my skills in this area:

- Correspondence English Usage, Kessler AFB, Mississippi
- Legal Terminology, Kessler AFB, Mississippi
- Legal Composition, Andrews AFB, Maryland
- Building a Professional Image, Andrews AFB, Maryland

MELANIE T. EUBANKS

SSN: 000-00-0000

LEGAL ASSISTANT, GS-09 ANNOUNCEMENT #XYZ123

KSA #2: Ability to communicate in writing.

In my most recent position as a Legal Assistant for the Department of Defense, I composed and prepared all correspondence for the office. Demonstrated my understanding of legal terminology as I carefully proofread and edited this material, making necessary changes to ensure precision of language, correct grammatical usage, and compliance with the appropriate format under the rules and regulations of correspondence. Also prepared all personnel actions for the office, to include personnel action requests, travel orders, transportation and training requests, and performance appraisals and incentive awards. Used style manuals, technical and non-technical dictionaries, and other references to ensure correctness of grammar and usage as well as precision of language. This position involved writing, editing, proofreading, and final printing of a large volume of letters, memos, reports, and other correspondence, as I posted transactions for over 35 attorneys and more than 150 program managers. Was known for my sound judgment, exceptional communication and organizational abilities, and attention to detail.

LEGAL ASSISTANT will use these KSAs in order to apply for a federal government position.

In earlier positions as the Secretary and Stenographer to the Chiefs of the Plans and Operations Division and Logistics Communication, I composed all office correspondence, including letters, memos, reports, and personnel actions. Using style manuals, technical and non-technical dictionaries, and other reference materials, ensured correctness of grammar and usage, precision of language, and adherence to proper formats according to the rules and regulations of correspondence. I composed and prepared initial drafts of all correspondence, proofread and edited the initial draft, made necessary changes and prepared the final documents. As I worked closely with a senior rater, this position involved preparing a heavy volume of personnel recommendations for awards, and civilian employee appraisals. Performed stenography duties, recording minutes of weekly staff meeting and other information which I then compiled, edited, and modified for use in memos, reports, letters, and other correspondence. Prepared, edited, and finalized a wide range of classified and non-classified documents, including staff papers, directives, and other military and non-military reports.

In an earlier position as Legal Assistant to the Commander of the 23rd Intelligence Division, I prepared, edited and finalized all correspondence, to include OERs, APRs, military awards and decorations, letters, reports, and memos. I proofread and edited all materials submitted for publication in a newsletter, ensuring correctness of grammar and usage, precision of language, and adherence to length requirements, and styles.

Education and Training Related to This KSA:

In addition to the Certificates I received from Central Florida Community College and the Bethune-Cookman College, the following courses have been helpful in refining my skills in this area:

- Correspondence English Usage, Kessler AFB, Mississippi
- Legal Terminology, Kessler AFB, Mississippi
- Legal Composition, Andrews AFB, Maryland
- Building a Professional Image, Andrews AFB, Maryland

ABOUT THE EDITOR

Anne McKinney holds an MBA from the Harvard Business School and a BA in English from the University of North Carolina at Chapel Hill. A noted public speaker, writer, and teacher, she is the senior editor for PREP's business and career imprint, which bears her name. Early titles in the Anne McKinney Career Series (now called the Real-Resumes Series) published by PREP include: *Resumes and Cover Letters That Have Worked, Resumes and Cover Letters That Have Worked for Military Professionals, Government Job Applications and Federal Resumes, Cover Letters That Blow Doors Open,* and *Letters for Special Situations.* Her career titles and how-to resume-and-cover-letter books are based on the expertise she has acquired in 25 years of working with job hunters. Her valuable career insights have appeared in publications of the "Wall Street Journal" and other prominent newspapers and magazines.

PREP Publishing Order Form
You may purchase our titles from your favorite bookseller! Or send a check, money order or your credit card number for the total amount*, plus $4.00 postage and handling, to PREP, 1110 1/2 Hay Street, Fayetteville, NC 28305. You may also order our titles on our website at www.prep-pub.com and feel free to e-mail us at preppub@aol.com or call 910-483-6611 with your questions or concerns.

Name: _____

Address: _____

E-mail address:_____

Payment Type: ☐ Check/Money Order   ☐ Visa   ☐ MasterCard

Credit Card Number: _____ Expiration Date: _____

Put a check beside the items you are ordering:

☐ $16.95—REAL-RESUMES FOR RESTAURANT, FOOD SERVICE & HOTEL JOBS. Anne McKinney, Editor

☐ $16.95—REAL-RESUMES FOR MEDIA, NEWSPAPER, BROADCASTING & PUBLIC AFFAIRS JOBS. Anne McKinney, Editor

☐ $16.95—REAL-RESUMES FOR RETAILING, MODELING, FASHION & BEAUTY JOBS. Anne McKinney, Editor

☐ $16.95—REAL-RESUMES FOR HUMAN RESOURCES & PERSONNEL JOBS. Anne McKinney, Editor

☐ $16.95—REAL-RESUMES FOR MANUFACTURING JOBS. Anne McKinney, Editor

☐ $16.95—REAL-RESUMES FOR AVIATION & TRAVEL JOBS. Anne McKinney, Editor

☐ $16.95—REAL-RESUMES FOR POLICE, LAW ENFORCEMENT & SECURITY JOBS. Anne McKinney, Editor

☐ $16.95—REAL-RESUMES FOR SOCIAL WORK & COUNSELING JOBS. Anne McKinney, Editor

☐ $16.95—REAL-RESUMES FOR CONSTRUCTION JOBS. Anne McKinney, Editor

☐ $16.95—REAL-RESUMES FOR FINANCIAL JOBS. Anne McKinney, Editor

☐ $16.95—REAL-RESUMES FOR COMPUTER JOBS. Anne McKinney, Editor

☐ $16.95—REAL-RESUMES FOR MEDICAL JOBS. Anne McKinney, Editor

☐ $16.95—REAL-RESUMES FOR TEACHERS. Anne McKinney, Editor

☐ $16.95—REAL-RESUMES FOR CAREER CHANGERS. Anne McKinney, Editor

☐ $16.95—REAL-RESUMES FOR STUDENTS. Anne McKinney, Editor

☐ $16.95—REAL-RESUMES FOR SALES. Anne McKinney, Editor

☐ $16.95—REAL ESSAYS FOR COLLEGE AND GRAD SCHOOL. Anne McKinney, Editor

☐ $25.00—RESUMES AND COVER LETTERS THAT HAVE WORKED. McKinney. Editor

☐ $25.00—RESUMES AND COVER LETTERS THAT HAVE WORKED FOR MILITARY PROFESSIONALS. McKinney, Ed.

☐ $25.00—RESUMES AND COVER LETTERS FOR MANAGERS. McKinney, Editor

☐ $25.00—GOVERNMENT JOB APPLICATIONS AND FEDERAL RESUMES: Federal Resumes, KSAs, Forms 171 and 612, and Postal Applications. McKinney, Editor

☐ $25.00—COVER LETTERS THAT BLOW DOORS OPEN. McKinney, Editor

☐ $25.00—LETTERS FOR SPECIAL SITUATIONS. McKinney, Editor

☐ $16.95—REAL-RESUMES FOR NURSING JOBS. McKinney, Editor

☐ $16.95—REAL-RESUMES FOR AUTO INDUSTRY JOBS. McKinney, Editor

☐ $24.95—REAL KSAS--KNOWLEDGE, SKILLS & ABILITIES--FOR GOVERNMENT JOBS. McKinney, Editor

☐ $24.95—REAL RESUMIX AND OTHER RESUMES FOR FEDERAL GOVERNMENT JOBS. McKinney, Editor

☐ $24.95—REAL BUSINESS PLANS AND MARKETING TOOLS ... Samples to use in your business. McKinney, Ed.

☐ $16.95—REAL-RESUMES FOR ADMINISTRATIVE SUPPORT, OFFICE & SECRETARIAL JOBS. Anne McKinney, Editor

☐ $16.95—REAL-RESUMES FOR FIREFIGHTING JOBS. Anne McKinney, Editor

☐ $16.95—REAL-RESUMES FOR JOBS IN NONPROFIT ORGANIZATIONS. Anne McKinney, Editor

☐ $16.95—REAL-RESUMES FOR SPORTS INDUSTRY JOBS. Anne McKinney, Editor

☐ $16.95—REAL-RESUMES FOR LEGAL & PARALEGAL JOBS. Anne McKinney, Editor

_____ TOTAL ORDERED

_____ (add $4.00 for shipping and handling)

_____ TOTAL INCLUDING SHIPPING *PREP offers volume discounts on large orders. Call us at (910) 483-6611 for more information.

Would you like to explore the possibility of having PREP's writing team create a resume for you similar to the ones in this book?

For a brief free consultation, call 910-483-6611
or send $4.00 to receive our Job Change Packet to
PREP, 1110 1/2 Hay Street, Fayetteville, NC 28305. Visit our
website to find valuable career resources: www.prep-pub.com!

QUESTIONS OR COMMENTS? E-MAIL US AT PREPPUB@AOL.COM